Winter Love

Also by Jacob Korg:

George Gissing: A Critical Biography

Dylan Thomas

Language in Modern Literature

Browning and Italy

Ritual and Experiment in Modern Poetry

Winter Love

Ezra Pound and H.D.

Jacob Korg

THE UNIVERSITY OF WISCONSIN PRESS

Publication of this book has been made possible in part by the generous support
of the Anonymous Fund of the University of Wisconsin-Madison.

The University of Wisconsin Press
1930 Monroe Street
Madison, Wisconsin 53711

www.wisc.edu/wisconsinpress/

3 Henrietta Street
London WC2E 8LU, England

1   3   5   4   2

Printed in the United States of America

Library of Congress Cataloging-in-Publication Data
Korg, Jacob.
Winter love : Ezra Pound and H.D. / Jacob Korg.
p.   cm.
Includes bibliographical references and index.
ISBN 0-299-18390-4 (alk. paper)
1. Pound, Ezra, 1885-1972.   2. H.D. (Hilda Doolittle), 1886-1961.
3. Pound, Ezra, 1885-1972—Friends and associates.
4. H. D. (Hilda Doolittle), 1886-1961—Friends and associates.
5. Poets, American—20th century—Biography.
6. Modernism (Literature)—United States.
I. Title: Ezra Pound and H.D.   II. Title.
PS3531.O82 Z7142   2003
811´.52—dc21   2002010205

Contents

Preface

In this study, I have examined the careers of Ezra Pound and
H.D. as a lifelong dialogue. There were actually two dialogues—
one on the level of life, and the other on the level of poetry. I have
attempted to follow these exchanges in ways that will clarify the
relationships between the poets and their works, using unpublished letters and manuscript sources as well as the extensive biographical material now available. Although they rarely saw each
other after their twenties, the two poets continued to exchange
letters throughout their lives (except for wartime interruptions),
never quite dropping their old friendship. As Michael King has
observed in his introduction to H.D.'s memoir of Pound, *End to
Torment*, "Throughout the memoir runs H.D.'s conviction that
her life and Ezra's had been intertwined irrevocably since those
early days when they walked together, 'maenad and bassarid,' in
the Pennsylvania woods."[1]

Susan Stanford Friedman has noted that H.D. conducted a
"dialectical interaction" with many men, including Pound, and
Pound himself was often responsive to H.D. The two poets were
collaborators early in their lives, but afterward their works display
an intermittent pattern of give-and-take, where stylistic and thematic influences sometimes come together and sometimes di-
verge, and where H.D., particularly, continues to include Pound
and figures based on him in her prose and poetry.

There are sharp contrasts between the publishing histories and critical reputations of the two poets. Pound had been a prominent figure in the literary scene continuously from the time he went to England in 1909, and he published prolifically in a variety of forms throughout his life. Most of H.D.'s publications, on the other hand, were limited editions privately subsidized, and some of her books were published posthumously or never published at all, so that it was not until after her death that the full range of her writing began to appear. Although her friends and readers were enthusiastic about her work (and this occasionally included Pound), she was generally neglected by critics until the 1980s, twenty years after her death. At that time, her *Collected Poems 1912–1944,* edited by Louis L. Martz, the biographies by Janice Robinson and Barbara Guest, and the criticism of Susan Stanford Friedman began a vigorous revaluation of H.D. as a poet and literary figure. This posthumous recognition has continued with the appearance of numerous books and articles devoted to her work.[2]

The two poets differed widely in temperament. H.D. was reticent, self-absorbed, vulnerable, always dependent on others. Pound, on the other hand, was ebullient, self-promoting, arrogant, contentious, and feverishly energetic, publishing his criticism and poetry at a furious pace. Both poets underwent psychiatric analysis, Pound as a reluctant patient in St. Elizabeths, the Washington, D.C., mental hospital, and H.D. as an eager subject who sought help from many sources. Pound's doctors examined him frequently, and while they never produced a final diagnosis, they recorded very different opinions about his condition. He was found by some to be both paranoid and schizoid, but not psychotic, while others thought his disorders rose to the psychotic level, or considered him merely delusional, narcissistic, neurotic, or not mentally disturbed at all.

H.D. consulted a series of psychiatrists throughout her life, the most notable being Freud, but some critics have continued to explore her unconscious, apparently trying to complete the work the therapists left unfinished. Susan Stanford Friedman, in *Psyche Reborn,* has offered a detailed analysis of the family relations that she regards as the source of H.D.'s sexual ambivalence. Freud told her that she was fixated on her mother and was a "perfect bisexual." A number of male critics have maintained that her work exhibits penis envy, a view repudiated with vigor by female critics. On the other hand, it has been argued that she overcame the Lacanian "lack" characteristic of the female through her bisexuality, and this feature of her psyche has been used to observe that she did not sharply differentiate the genders. In the light of these abundant and often conflicting analyses, I have preferred to let the two poets speak for themselves, instead of adding further speculation about their unconscious motives. Claire Buck has wisely observed that the psychological analyses offered by critics of H.D. are often forestalled in her poems. "Their resistance to theoretical explanation, interpretation or taxonomies is . . . in part a strategy of H.D.'s writing."[3] Pound's political and cultural ideas and the gender themes of H.D.'s work have also generated interesting controversies. Although they cannot be ignored, they are not central to my subject, and I deal with them only as they enter into the relationships between the two poets.

While there were many divergences in the development of the two poets, there were also parallels, such as the reform of poetry stemming from Imagism and topics that they had in common, such as war, the occult, sexuality, religion, and the Homeric legends. H.D. is the more prominent partner because she had much to say about Pound in her novels and responded to his work with poems of her own, while Pound, although he was strongly influenced by the Imagist H.D. and continued to correspond with her, referred to her only infrequently in his published work. Biographical facts are indispensable to an understanding of these connections, but I have not attempted to cover these fully, since many good treatments of both poets' lives are available.

Some years after the deaths of both poets, the winter 1968 issue of the *Yale Review* opened with an unpublished poem by each: Pound's "Fragment," a preliminary draft of a passage in Canto 74, and "Other Sea-Cities" by H.D. Pound's lines lament the fall of Italy in World War II, accompanying the lament "Rome is down," with fragmentary phrases that juxtapose such unrelated particulars as Mount Fuji and a cat seen walking on a railing. These incohesive details are enclosed within "the stillness outlasting all wars." H.D.'s "Other Sea-Cities" praises a surviving "sea-city" while lamenting the fall of others. The style of her poem contrasts with that of Pound's, since it is written in complete sentences spread over her characteristic short lines, and organizes images into a perfectly coherent message.

But there are also affinities between the two poems. H.D.'s reference to fallen cities is thematically linked with Pound's allusion to Rome. Her "sea-city" is no doubt Venice, where Pound had once acted as guide for H.D. and her mother. It was also the place where Pound lived, died, and is buried. He published his first book of verse there, and the city has a prominent place in the *Cantos*. H.D.'s lines, "ah sea-light, that touched marble, / till it quivered like live flesh," reflect a sensuousness she shared with Pound that appears in such examples from the *Cantos* as: "And in the water, the almond-white swimmers. / The silver water glazes the upturned nipple." On the other hand, Pound's lines, "Now that the world's walls are falling, / world's word must stand alone," parallel the imagery of H.D.'s World War II poem "The Walls Do Not Fall" and echo its theme of the enduring value of poetry.

Acknowledgments

My indebtedness to previous critics and literary historians is recorded mainly in my bibliography. Like everyone who writes on H.D., I owe a great deal to the work of Susan Stanford Friedman, whose analyses of the relations between the works of Pound and H.D. are pioneering anticipations of my study. Humphrey Carpenter's biography of Pound, *A Serious Character*, was a useful guide to Pound's life and thought, and *Herself Defined* by Barbara Guest was an invaluable source of facts about H.D.

My research was aided by a grant from the Graduate Research Fund of the University of Washington. I am indebted to the staffs of the Beinecke Library of Yale University and the Lilly Library of Indiana University for access to letters of H.D. and Ezra Pound, and for their indispensable services; to the staff of the Libraries of the University of Washington; to New Directions and the Poetry/Rare Books Collection of the State University of New York at Buffalo for access to material by H.D. and William Carlos Williams; and to Professor A. Walton Litz and the late Perdita Schaffner for permitting the use of manuscript correspondence.

I am grateful to Wendy Stallard Flory for saving me from errors and to Alison Carb Sussman for helpful suggestions.

Grateful acknowledgement is given to New Directions Publishing Corporation and Faber and Faber Ltd. for permission to quote from the following copyrighted works of Ezra Pound:

The Cantos (Copyright © 1934, 1937, 1940, 1948, 1956, 1959, 1962, 1963, 1966, and 1968 by Ezra Pound)
Collected Early Poems (Copyright © 1976 by the Trustees of the Ezra Pound Literary Property Trust)
Personae (Copyright © 1926 by Ezra Pound)

Grateful acknowledgement is given to New Directions Publishing Corporation for permission to quote from the following copyrighted works of H.D.:

Collected Poems 1912–1944 (Copyright © 1925 by H.D., Copyright © 1957, 1969 by Norman Holmes Pearson. Copyright 1982 © by the Estate of H.D., Copyright © 1983 by Perdita Schaffner)

Acknowledgment is also given to the Lilly Library, Indiana University, Bloomington, Indiana, for permission to cite and quote from letters by H.D. to Ezra Pound.

Winter Love

1

Two Poets

Why had I ever come down out of that tree?
H.D., *End to Torment*

An important chapter in the history of Anglo-American poetry began at a Halloween party in suburban Philadelphia in 1901. Hilda Doolittle, aged fifteen, and Ezra Pound, just turned sixteen, met there for the first time. A close relationship began a few years later and lasted, with many intermissions, for over half a troubled century, until the death of H.D. in 1961. It began as friendship and adolescent love marked by erotic passion, became an engagement to marry that was broken, and passed through successive phases of collaboration, alienation, betrayal, filial affection, distrust, and pity to end in a final reconciliation. As mature poets, the two went different ways, but they remained conscious of each other's work, sometimes agreeing, sometimes quarreling, and sometimes responding to each other's writing. Each was an active figure in the imaginative life of the other, and each appears in the work of the other, sometimes as a prominent subject or stylistic influence, and sometimes as an obscure responding echo.

H.D. and Ezra Pound were among those American writers of the early century whose lives and work were shaped by their discovery of Europe, for they spent most of their lives and did their most significant work there. Pound, as a lad of thirteen and sixteen,

3

had already seen most of the capitals of Western Europe during two trips with family members, and had gone to Spain, Paris, and London in the summer of 1906 as a graduate student researching Romance literature on a fellowship from the University of Pennsylvania. Hilda's life as an expatriate began in the spring of 1911 when, after a tour of the Continent with a friend and her mother, she settled in London and committed herself to exile by marrying the Englishman Richard Aldington in 1913.

The friendship between Pound and H.D., which began in a conventional American setting, grew into a pair of parallel poetic careers that traversed the political and cultural turmoil of Europe in the first half of the twentieth century. The lives and work of the two poets were influenced by such historical forces as two world wars, science and technology, Fascism, Freudianism, modern versions of the occult, and the sexual freedom of the time. Their writings are hardly reliable records of those times, but rather transformations of their experiences into poetry and poetic doctrines that had the effect of revolutionizing Anglo-American poetry.

The Ezra Pound of the Pennsylvania period was an energetic young polymath with a great bush of red hair and an air of self-confidence indistinguishable from arrogance. He had been a precocious and wide reader, had written verses at an early age, and filled several notebooks with his efforts before and during his college years. He enrolled for two years at the University of Pennsylvania, but then transferred to Hamilton College in order to study Romance languages, where he laid the groundwork for the emphasis, both in his criticism and poetry, on medieval French and Italian materials. He and William Carlos Williams were pals at the University of Pennsylvania in Pound's freshman year, 1902–3, and Williams thought him to be intelligent and fascinating, but also insufferably pretentious, "brilliant but an ass," intolerable except in small doses.[1] Like Hilda's parents, Gertrude Stein, and many others afterward, Williams found that Ezra was a nuisance who could not be ignored and was likely to change your life. Before and after meeting Pound, he said, was "like B.C. and A.D."

In his *Autobiography,* Williams reports that Ezra took him to visit the Doolittle home in order to introduce him to Hilda (not yet "H.D."). Williams found her to be a tall, nervous, awkward, reclusive beauty, with a certain wild and untamed manner, and saw that Ezra was "wonderfully in love with her." The two young men seem to have been rivals for Hilda's attention for a time, but Williams eventually became a friend rather than a lover.

The remarkable group of young people who were to become leading poets socialized with each other at parties and dances and strolled through the suburban woods and fields. Hilda was "indifferent to rule and order," and Williams observed this resistance to convention during a country walk the two took together. Ignoring appearances, Hilda dragged her long skirt over the grass and fences, refused to turn back in the face of a threatening storm, and when the storm arrived, sat down in the grass and held her arms out to the rain, exclaiming, "Come beautiful rain. Beautiful rain, welcome." On another occasion, she walked out into the surf as if she wanted to immerse herself in the sea, was knocked over and taken by the undertow, and had to be dragged unconscious out of the water and resuscitated.[2] Pound recalled this incident, or one like it, about fifty years later, in a letter to H.D. that briefly recalled some scenes of their youth.

What she had in mind in performing these feats is more fully explained in her 1927 novel, *HERmione,* whose autobiographical heroine, Hermione Gart, thirsts to bury herself in nature in a paradoxical effort to escape it. Water is a favored medium for this dream: "she wanted the inner lining of an Atlantic breaker . . . Water was transparent . . . she wanted to see through the reaches of sea-wall, push on through transparencies. She wanted to get away, yet to be merged eventually with the thing she so loathed." Perhaps H.D. was recalling her own youthful state of mind when she attributed to Hermione a confused sense that she was neither in the world nor out of it, together with an urge to "clutch toward something that had no name yet." If her character's desire to reach an invisible realm of freedom beyond a world where she felt unwanted and worthless does reflect the youthful Hilda's feelings, the behavior Williams observed might be taken as an early expression of her later mysticism.

Ezra and Hilda, with Williams often present, saw much of each other after 1905, and the friendship between the two soon developed into a passionate and intense love affair. The attitudes the two young lovers adopted toward each other were prototypes of their future patterns of behavior. Ezra dominated Hilda as her guide and teacher, introducing her to new books and ideas, giving her new eyes (in a phrase he was later to use), helping and controlling her at once. He was to adopt this rôle toward numerous disciples and fellow writers throughout his life, counseling them, imposing his tastes on them, assigning them various tasks, and advancing their interests. For Hilda, Ezra was the first of a long series of powerful male figures whom she idealized, whose dominance she willingly accepted, and who ultimately disappointed her.

At this time, the fall of 1905, Ezra, having completed his degree at Hamilton, was returning as a graduate student to the University of Pennsylvania, where he had spent his freshman and sophomore years. Hilda was studying at Bryn Mawr as a day student who lived at home. They were considered to be engaged, and Ezra and his family came to Sunday dinner with the Doolittles. But Hilda's relationship with Ezra was not a tranquil one. It somehow caused the troubled Hilda to leave college, and years later she wrote: "My second year was broken into or across by my affair with Ezra Pound, who, after all, at that time, proved a stimulus and was the scorpionic sting or urge that got me away."[3]

The profound effect of this youthful love affair on H.D.'s psyche cannot be stressed enough. In her memoir of Pound, *End to Torment*, written at her analyst's direction more than fifty years after their Pennsylvania youth, she wrote, "no 'act' afterwards, though biologically fulfilled, had had the significance of the first *demi-vierge* embrace." Vivid memories of that interval remained with her until she was past seventy, for when she then recalled how Pound kissed her in the snow, she could not find the right language to convey this image and said poetically, "perhaps in the frost of our mingled breath, the word was written." This seems to be H.D.'s acknowledgment, in her old age, that they were fated to be linked throughout their lives. Pound's kisses were "Electric, magnetic, they do not so much warm, they magnetize, vitalize. We need never go back." Like others, she felt that after meeting Pound a gap had been crossed. However, she adds that their feelings are numbed by the cold and asks if this is the beginning of *rigor mortis*—a symbolic suggestion that their love relationship would die.[4]

End to Torment also mentions an embrace in an armchair, where they were discovered by her father, "fiery kisses" in a secluded room during a dance, and kisses in a tree house. When she spoke to her analyst about the "fiery moment" of this affair with Pound, he recognized that it had mythic significance for her: "It has no time. It's out of time, eternal." Once she urged Ezra to leave the tree house to run for his trolley: "'No Dryad,' he says. He snatches me back. We sway with the wind. There is no wind. We sway with the stars. They are not far." The elderly H.D. mournfully asked, "Why had I ever come down out of that tree?"

Judging from these recollections, H.D.'s love affair with Ezra had been a magic enclosure formed of affection and eroticism on the one hand, and reading and literary discussion on the other. Hilda, like Ezra, had a knowledge of Latin and Greek, and he took her as the first of his many disciples, introducing her to a wide range of books and ideas. At the same time, he became her first lover, with those electrical, magnetic, vitalizing kisses. Looking back in her old age, she acknowledged that Pound had occupied a dominant place in her imaginative life. Recalling these sexual and intellectual influences, she wrote, "He drags me out of the shadows."[5]

Susan Stanford Friedman has shown how H.D. equated "erotics and poetics" in her later writing; this identification was present in the minds of both young people from the beginning and remained the knotted root of their relationship.[6] The love-play between Ezra and Hilda in real life was accompanied by readings and recitations, mainly instigated by Ezra, who approached Hilda with books and ideas as well as passion. He introduced her to Shaw, Maeterlinck, Bertrand de Born, and the *Morte d'Arthur,* lent her works by Blake, Balzac, Ibsen, and Whistler, and recited poetry by Browning, Willliam Morris, Swinburne, and Rossetti. In their maturity, both poets rebelled against the verbose styles of the Victorian poets, but these early readings nevertheless had a lasting influence on them, though each recalled them in his or her own way. Pound's early poetry echoed Rossetti and the Pre-Raphaelite mood, and Browning's versification and linguistic inventiveness became important models in his mature poetry. H.D. found in Swinburne's erotic poetry echoes of her own feelings, introduced lines recollected from her readings with Pound into her autobiographical fiction, and later wrote a novel about the Pre-Raphaelites.[7] The atmosphere of these scenes is suggested in a letter to Pound that H.D. wrote about forty years later from her hotel in Switzerland: "I am re-reading Jason; I remember first hearing *Ah, quelle est belle, La Marguerite* under some apple-trees and you shouting the *Ha-Ha* and the *Two Red Roses* at the same session—my first introduction to William Morris."[8]

They also read the story of Tristram and Iseult, and Ezra thought of Hilda as an idealized figure out of myth or literature, dubbing her "Bellissima," "Is-Hilda" (a variant of Iseult), and finally "Dryad" (or wood-nymph), a name from Greek mythology that both used for the rest of their lives. Richard Aldington, H.D.'s future husband, used "Dryad" as one of her many nicknames, an implicit acceptance of her bond with Pound.

H.D.'s records of this early courtship show that while she was hesitant to accept Pound as a lover or husband, he helped to lay the basis for her literary achievement and found a permanent place in her feelings. When she was undergoing analysis in her seventies, she was asked what she was hiding, and admitted that "It was all *that* [by which she meant "the early American scene"], my deep love for Ezra . . . I *did* have a life in U.S."[9]

Apart from "Hilda's Book," the collection of poems written between 1905 and 1907 while he was a graduate student, Pound wrote little or nothing about this youthful episode. His erotic attachment to the young Hilda was transformed into a firm respect for the poetry she was later to write.[10] Most of the poems in "Hilda's Book" are not much better than what might be expected from an overeducated and uncritical young mind. Archaizing, pretentious, and intolerably literary, they display a wide knowledge of fossilized poetic styles and a facility for imitating them. They reflect Ezra's studies in Old French and Provençal, and his enthusiasm for traditional poets. The young poet enclosed his idol in a world of Victorian medievalism, projecting his love for Hilda over a realm of castles, secluded woods, elves, and banners, patched together with influences from Dante, William Morris, Chaucer, and Keats. Nevertheless, Pound thought three of these poems worth publishing in his first book of verse, *A Lume Spento,* and one of these, "The Tree," became a permanent item in his canon.

Their youthful flirtations imprinted on the minds of both poets impressions of the opposite sex that lasted throughout their lives and became central parts of their poetry. The artificiality of the "Hilda's Book" poems no doubt confirms H.D.'s feeling that the young Ezra was in love with her image. His poetic idealization of Hilda is the source of some of his prominent themes. As "Hilda's Book" shows, she inspired in the young Ezra a reverence that he identified with the medieval religion of love. The figure he addresses, the idealized "Is-Hilda" named after Iseult of the chivalric tradition, is enfolded in a religious aura, for the poet feels a "wondrous holiness" as the beloved's fingers touch his, and "Saint Hilda" is asked to pray for him.

This worship of a female figure, strongly encouraged by Pound's reading of Dante and the troubadour poets, is the basis of his later theory that the troubadour love poems encoded a secret pagan religion of love. The posture of veneration first directed toward Ezra's idealized image of Hilda takes the form of goddess worship in the *Cantos* and is the germ of the eclectic religious sensibility seen in Pound's later poetry. Through the numerous female figures, mortal and divine, who appear in the *Cantos,* this theme developed into the concept of "amor" that encompassed for Pound both the fertility of nature and the enlargement of the soul through the contemplation of beauty.

In spite of its immaturity, "Hilda's Book" made a lasting impression on the girl to whom it was addressed. As we will see, twenty years later, H.D.'s *HERmione* makes use of imagery recollected from these poems. Pound's effect on Hilda's psyche was even more pronounced than his influence on her writing. Their friendship set a pattern that she was to relive many times, for her lesbian tendencies did not prevent H.D. from attaching herself to authoritative men as a disciple and sometimes as a lover, eventually coming to distrust them, and ultimately to feel that she was rejected. The story was retold with her husband, Richard Aldington, the writer D. H. Lawrence, the composer Cecil Gray, the psychologist Havelock Ellis, the air marshal Lord Dowding, and the journalist Lionel Durand. Her analysts, Erich Heydt and Freud, could also be added to this list, except that her relationships with them ended without pain.

H.D.'s relationships with many different men were based on her belief that her life followed the pattern of the Egyptian myth of Isis and Osiris. In one part of the myth, Osiris, regarded as a god of vegetation and agriculture, was murdered by his brother, Seth, and his body was set adrift in the Nile. Isis, his sister as well as his wife, recovered the body, brought it back to Egypt and, after reviving it, was impregnated by Osiris and gave birth to a son, Horus. But Seth discovered the body, cut it into fragments, and scattered the parts in different places. Isis then traveled far and wide in a search for the fragments, assembled them, and wrapped them in cloth so that they became the first mummy.

H.D. referred to these deities in her later poetry, and took the view that her life was a parallel "legend," a search, like that of Isis, for an Eternal Lover. Pound was the first man to be the hero or Eternal Lover of H.D.'s personal myth, and no doubt its defining figure. But fifty years later, when she wrote *End to Torment*, the aged H.D. realized that "I was not equipped to understand the young poet."[11] The men she encountered in her Isis-like quest influenced her poetry and prose works, many of them appearing under pseudonyms as prominent figures in her stories or as subjects of her poetry. When we recall that Pound was their prototype, we can understand the profound effect her youthful friendship with him had on her imaginative life.

The Pennsylvania love affair did not last but changed into something else. Hilda learned that Ezra had shown serious interest in other girls, especially Mary Moore, to whom his 1909 volume, *Personae,* was dedicated. In a letter of February 1908, she told Williams that she was going to marry Pound, whom she described as a lonely, suffering altruist—a description whose wild inaccuracy must have amused Williams, but which suited Hilda's tendency to sympathize with the downtrodden. Ezra, she said, was one who would "crucify" himself for others, and she dramatically observed, with a misspelling that is perhaps significant, that "All great love is a crucifiction [*sic*] of self." The error, unintentionally suggesting the artificiality of Ezra's "great love," acquires authority from a letter written less than a month later in which Hilda informed Williams that the engagement had been broken off.[12]

According to a recollection in *End to Torment,* a friend let them make use of her father's study at a school, where "[t]here were fiery kisses."[13] Hilda was embarrassed when their lovemaking was interrupted, and they learned that the schoolgirls had been peeping at them. H.D. recalled those days in a few pages of her unpublished novel, "The Sword Went Out to Sea," written in the winter and spring of 1946-47. Her clipped, noncommittal sentences report that when she was sixteen and seventeen she had been in love with "Allen Flint," as she called the Pound character. He brought her books, they took walks together, and they were discovered in the armchair. Flint was "clever," "a misfit," and "very fascinating." Everything went wrong, he could not keep a job, and when he asked her to go to Europe with him, she refused. When Ezra did, in fact, sail for Europe in 1908, it was Mary Moore, not Hilda, who saw him off at the pier in New York.

In spite of her ambivalent attitude toward Pound, the parting was traumatic for Hilda, and she never recovered from the pain it caused her; it aroused such intense distress that she mentioned it repeatedly in later years as an injury inflicted by Pound that could never be forgotten. She declared that the depression she felt at the time of his departure carried into her relations with others throughout her life. Fifty years later, after hearing of the elderly Pound's friendship with the young Bohemian, Sheri Martinelli, Hilda recalled "my own shock at Ezra leaving for Europe—1908?"[14] When she learned that Pound had abandoned Martinelli, she thought of it as a "super-imposition" on the event of 1908. And when Pound, after his release from the mental hospital to which he had been confined, left with his wife for Italy in 1958, H.D. attributed her feeling of frustration to her memory of that earlier departure.

During Pound's absence the two continued to exchange letters, but H.D. turned to another friend, Frances Gregg, for love and companionship. Her account of this relationship in *HERmione*—where Frances bears the name of Fayne Rabb, and Pound is George Lowndes—is a complex, sensitive narrative that corresponds, in the main, with the known facts. The story of the heroine's visit to Fayne's home in a modest Philadelphia neighborhood is especially convincing, and the conversations between the two girls embody a love-hate relationship that seems to record a recalled reality. In the novel, the two rivals for Hermione's love, George and Fayne, at first make disparaging observations about each other. Fayne tells the submissive Hermione that she is too good for George and dismisses his influence by telling her, "Your writing is nothing really." But later, after Hermione has become her captive, Fayne treacherously tells her that she herself is now deeply in love with George. (Can the name Fayne Rabb echo "feign" and "rob"?) In actual fact, Ezra had made love to Frances, and she became passionately and hopelessly attached to him. Her recollections of this affair in her memoir, *The Mystic Leeway* (posthumously published), are eloquent. She wrote that Pound taught that love was an art: "Pound was beautiful in a blunt, unfinished, exciting way that a young artist might sculpt a young god . . . He corrupted us all to his way of thinking." Speaking again of Pound, she wrote: "What happens the first time one is kissed? What gate is that which opens? What mystery is revealed?"[15]

Ezra also encouraged Frances's writing, as well as Hilda's, intensifying the rivalry between them. It was probably Pound's influence that led the *New Freewoman* to publish her three short, extremely gruesome stories, "Contes Macabres," in its issue of 1 December 1913. What must have been a painful situation for the two young women was eased when the man both loved left for Europe again in 1911, and their relationship intensified as they turned to each other.

Hilda's friendship with Frances Gregg, her first lesbian attachment, was to be continued intermittently for some years, and her position between Ezra and Frances foreshadowed her future emotional life. She was to have both male and female lovers, but they occupied different levels in her mind. In spite of some initial conflicts, her relations with women, especially Bryher, were to be relatively long-lasting and satisfying. But her affairs with men, including her husband, Richard Aldington, were stormy, painful, and often came to some abrupt end. The male figures obsessed her imagination, and her feelings about them generated much of her poetry, as well as her novels, where they appear in a variety of disguises. Her women friends did not, after her early poems, strongly influence her poetry, though they appear in her autobiographical novels. The female figures and the powerful expressions of female consciousness in H.D.'s poetry are not, in general, related to the women she knew. They are drawn from within herself, emerging from that quarrel with ourselves that Yeats identified as the source of poetry.

Pound's romantic interests at this time, while firmly heterosexual, were also ambiguous. They formed a pattern that was to recur in his later life, as he maintained relationships, not always Platonic, with several women at a time. While Hilda's friendship with Frances Gregg represents at least a partial withdrawal from Pound's influence, Pound himself, during his two years in London and even earlier, was clearly freeing himself, at least temporarily, from his attachment to Hilda. However, as the two continued to write to each other during this time, Hilda apparently hoped that their engagement might be renewed.

Pound's literary career had been germinating before he left for Europe. He had published a number of erudite contributions on Renaissance Latin poetry and other esoteric matters in *Book News Monthly* in 1906 and 1908 that included some translations from Latin, a significant anticipation of his future interest in cultural transmission. After landing at Gibraltar and spending some time in Spain, he went to Venice and hired a printer to publish his first book of verse, *A Lume Spento,* sending a copy to Hilda. He proceeded to London in the summer of 1908, where major advances in his career and changes in his personal life occurred.

He began by approaching Elkin Mathews, a publisher and bookseller who had published prominent figures of the 1890s and who agreed to display some copies of *A Lume Spento* in his shop. Mathews later published Pound's next books, *A Quinzaine for This Yule* and the augmented edition of *A Lume Spento* called *Personae.* Perhaps equally important, he introduced Pound to writers who gradually passed him on to their more famous acquaintances. As a result, Pound climbed a kind of ladder that led him to become intimate with some of the major writers and editors of the time, including May Sinclair, Ford Madox Ford, and ultimately his idol, Yeats. Through his publications and the obvious talent he displayed, the brash, intrusive young American—who rankled the sensibilities of even less conventional English people by appearing in a wide-brimmed hat, a velvet jacket, and a single earring— became a prominent figure in the London literary scene.

There were signs of original temperament in the poems of this period, but no foreshadowings of the coming poetic revolution generated by Imagism and Vorticism. Occasionally, an exceptional vigor or directness breaks through, as in "Sestina: Altaforte" or "Mesmerism," but most of these poems are mannered and artificial, as Pound seeks to capture the tone of various historical periods. His language is conventional, even deliberately archaic, imagery is traditional, even Romantic, and much of the material is drawn from myth and history with many invocations to gods and goddesses. Such imagery as heavenly spheres, astral souls, and figures seen in dreams anticipate the mysticism that became one of his themes. An overt statement of this commitment occurs in "Redondillas," an awkward Whitmanesque effort where Pound speaks in his own voice and declares, among a great many other claims:

> I sing of risorgimenti,
>   of old things found that were hidden,
> I sing of the senses developed,
>   I reach towards perceptions scarce heeded.[16]

The change in his style came about when Ford Madox Ford, after reading the poems in *Canzoni,* displayed his pain by rolling on the floor of his hotel room in Germany, a scene recorded in Pound's obituary essay of 1939. Pound acknowledged that Ford had consistently impressed him with the need for simple, natural, contemporary language, and the poems in his next volume, *Ripostes* (1912), reflect Ford's advice. *Ripostes* included some poems in the earlier style as well as "The Seafarer," a triumphant demonstration of Pound's talent for capturing the tone of an earlier period, but he showed that he was on the way to change in such lines as:

> Your mind and you are our Sargasso sea . . .
> No! There is nothing! In the whole and all,
> Nothing that's quite your own.
>   Yet this is you.[17]

Pound, now well known in London literary circles, gained a new level of notoriety in November 1909 when the American *Literary Digest* devoted a page and a photograph to "An American Poet Discovered in England," with some quotations from Pound's verse.

Hilda is absent from the five books of verse Pound published between 1908 and 1911. However, the themes of chivalric love treated in many of these poems are offshoots of the poems in "Hilda's Book" and Pound's idealization of Hilda. His feelings for her were transposed into poems following the literary tradition of romantic love, a tradition he attempted to extend during this phase of his poetic development.

While Pound was developing as a poet, there were also changes in his personal life, for he befriended Olivia Shakespear, who had been Yeats's lover years before, and her daughter, Dorothy, who promptly fell in love with him and ultimately became his wife. Thoughts of Hilda undoubtedly receded to the background during his busy time in Europe and his visit to America in June 1910. Pound, who was occupied with editorial contacts and his writing during this visit, paid little attention to her, although she did spend time with him in the Philadelphia area and followed him to New York that summer. It seems to have been agreed at this time that she would join Pound in London, and Hilda, apparently unaware of his attachment to Dorothy Shakespear, went home with the impression that she and Pound were engaged again. But it is clear that from Pound's point of view, at least, their relationship had entered a new phase whose exact tone was not yet clear. It was, in fact, becoming painfully complex, for this was the time when H.D. fell in love with Frances Gregg, who had received advances, as she knew, from Pound; also, Pound was sufficiently interested in Dorothy Shakespear to dedicate his volume, *Provença*, to her and her mother when it was published in November 1910.

There were two important developments in Hilda's life between Pound's arrival in America in the summer of 1910 and his return to London in February 1911. First, she had been writing poems and translations since college, but now she began to focus more seriously on her own poetry, an effort perhaps connected with her trip to New York, which was supposed to lead to work as a writer. Second, she decided to join Pound in London. She accompanied Frances Gregg and her mother on a tour of the Continent in 1911, and when the others went home, she stayed behind in London to be with Pound.

The scene of their friendship was now London, not Pennsylvania, and although they did not know it, the two had left America behind forever. Pound took Hilda around, introduced her to women writers and other friends, and reassured her about the impression she was making. His letters to his parents at this time often include a sentence about H.D.'s whereabouts and activities: "Am having Hilda to tea this P. M." or "Hilda is in Florence with her family." The two frequented the British Museum's reading room together with Richard Aldington. H.D., on her part, wrote frequently to Pound's mother, reporting on her son's activities as if she were still engaged to him, an impression that Pound apparently did little to discourage, in spite of his growing commitment to Dorothy Shakespear.

When H.D. joined Pound in London in the fall of 1911, she entered an environment where literary questions and the future of poetry were being vigorously debated in periodicals and informal meetings of poets and critics. The effort to free English poetry from the stifling influence of its Romantic and Victorian predecessors had begun as far back as the 1890s with such Decadent poets as Arthur Symons and Ernest Dowson, and took on new directions in the new century in the work of Rudyard Kipling, John Masefield, Gerard Manley Hopkins, A. E. Housman, and Thomas Hardy. These poets introduced innovations such as metrical experiments, subjects from contemporary life, natural language, and regional dialects. At the same time, the avant-garde Continental movements of Symbolism, Futurism, and Cubism were opening new possibilities to English poetry, which was nevertheless dominated by Yeats. Although there was a general movement toward a Modernism involving simplification and directness in the work of such figures as Ford Madox Ford, T. S. Eliot, and Robert Frost, the Imagist emphases on concrete imagery and strict verbal economy were yet to come.[18]

This contentious milieu was perfectly congenial to Pound, who knew many literary figures and editors, wrote for various periodicals, and was robustly sponsoring one cause or aspiring writer after another. But H.D. preferred the quieter relationships with the women writers she met through Pound during her first months in London. She remained unpublished but continued to experiment with poetry and translations from the Greek. In 1911–12 she talked with Pound, Richard Aldington, and F. S. Flint in Pound's room and various tea shops as they developed together the poetic style called Imagism.

Aldington had a father who was a Portsmouth solicitor and a mother who wrote novels. He had been to a public school and had spent some time at University College, London, where A. E. Housman was one of his teachers, and he learned much by random reading in his father's library. Aldington was enthusiastic about poetry and poets as a boy, and he published creditable verses in several periodicals when he was sixteen. He was well grounded in Greek and Latin and later became a novelist and, like Flint, a significant critic of French literature. H.D. was introduced to him, not by Pound, who knew him, but by Brigit Patmore, one of the women H.D. had befriended through Pound.

F. S. Flint was a Londoner who specialized in contemporary French poetry and wrote poetry reviews. He joined the poetic revolution early, as a member of the 1909 Poets' Club, and became one of the original Imagists. Although he wrote and published poetry of his own, his main contribution was the influence he exerted through his reviews of French poetry and his association with Hulme and Pound. It was through Flint's influence, as well as the visits of Pound, Aldington, and H.D. to Paris in the summer of 1912, that the Imagists became aware of such intellectual currents as Symbolism and Unanimism, the philosophy of Henri Bergson, the merits of *vers libre,* and the works of the French poets.

At this time, H.D.'s relation to Pound was thoroughly unsettled. In December 1911, she wrote from London to Pound's mother that while he had given her a pearl ring, they were not engaged. In her fictional treatments of this period, her heroines are confused about the state of their engagement. The heroine of her autobiographical novel, *Asphodel,* describes "George," a character obviously based on Pound, as "beautiful" and recalls his kisses as "Famished kisses like a desert wind full of sand." In reply to insistent questioning, the heroine acknowledges that she can't marry him, thinking, "She should have known that from the start," but adding, "she had to keep him on."[19]

It seems likely that at this time, early 1912, H.D. had already met Aldington and developed an interest in him, since the heroine of *Asphodel* looks to "Darrington" for understanding. Their friendship soon became a love relationship that included a shared passion for literature, like the earlier tie between H.D. and Pound. Since Aldington could not gain access to the Greek and Latin texts he needed in the British Museum library because he was under twenty-one, the age required for admission, H.D. transcribed them for him so that he could produce the translations he published in *New Age*.[20] And, if *Asphodel* reflects H.D.'s feelings at the time, she really did not know whether she was to marry Aldington or Pound or neither.

Nevertheless, Pound continued to be a significant presence. He was a near neighbor at 10 Church Walk in 1911–12 when H.D. and Aldington lived in separate rooms at No. 6 across the courtyard, and the three haunted the British Museum and London tea shops together to discuss poetry. In 1912–13 the three, together with Brigit Patmore, met for tea "nearly every afternoon."

H.D. and Aldington were sufficiently attached to each other to spend the spring and summer of 1912 together in Paris, visiting museums and exploring the city. They were joined for at least part of the time by Pound, who was gathering material on the troubadour poets at the Bibliothèque Nationale. He maintained a paternal or avuncular authority over H.D., describing himself as her "nearest male relation." Aldington, who admired Pound and learned much from him, nevertheless regarded his presence in Paris and during their later travels as thoroughly unnecessary.

In *End to Torment,* H.D. says that when she heard of Pound's interest in other girls, "The engagement, such as it was, was shattered like a Venetian glass goblet, flung on the floor."[21] But it was probably not until this Paris visit, when she learned that Pound was engaged to marry Dorothy Shakespear, that she finally had to give up the idea that they might be married. Although she had been friendly with Dorothy and her mother, H.D. had had no inkling of the fact that Pound and Dorothy were lovers and were planning to marry. She still felt possessive about Pound in spite of her new friendship with Aldington, for she says in *End to Torment* that when her psychiatrist asked her how she felt on learning the news, she replied: "Look—it's impossible to say. I felt bleak, a chasm opened—"[22]

The diary H.D. kept during her Paris visit offers evidence of an important step in her poetic development.[23] She drafted a number of poems in it, most of them crossed out, incomplete, or largely illegible. Those written up to 31 May 1912 (not all of which are dated, however) are conventional sonnets with conventional syntax, and some even show the conventional break between octave and sestet. A poem dated 10 June, however, is written in short lines of free verse with no rhyme, a form she continued in the few remaining pages of the diary, with one reversion to the sonnet form. Free verse was to be a major feature of Imagist doctrine and the form H.D. used almost without exception throughout her career.

The change may have been motivated by the time and place. In Paris, H.D. was far from the restrictive atmosphere of her home or London, traveling unchaperoned with a lover, apparently asserting her freedom from convention openly for the first time. *Vers libre* as it was called, was also regarded as a daring departure from convention, a parallel to her behavior that might well have suited her Paris mood. As its name suggested, Whitman was less important as an influence on the emergence of free verse than the French poets admired by Pound, Aldington, and Flint. It was not an absolute novelty in English poetry. H.D. herself had written free verse poems before this time, but it seems fair to say that the examples in this diary, casual and fragmentary as they are, foreshadow the break with conventional verse represented by H.D.'s distinctive poetic style.

Another insight into the emergence of H.D.'s style, and an important key to the Imagist spirit, appears in a letter written years later to Norman Holmes Pearson. She describes writing she did in London in 1912, probably before the Paris summer: "I let my pencil run riot, in those early days of my apprenticeship . . . Then I would select from many pages of automatic or pseudo-automatic writing, the few lines that satisfied me."[24] H.D.'s method here brings to mind Pound's account of the composition of his two-line poem "In a Station of the Metro." He says that after seeing attractive faces in an Underground entrance, he tried for weeks to write a poem expressing his feelings. But then he thought of the economy of Japanese poetry, and evidently rejected whatever he had written in favor of a brief, hokku-like poem that perfectly embodies Imagist principles. Like the selected lines of the young H.D., the clipped language of the Imagist poem must be regarded as the visible edge of unexpressed ideas floating freely in the poet's imagination.

Aldington now far surpassed Pound as an influence on H.D.'s poetic work as well as her personal life. His early poems, like hers, are indebted to the *Greek Anthology* both had studied at the British Museum. They are in free verse, employ flower and landscape imagery, are often set in Greek backgrounds, and sometimes consist of fervent prayers to the Greek gods. One poem, "Imagery," consists of a series of images, but fails to qualify as Imagism because each image is discursively related to a lover.

In spite of their embittered relations after the failure of their marriage, Aldington always insisted on H.D.'s exceptional gifts. In his memoir, *Life for Life's Sake*, he says that she was more "distinguished" than Pound, "both as a person and as a mind." He adds: "To look at beautiful things with H.D. is a remarkable experience. She has a genius for appreciation, a severe but wholly positive taste. She lives on the heights, and never wastes time on what is inferior or in finding fault with masterpieces. She responds so swiftly, understands so perfectly, re-lives the artist's mood so intensely, that the work of art seems transformed."[25]

Pound still considered himself to be the protector of the girl he had known and courted in the Philadelphia suburbs, as he showed when, in 1912, he interfered in H.D.'s affairs by preventing her from accompanying the newly married Frances Gregg and her husband, Louis Wilkinson, on a journey to Venice. H.D.

was deeply wounded by her friend's sudden marriage, but she accepted the situation after meeting the new husband. The Wilkinsons had arranged for H.D. to accompany them to the Continent without first consulting her. Pound justified his right to stop her with the familiar claim that he was her "nearest male relation." H.D. seems to have accepted this claim, for nearly ten years later she threw his words back at him in a letter complaining that she should have been informed about the birth of Pound's daughter, Maria, on the ground that she was "Ezra's oldest femaile [*sic*] relative."[26]

The Gregg-Wilkinson event is fictionalized in two of H.D.'s novels, *Asphodel* and *Paint It Today*, in somewhat different ways. Pound forbade H.D. to accompany the Wilkinsons on the ground that she would spoil Frances's chance for happiness in her marriage. He had apparently warned H.D. that the Wilkinsons' union was to be a *mariage blanc*, and that Frances was really in love with another man. He acted vigorously, went to Victoria Station, bought H.D.'s ticket back from Wilkinson, and took her back to her room in a taxi.

Although H.D. thought all this was a product of Pound's fertile imagination, his explanation of the Wilkinsons' situation, as filtered through H.D.'s novelistic accounts, approximates the real state of affairs and testifies both to Pound's perceptiveness and H.D.'s naïveté. Wilkinson was an old friend of the writer John Cowper Powys, who had become infatuated with Frances Gregg. Being already married, Powys could not marry her, but he arranged for her to marry Wilkinson. The wedding took place two weeks after Wilkinson and Frances had met, and the three sailed for England ten days later, in April 1912. The group formed a circle that was totally indifferent to the principle of marital fidelity and entertained some highly unconventional ideas about sex in general. Wilkinson told his future bride that he did not believe in being faithful, and they formed an understanding that they would not have sexual relations with each other for a year, an agreement in which the influence of Powys might well have played a part.[27] Pound knew that the Wilkinson marriage was a cover for Powys's interest in Frances. In fact, after the married couple went to Venice without H.D., Powys and his brother, Llewelyn, who had also fallen in love with Frances, joined them.

Pound's feelings about H.D. during this period can only be guessed. It is clear that he had a continuing interest in her, although he was engaged to Dorothy Shakespear. He told H.D. that he was trying to save her, apparently from Wilkinson's attentions. His flirtation with Frances lurked in the background of the affair, for Frances often wrote to him after she left for Europe but did not write to H.D. According to H.D.'s novel *Paint It Today*, Pound never answered but turned the letters over to H.D., a move that no doubt intensified her suffering at the infidelity of a woman to whom she was passionately attached.[28]

There were some prolonged periods of separation, as well as close association, between Pound and H.D. during the time that the doctrines of Imagism were being formulated. While Pound accompanied H.D. and Aldington in Paris in the summer of 1912, he left to go south for a walking tour of sites in Provence connected with the troubadour poets he was studying, but he came back to Paris briefly after learning that his friend and benefactor, Margaret Cravens, had committed suicide.

Cravens, an American pianist from Indiana, had been living in Paris since 1907. When she met Pound in 1910, she was so strongly impressed by him that she offered to support him financially so that he could concentrate on his writing. Pound accepted, and maintained a correspondence with her. H.D. met her about a month before her death and used her as a model for the character of Shirley Thornton in her novel *Asphodel*. Her suicide at the age of thirty-one sent a profound shock through the circle of her American friends.[29]

In later years, H.D. reported a moment of intimacy with Pound that took place at this time. While walking together, they stopped on one of the bridges leading to the Île-St.-Louis, and the despondent Pound "waved his somewhat Whistlerish stick towards the river, the bridge, the lights, ourselves, all of us, all that we were and wanted to be and the thing that I wanted to say and couldn't say he said it before he dismissed me: 'And the morning stars sang together in glory . . . ,'" a biblical echo that somehow

contradicts the "vague, helpless sort of manner" of his gesture.
H.D. seems to interpret Pound's behavior as an assertion of ambi-
tion against the possibilities of such tragedies as Margaret Cravens's death. But she felt that Pound then "dismissed" her. It appears that, while H.D. shared his feelings as she understood
them, he did not care to share them with her. At this moment,
said H.D., "I myself did once see Ezra plain too."[30]

When Pound joined H.D. and Aldington in Paris in 1912 and
in Venice in 1913, he noted approvingly that they were falling in
love with each other. By this time, he seems to have given up his
rôle as her "nearest male relative" and guardian. Before the end of
the year, he wrote to his mother that the two were "decently married." Pound had been a witness at their wedding.

2

Imagism

Poetry constantly requires a new relation.
                        Wallace Stevens, "Adagia"

Imagism was invented, named, and organized by Pound, but was
best embodied in the early poetry of H.D. She had little to do
with the development and doctrinal underpinning of the movement, but she was present throughout its genesis, and her poetry
displayed a perfect assimilation of its revolutionary intentions.
At this time, the opening of their poetic dialogue, she and Pound
were in perfect agreement about the path Modern poetry should
take.

There has been some difference of opinion as to whether
Pound or H.D. should be given priority for the invention of
Imagism. Richard Aldington, who was intimate with both poets
at the time, wryly wrote: "The fame or otherwise of Ducedom
must go to Ezra, who invented the 'movement.'"[1] In her examination of the origins of Imagism, Cyrena N. Pondrom has argued
that Pound developed the Imagist doctrines in response to H.D.'s
poems. Actually, the emergence of Pound's ideas and H.D.'s Imagist poems are so nearly simultaneous that it might be best to regard them as representing a moment of unanimity in their poetic
interchange, when Pound sponsored certain poetic principles and
H.D., either spontaneously or in reply, wrote poems embodying

them. Perhaps the situation is best described by what Aldington wrote to H.D. nearly fifteen years later, especially if his ironic quotation marks are noted: "Ezra may have 'invented' Imagism but, after all, you wrote the poems."[2]

As early as December 1911, Pound had published a "Prolo-gomena" [*sic*] including a "Credo" that looked forward to Imag-ism by declaring a belief in poetry that "corresponds exactly to the emotion"—a counterpart of Eliot's "objective correlative"—and in the effectiveness of the "natural object" as a symbol.[3] Pound seems to have picked up the idea of a poetic movement during his time in France between May and July 1912, as his original French form of "Imagiste" suggests, for French poets were Parnassian and "Symboliste," and artists were Impressionist or Cubist. This was soon followed by the emergence of H.D.'s Imagist poems, and the movement was launched.

Pound's "The Return," written as early as April 1912, obeyed Imagist principles that had not yet been formulated. It appeared in the *English Review* in June, while Pound was in France. At nearly the same moment, on 10 June, H.D. was experimenting with a new style by writing in free verse in her Paris diary. The first recorded use of the term "Imagist" occurs in a letter of Au-gust 1912 to Harriet Monroe from Pound, where he describes one of his poems, "Middle-Aged," as "an over-elaborate post-Browning 'Imagiste' affair," without explaining what he meant by the comment.[4] At a historic meeting with Aldington and H.D. in the tearoom near the British Museum, Pound recognized that the poems H.D. had been writing fulfilled the aspirations for the re-form of poetry he had been promoting. H.D.'s account of this scene is famous:

> Meeting with him alone or with others at the Museum tea room. We all read in the British Museum reading room . . . "But Dryad," (in the Museum tea room), "this is poetry." He slashed with a pencil. "Cut this out, shorten this line. 'Hermes of the Ways' is a good title. I'll send this to Harriet Monroe of *Poetry*. Have you a copy? Yes? Then we can send this, or I'll type it when I get back. Will this do?" And he scrawled "H.D. Imagiste" at the bottom of the page.[5]

Many years later, H.D. told Norman Holmes Pearson that Pound had attacked her poems with "slash, slash, slash. 'That line, you know, was Ezra's. He made it; it wasn't there as such, until he showed it to me within it.'" Aldington, who reported that Pound had been in the habit of "butting in on our studies and poetic productions," recalled this event or one like it. He wrote: "Ezra was so much worked up by these poems of H.D.'s that he removed his pince-nez and informed us that we were Imagists . . . H.D., looked very much pleased by the praise Ezra generously gave her poems."[6] By recognizing the merits of H.D.'s poems and securing their publication, Pound, in effect, opened her poetic career.

Both Aldington and H.D. objected to the signature Pound decreed, but "Ezra was a bit of a czar in small but irritating ways," and the initials remained, to become a part of literary history. According to the account H.D. gave to Pearson, she had already signed the drafts with her initials, and Pound accepted them and added "Imagiste." H.D. herself came to value them as an identification of her poetic identity, giving the letters conspicuous positions in such titles as *Hedylus* and *Hermetic Definition*. When he sent the poems to Harriet Monroe, Pound reported that H.D. had lived with the "laconic speech of the Imagists" and her classical subjects "since childhood," and he said the poems were: "Objective—no slither; direct—no excessive use of adjectives, no metaphors that won't permit examination. It's straight talk, straight as the Greek!"[7] These were virtues to which English and American poetry would aspire for decades to come. Richard Aldington, who soon left Imagism and was out of sympathy with Modernism, nevertheless acknowledged that "the early Imagist discipline was an excellent thing. It gave us power over words and confidence in using them."[8]

H.D.'s account tells us much about their relationship at the time. We see Pound as overbearing, H.D. as submissive. Pound did not hesitate to make sweeping cuts in another's verse—as he was later to do on a grand scale with T. S. Eliot's *The Waste Land* manuscript—and H.D. accepted them. But he was also helpful in promoting publication—a step she was probably too diffident to attempt herself—by labeling the poems in a way that he thought would improve their chances and advance his new movement.

Pound's term "Imagiste" first appeared in print in October 1912, in a note appended to a group of six short poems titled "The Complete Poetical Works of T. E. Hulme," which Pound generously reprinted in his volume *Ripostes*. The note made fond reference to dull meetings of two years before that were nevertheless pleasant to recall, and to the principles of a "School of Images" and stated that "Les Imagistes" were the descendants of the "forgotten school of 1909."[9] However, he did not at first explain what "Imagiste" meant, and this led to some confusion, for when a group of Aldington's poems appeared in the November 1912 issue of *Poetry,* he was described as "a young English poet, one of the 'Imagistes,' a group of ardent Hellenists who are pursuing interesting experiments in vers libre."[10]

The "school" of 1909 that Pound regarded as the source of the Imagist illumination first met on 15 March 1909, when a group of writers interested in poetic reform came together at the Café Tour d'Eiffel near Charlotte Street. Pound joined them on 22 April and read his poem "Sestina: Altaforte" so loudly that the waiters put a screen around their table to shield the other diners. Pound, F. S. Flint, and Richard Aldington came to some of these meetings, but the group broke up after about a year, and became "the forgotten school of 1909."

Its most prominent figure was Thomas Ernest Hulme, a Cambridge dropout of violent tendencies and rude manners who had published translations of French philosophy and whose poems Pound had included in *Ripostes*. Hulme's criticism, which was not published until long after his death on the battlefield in 1917, contains the seeds of Imagism, and Pound must have learned much about his ideas when he heard Hulme lecture during the course of their friendship. He seems to have regarded the handful of poems Hulme wrote as the first examples of Imagism. They were, significantly, in free verse, and conveyed fleeting impressions through such unconventional images as "the ruddy moon . . . Like a red-faced farmer" and "the star-eaten blanket of the sky."

Hulme had developed the theories behind these unpretentious poems in notes written about 1907 and in a lecture he delivered in 1908. In his poetic theory, people, as limited beings, cannot aspire to the infinite insight envisioned by the Romantics, but can exploit the beauty of "small, dry things" in language that must achieve unprecedented precision and accuracy if it is to escape banality. He declared that the imagery of poetry is directly expressive of physical experience, while the words of prose discourse are only abstract "counters"—that is, signs with conventional meanings, like algebraic symbols, which can be used without any sense of their relation to actuality. In an essay written at the time Pound's little group was meeting to devise the rules of Imagism, Hulme was saying:

> [Poetry] is not a counter language but a visual concrete one. It is a compromise for a language of intuition which would hand over sensations bodily. It always endeavours to arrest you, and to make you continuously see a physical thing, to prevent you gliding through an abstract process. It chooses fresh epithets and fresh metaphors, not so much because they are new, and we are tired of the old, but because the old cease to convey a physical thing and become abstract counters. . . . Images in verse are not mere decoration, but the very essence of an intuitive language.[11]

The germ of Imagism appears in such notebook jottings as: "Each *word* must be an image *seen*, not a counter"; "each sentence should be a lump of clay, a vision seen"; and "A man cannot write without seeing at the same time a visual signification before his eyes." Hulme adds, "Never should one feel light vaporous bridges between one solid sense and another. No bridges—all solid."[12] This would achieve the effect of "a visual chord . . . an image which is different to both,"[13] a rule which anticipates a central principle of Pound's poetics: the device called "superposition," the juxtaposition of images without comment or linkage.

According to Pound, he, H.D., and Aldington in "the spring or early summer of 1912" agreed to the three Imagist principles that became familiar, either directly or indirectly, to future generations of poets and critics:

1. Direct treatment of the "thing," whether objective or subjective.
2. To use absolutely no word that does not contribute to the presentation.
3. As regarding rhythm: to compose in sequence of the musical phrase, not in sequence of a metronome.[14]

There are some significant words here. "Subjective"—feelings, emotions, and states of mind are not ruled out, but they must enter in the form of "treatment." "Presentation"—this recalls Pound's advice in a letter to Iris Barry—"Don't represent—present," a reaffirmation of "direct treatment." The third rule seems to call for the flexible employment of free verse.

The articles titled "Imagisme," signed by F. S. Flint, and "A Few Don'ts by an Imagiste," by Pound, which appeared in the March 1913 *Poetry*, published these rules and declared that the Image—"that which presents an intellectual and emotional complex in an instant of time"—generated the sense of liberation one experienced in the presence of great art. Modestly acknowledging that these ideas were open to debate, the article went on to advise strict verbal economy, avoidance of abstract language, attention to the musical resources of poetry, and the practice of translation.

The Imagist principles, together with the poems by the Imagist circle Pound placed in the early issues of *Poetry*, clarified the meaning of Pound's new term and launched his "school." They gained powerful authority with later poets, though Flint and Pound denied that they were dogmatic, and ended by reminding the reader: "Mais d'abord il faut être un poète."[15]

It is hard to say how much H.D. contributed to these and the other theoretical statements of Pound and Flint. Her contribution to Imagism, however, was decisive. It initially consisted of the three poems published under Pound's sponsorship in the January

1913 issue of *Poetry*. These, together with the poems of her first volume, *Sea Garden*, written with the encouragement of Pound and Aldington, have come to be regarded as the definitive examples of Imagism. It is clear that at this point Aldington had replaced Pound in H.D.'s emotional and literary life, for he and H.D. were lovers, and her poems resemble the verses Aldington was writing at this time far more than they resemble Pound's. Their poems, derived from the *Greek Anthology*, observe the Imagist principles of economy, concrete imagery, and metrical freedom, but they express feelings more directly than examples by Pound or Hulme.

H.D.'s first published poems, "Priapus: Keeper of Orchards" (later retitled "Orchard"), "Hermes of the Ways," and "Epigram," are characteristic. "Orchard" opens:

> I saw the first pear
> as it fell—
> the honey-seeking, golden-banded,
> the yellowswarm
> was not more fleet than I,
> (spare us from loveliness)
> and I fell prostrate
> crying:
> you have flayed us
> with your blossoms,
> spare us the beauty
> of fruit-trees.[16]

At about the same time, Aldington, using a similar poetic idiom, addressed Hermes, another Greek deity:

> Bear us upon thy winged flight
> Down the dark blue ways unto Orcus
> Make us stabile
> With thy imperishable hands,
> For our feet stumble and age . . .[17]

H.D. did not welcome the Imagist label that Pound had attached to her poems in the tea shop conference. She was identified as "H.D., Imagiste" both at the end of the first *Poetry* poems and in the table of contents. Although the term came to define a style that was of great importance in Modern poetry, some of the original Imagists did not approve of it. H.D. soon wrote to Harriet Monroe that she wanted the label dropped. Aldington, many years later, declared: "it was a 'label' which should never have been attached. It gave a little temporary réclame and a lasting misunderstanding. I have never forgiven [Ezra] for pinning that second-rate tag on you." H.D. herself, however, eventually mellowed. When Aldington wrote, as late as 1953, that he regretted his involvement in the Imagist episode, H.D. said that his attitude saddened her, and that now, at the age of seventy-two, she regarded "the Imagist saga" as "part of my youth."[18]

Though they share the spirit of Pound's movement, H.D.'s early poems represent an independent development in Modern poetry. They depart from Pound's doctrine mainly by expressing emotions through their imagery. Pound, who favored treating emotion objectively, acknowledged this difference in a footnote appended to his essay "Vorticism" by observing that certain poems by Aldington and H.D. expressed much stronger feelings than the bare imagery of his own "In a Station of the Metro."[19]

If H.D.'s poems do not invariably adhere to Imagist principles, the same might be said of Pound's superb "The Return." It is Imagist in being free in its rhythms and severely economical in language, but its imagery is only vaguely visual. Its effectiveness arises from the mood of defeat suggested by the shadowy figures of the returning hunters or warriors and their hounds. Nothing could be further from the clipped, limited ironies of Hulme's small poems than the powerfully suggestive Imagism of Pound and H.D.

H.D. and Aldington may have been more successful than Pound as practicing Imagist poets, but they did not share Pound's revolutionary fervor. The rhetorical idiom they adopted avoided the prolixity of conventional poetry, but it displayed little awareness of the changes going on in the contemporary cultural scene. In fact, Aldington, in later years, denied that he consciously took part in the poetic revolution of the time and distanced himself from the emphasis on "technique" that characterized it. The fact that his poems met with approval (by Pound, of course, though he is not mentioned) was purely accidental, not the result of any theoretical agreement.

H.D. told John Gould Fletcher, who was seeing much of the Imagists at this time, that, while she was uncertain of the value of her work, Pound encouraged her, and Fletcher reported that Pound regarded her poetry as the best examples of Imagism. Pound also considered himself responsible for her development, if she is indeed the subject of the brief lyric "Ortus," written in 1913, the year in which he placed her first poems in *Poetry*. The title means "birth" or "origin," and the poet asks:

> How have I laboured?
> How have I not laboured
> To bring her soul to birth,
> To give these elements a name and a centre!

While he feels that she is unformed and uncertain, he nevertheless expresses a love that seems to have survived since the "Hilda's Book" days in Pennsylvania:

> She is beautiful as the sunlight, and as fluid.
> She has no name, and no place . . .
> Surely you are bound and entwined,
> You are mingled with the elements unborn;
> I have loved a stream and a shadow.[20]

Pound suspected that H.D. might not continue the success of her good first poems and was critical of her immersion in Hellenistic lyrics. In the spring of 1913, soon after Aldington and H.D. had arrived in Venice, he wrote to Dorothy: "H. & R. are submerged in a hellenism so polubendius and so stupid that I stop in the street about once in every 15 minutes to laugh at them . . . I don't know—Hellenism? True, they have attained a dullness almost equal to the expression *(facial)* of gk. statuary."[21]

His poem "Tempora," written at about this time, is particularly unkind, for in it he reports: "The Dryad stands in my courtyard / With plaintive, querulous crying . . . 'May my poems be printed this week?'" (It was accompanied, when first published, by a poem titled "The Faun," Pound's name for Aldington, which opened "Soul of a dog," and complained of ignorant meddling. The final version of this is much revised.) Nevertheless, he did admire H.D.'s poems, and predicted that she and William Carlos Williams "Ought to produce really fine things at great intervals."[22] He included her first published poems on the list of the few "that still ring in my head." Pound continued to press H.D.'s poems on the editors of *Poetry* and *The Little Review,* and while commenting favorably on the poetry she was writing, warned Margaret Anderson, the editor of *The Little Review,* "H.D. is all right, but shouldn't write criticism."[23]

The Imagist moment of Pound, H.D., Aldington, and Flint lasted from 1912 to 1916. It reached its high point in the winter of 1914 with the publication of an anthology of Imagist verse. The time—half a year after the outbreak of World War I—was not convenient, but Pound succeeded in having it published in New York as a volume of a journal called *The Glebe,* which was reprinted in England. It was titled, awkwardly, *Des Imagistes: An Anthology.* (The French title pretentiously adopted by Pound means "of the Imagists," as Aldington observed, not "some Imagists," as he must have intended.) It contained a generous representation of poems by H.D., Aldington, and Pound himself, many of them reprinted from *Poetry.*

There had been prolonged periods of separation between Pound and H.D. when she traveled on the continent with her parents, and Pound spent the winters with Yeats at Stone Cottage. The H.D. marriage to Aldington on 18 October 1913 and the Pound marriage to Dorothy Shakespear on 20 April 1914 naturally drew the two poets apart. There was a further distancing in January 1915, when the Aldingtons left Kensington and moved to Hampstead.

Another poetic influence, besides Aldington's, to which H.D. now turned was that of Amy Lowell, who had befriended Pound on a visit the year before, and, responding to his poetic doctrines, came to England in July 1914 to join the Imagists. Pound invited Lowell to a dinner celebrating the appearance of the new Vorticist journal, *Blast* at the Dieudonné restaurant. Lowell responded with a dinner of her own, supposedly to mark the publication of *Des Imagistes*.

John Gould Fletcher has given a good account of this occasion, which was attended by H.D. and Aldington as well as Dorothy Shakespear and other members of Pound's circle. Henri Gaudier-Brzeska was there, and Pound recalled the sculptor's observation of the obese Lowell in Canto 77: "Gaudier's eye on the telluric mass of Miss Lowell."[24] Although the dinner was supposedly a celebration of the Imagist anthology, the successive speakers rose to say that they did not know what Imagism was. An altercation broke out between Aldington and Gaudier-Brzeska, which was interrupted when Pound left the room and reappeared carrying a "large tin bathtub." Employing a terrible French pun, he announced that the tub was intended to refer to a line from one of Lowell's poems mentioning bathing as the symbol of a new school of poetry. Fletcher thought that Lowell accepted this calmly, but her break with Pound was imminent.[25]

Lowell, who was wealthy, intended at first to support the Imagists by funding anthologies of their work, but when she would not allow Pound to control the choice of poems, he refused to take part. Accepting his defection, Lowell then excluded Pound from a dinner in her rooms at the Berkeley Hotel, inviting only the Aldingtons, Lawrence, and John Gould Fletcher. These would be the nucleus of the heretical movement that led to Lowell's control of a new path in Imagism and to the series of anthologies published in America, *Some Imagist Poets*.[26]

H.D. and Aldington were present at all of Lowell's meetings, and, together with the others, collaborated trans-Atlantically with her in planning the anthologies. Pound stood aside, refusing to cooperate, but grudgingly admitted the usefulness of the new development and denied that he felt hostility toward it, saying that a family rivalry between himself and the new Imagists might be beneficial. Some years later, lamenting the theft of the Imagist label by these poets, he said that he had meant to announce that the Imagist movement was concluded with the publication of *Des Imagistes*. "Like a damn fool I didn't."[27] In any event, he had now moved on to a new doctrine, Vorticism, which incorporated and extended the Imagist doctrines, but involved a completely new set of collaborators. Together with them, he produced the sensational new journal *Blast*, which announced its aggressive Modernism by placing its title diagonally on its purple cover in huge letters and featuring angular abstractions by Wyndham Lewis.

In August 1915, Pound was now finding other sources of revolutionary ideas in his relations with Wyndham Lewis, Henri Gaudier-Brzeska, and T. S. Eliot. He wrote to Alice Corbin Henderson, the associate editor of *Poetry*, that his Imagist friends were jealous of these new connections and that the Aldington marriage had made it difficult for him to evaluate their work. "At any rate, I wash my hands of the lot of 'em."[28] But he continued to approve of what H.D. was writing and even reprinted her poem "Oread" in the pages of *Blast* in order to illustrate the point that the image was the "primary pigment" of poetry in accordance with Vorticist doctrine.

In later years, Pound freely acknowledged that H.D.'s poems were crucial in the founding of Imagism. He wrote to Glenn Hughes, who was writing a book on the Imagists, that "the name was invented to launch H.D. and Aldington before either had enough stuff for a volume."[29] He later declared that Imagism was formulated to foreground the qualities of H.D.'s poetry, which displayed "a profound, true mytho-poetic sense of nature."[30] H.D.'s comments on the work of Marianne Moore expose a somewhat different idea of poetry and apply perfectly to her own style. She found in Moore's poetry "direct presentation of beauty, clear, cut in flowing lines, but so delicately that the very screen she carves seems meant to stand only in that severe palace of her own world of inspiration—frail, yet as all beautiful things, are, absolutely hard."[31] At about this time, Pound was laying down principles on which he and H.D. would agree for the young poet, Iris Barry. He recommended "compression"—"The force of phrase, and of the single line." In rules similar to the original Imagist statement, he said that "the whole art" was a matter of "concision . . . saying what you mean in the fewest and clearest words" and the need "for creating or constructing something; of presenting an image, or enough images of concrete things arranged to stir the reader." In addition, "simple emotional statements of fact" were permitted.[32]

While Pound and H.D. were in agreement about the general direction poetry should take during the Imagist period, their poetic practices quickly diverged. Pound rarely followed the Imagist principles at this time, but adventured in many fields. In fact, his extremely eclectic output suggests that he lacked a clear sense of direction. He tried his hand at satire in the poems published in *Blast* and in the group, "Moeurs Contemporaines." Among the lyrics of *Lustra* (1913-14) are discursive personal statements, imitations of Japanese and Chinese poetry, and ironic glimpses of contemporary life. Only a handful of superb brief lyrics such as "In a Station of the Metro," "The Return," "April," and "The Coming of War: Actaeon" follow Imagism closely.

Both poets leaned heavily on ancient traditions, but while H.D. lingered in ancient Greece, Pound wandered far afield, investing much of his poetic energy in China with the translations of *Cathay* (1915), in Japan with *Certain Noble Plays of Japan* (1916), and in Rome with *Homage to Sextus Propertius* (1918). He also looked to medieval Provence and contemporary London as well as Greece for his poetic resources. He began work on the *Cantos* as early as August 1915, for in that month he wrote to Alice Corbin Henderson, "I am working on a long poem which will resemble the Divina Commedia in length but in no other manner."[33] The result of this early effort was the "Three Cantos" published serially in *Poetry* in 1917. One of these, the masterly rendering of a Latin version of Homer's account of Odysseus's descent to the underworld, survived to become Canto 1. The other two, written in a chatty Browningesque style, range over Browning's *Sordello*, Catullus, Confucius, Egypt, Botticelli, troubadour tales, Ignez of

Portugal, and a man from Indiana. This "rag-bag," to use Pound's term, often speaks in the first person in a kind of casual conversation with Browning, a style dropped in the final version of the *Cantos*.

All of this work of Pound's contrasts with the sharply restrained poetry H.D. was writing at the time. The poems in *Sea Garden* (1916) and the collection called *The God* hewed to the Imagist line, and Pound acknowledged that they were the best examples of the genre. They seem to confirm his dictum that "There must be intense emotion before language simplifies itself to the point of Imagism."[34] The language of the poems is natural, free of artificial constructions, using nothing, as Pound put it, that could not actually be said. The free verse rhythms do not follow patterns, but are irregular and resourceful, often displacing the stresses, as Pound's verse does, to avoid conventional iambics. H.D. finds it natural to follow Pound's rule "Don't represent, present" and betters his instruction with her inventories of flowers, rocks, branches, landscapes, seascapes, and human figures.

When the Imagist mode was misunderstood as a strictly objective one, Pound vigorously protested. "Imagism of the first book, 'Des Imagistes' NEVER never looking out rather than in."[35] His objection bears on the paradox that Imagist poems have been regarded as coldly impersonal on the one hand, and, especially in H.D.'s case, as suffused with underlying erotic passion on the other. Both views are possible because the poems combine a sharply focused visual effect with a strongly suggested but indeterminate emotional subtext. When the subtext is given priority, it casts a discursive veil over the poem or the image, conflicting with Pound's injunction "don't be viewy."[36]

But the poems published by the two at this time have much in common beyond Imagism. Both poets preferred to live in pagan worlds. They turned to remote and exotic sources of inspiration, pointedly rejecting Christianity. In writing their translations, they shared the view that it was better to capture the spirit of the original than to repeat its literal meaning. The poems of both display a taste for what Pound called "the intaglio method," such sculptural effects as the decisive cut and sharp edge. H.D. pictures a temple as "clean cut, white against white" and says of rose petals, "The night has cut / each from each."

This taste is also reflected in the innovative layout of H.D.'s poems on the page. In a device that recalls Mallarmé's "Un Coup de Dès," the thin printed stream of the poem forms a sharp line between the articulate world of language and the white space on the page, asserting itself bravely against the vacancy that surrounds it. This effect is less prominent in Pound's Imagist poems, but he employed a related one in his poem "In a Station of the Metro," which first appeared in *Poetry* with blank spaces between its phrases:

> The apparition   of these faces   in the crowd:
> Petals   on a wet, black   bough.[37]

Empty space is also eloquent in "Papyrus":

> Spring. . . . . . .
> Too long. . . . . .
> Gongula. . . . . . .[38]

This suggests the surviving fragments of a poem by Sappho and speaks, through its ellipses, of the sadness of loss.

Both poets, working within the Imagist framework, exploit the resources of silence. Situations are presented in sharp images without explanation, so that their significance is left to resonate in the mind of the reader and enters the world he or she inhabits. H.D. enigmatically completes "Hermes of the Ways" in this fashion:

> Hermes, Hermes,
> the great sea foamed,
> gnashed its teeth about me;
> but you have waited,
> where sea-grass tangles with
> shore-grass.[39]

A similar suspension of meaning is characteristic of Pound's image groups. An example appears in the first stanza of "Heather":

The black panther treads at my side,
And above my fingers
There float the petal-like flames.[40]

Pound was to make such abrupt juxtapositions a basic method of
the *Cantos,* while H.D. in her later poetry tended to smooth out
and connect them.

The suggestive juxtaposition of unrelated images, the trope
Pound called "superposition," is a legacy of the international
Modernism of the early century. It was to be one of the chief stylistic characteristics of the *Cantos.* By joining elements considered
irrelevant to each other, the Modernists meant to free language
from the restrictions of rational thought and to reshape the
world, or at least the world of cognition. The Dadaists, whose
movement was founded in 1916, the year *Sea Garden* was published, reacted to the ongoing war that conventional thinking had
produced. They ignored logical coherence and called for anarchic
behavior and works of art that linked things by chance. Their
movement was followed by Surrealism, which tried to outflank
rational thought by drawing fantastic images from such sources as
dreams and automatic writing. The contemporary Futurist movement advocated a fragmentary language that expressed itself
through "analogies" pairing images of totally different categories,
thus hoping, as its leader, F. T. Marinetti, said, to eliminate the
hostility between them.

H.D. titled the group of three novellas she published in 1926
Palimpsest, as if her volume presented a surface on which several
writings or paintings had been superimposed on each other. The
concept seems to refer both to the three separate and apparently
unrelated narratives and to the thought processes of her characters, but it also appears in the structure of her poems. Palimpsest-
like imagery consisting of overlaid but disconnected elements is
persistent in H.D.'s poetry and resembles Pound's superposition
as a technique for evoking new relationships and new unities.
While neither H.D. nor Pound was as radical in using enigmatic
imagery as their Dadaist, Surrealist, or Futurist contemporaries

were, their use of imagery owes something to the rebellious mood of the period.[41] The reader of the later *Cantos* often encounters unexplained spaces between the elements of a metaphor or juxtaposed words. This practice can be interpreted as a kind of tyranny, compelling the reader to accept the poet's eccentric connections, or, on the contrary, as a liberating device that gives the reader the freedom to make his or her own connections, perhaps multiple ones. The latter interpretation would make the *Cantos* a "writerly" text in Barthes's sense, one in which the reader collaborates with the author.

In his "H.D. Book," a series of essays published in various journals beginning in 1966, Robert Duncan dwells on this resemblance between the techniques of the two poets. Writing of the gaps and apertures in Pound's "In a Station of the Metro" and H.D.'s "Heat," Duncan says, "We must discover correspondences in ourselves." He regards imagery of this kind as an aspect of the mysticism he sees in these Imagist poems, saying that their meaning is hidden from the poet as well as the reader, and that they are "links that bind us to the unseen and uncreated." Duncan has this mysticism in mind when he puts such images within a general perspective: "The great art of our time is the collagists's art, to bring all things into new complexes of meaning."[42]

However, their early poems show that Pound and H.D. also shared a belief in the referential power of language, a conviction that places them at odds with postmodern views. Pound advised "Don't represent—present" and emphasized "the application of word to thing." The nondiscursive foregrounding of verbal images seen in the Imagist work of both poets asserts a direct relationship between the word and "the 'thing,' whether subjective or objective," as Pound said in the original "Imagisme" statement. The ambiguity of the New Criticism and the free play or indeterminacy that later deconstructive critics attributed to language are alien to the Imagist dispensation, which called for precision even, or especially, when the words refer to mystical or intuitive experience.

Pound's edition of Ernest Fenollosa's *The Chinese Written Character as a Medium for Poetry* foretells another aspect of the imagery in the early poems of the two poets. It shows that the Chinese characters express actions, that they perform the functions of verbs as well as nouns. In the Imagist poems of both Pound and H.D. the image is usually, though not always, moving or in process. The figures in Pound's "The Return" move "with slow feet . . . Wavering." In "The Coming of War: Actaeon," the sea, while "harsher than granite" is also "unstill, never ceasing." There is movement even in the abrupt, hokku-like "Fan-Piece, For Her Imperial Lord," for the fan and the speaker are "laid aside." H.D.'s Imagist poems are full of vigorous actions and processes, most of them destructive and threatening. Her images are nearly always changing or in motion and these early poems are rich in vivid verbs, many of them violent, such as "slashed," "hurl," trampled," and "splintered and torn." Imagist poems, normally considered static, usually have a subtle narrative element, capturing the dimension of time that Fenollosa attributed to the Chinese character.

What Pound found in Fenollosa's analysis of Chinese was a general idea of the image based on the principle of metaphor, the use of physical imagery to impart elusive relationships and ideas. "The known," wrote Fenollosa, "interprets the obscure, the universe is alive with myth."[43] The principle is perhaps best expressed in W. C. Williams's "No ideas but in things." Pound called this the ideogrammic method, and it appears in the innumerable particulars presented in the *Cantos* and in the actual Chinese characters that begin to confront the reader halfway through the poem.

H.D. also adopted a theory of imagery based on pictographic writing. She did not see Fenollosa's essay until Pound sent her a copy many years later, but she read it with enthusiasm and may well have felt that it corresponded with ideas of her own. But she had earlier found a parallel to her use of imagery in another source. She was strongly impressed by the mystical suggestiveness of the hieroglyphics she saw in Egypt, and regarded the image that conveyed thought through visible objects as a hieroglyph. Both poets found that these alien writing forms were sources of newly discovered meaning, that they were, as Fenollosa said, "alive with myth." Pound, taking the Chinese characters as pictographs, exploited the objects he thought they represented. For example, he treats the ideogram that can be translated as "display," in Canto 74, as a religious sign because it contains elements representing silk, the sun, and grain.

H.D. similarly finds suggested significance in Egyptian hieroglyphics, as she says, in Section 1 of "The Walls Do Not Fall," "the Luxor bee, chick and hare / pursue unalterable purpose . . . they continue to prophesy / from the stone papyrus."[44] In her late poem, *Helen in Egypt,* Helen, seeing the writing in one of the great temples at Luxor, cannot read the "indecipherable Amen-script," even though she recognizes the animal and flower forms in it. But she comes to feel that it tells her own troubled story because it is "as if God made the picture / and matched it / with a living hieroglyph" and that "the riddle of the written stone / suddenly weighs me down."[45] The writing is inscrutable, but it nevertheless says something of importance to the observer who cannot decipher it.

The concepts of ideogram in Pound's thinking and hieroglyph in H.D.'s do not match precisely, but they have much in common as entries to otherwise inaccessible realms of meaning. Their ideas no doubt account for the pictorial and often enigmatic images that characterize all of their work, including their later poems. They offered both poets a way of extending the original Image, which depended on referential language, so that imagery could both "present" (to use Pound's command) and also suggest what cannot be presented. If the details that characterize their styles sometimes seem to be lists of unexplained particulars, it is because they are following, deliberately or otherwise, some of Fenollosa's insights. Objects can be presented directly because they are not inert but parts of a process, and relations between things are more important than the things themselves, as Fenollosa said.

There is, however, a major difference of direction between the two poets, even at this early period. H.D.'s early poetry preserved a persistent style, even in her translations, a style that was immediately recognizable and underwent little variation, while Pound, who believed that the poet should master all the forms, ranged across the centuries and over wide geographical areas, imitating and experimenting with the successful works of the past.

Pound said that his early poetry involved trying out various "masks" or different poetic voices attributed to imagined figures, and the title he used for his volume, *Personae,* marks this as an integral part of a poetic method derived from Browning's dramatic monologues. H.D. used this form in poems titled "Pygmalion" and "Eurydice," and her *Sea Garden* poems are often regarded as impersonal, dissociated from the poet herself, and, as she said, "crystalline." However, their terse, intense surface readily suggests the presence of underlying emotion, as Pound and other critics recognized. H.D. maintained that, in writing poetry, she set her "real self" aside, and that the emotions are those of an imagined poet, a literary device not entirely different from Pound's "masks." However, it seems clear that they are drawn from the real woman's mind and are reflections of her own emotional experiences. Whether the feelings expressed are those of H.D. or her poetic self, she distances them by embodying them in landscape and flower imagery, and by attaching them to figures from the Greek myths.

These contrasts are perhaps related to the fact that the two poets had different relations to the literary and artistic revolutions of the time. In embracing Imagism, Pound was embarking on a reform of English poetry. He was far more responsive than H.D. to the revisionary Modernism that was sweeping the arts in the first two decades of the century. It was a time when artists of all kinds were feeling the validity of Clive Bell's doctrine that the essential quality of art was "significant form." Pound had conceived of Imagism as a Modernist "movement" that would rival the Symbolism and Cubism of France; he was deeply immersed in the work of such graphic artists as Wyndham Lewis, Jacob Epstein, and Gaudier-Brzeska, and he learned much from the work of other writers such as T. S. Eliot and James Joyce.

H.D., while fully sharing Pound's conviction that new forms were needed for the new times, did not include the contemporary world in her Imagist poetry. She did not observe the superficialities of social life, as Pound did, or, with few exceptions, take up urban themes, as Eliot did. The environment of her early poems is nearly exclusively that of ancient Greece, and it achieves a strange and effective blending of traditional Greek settings with the directness and individualism of the Modern spirit.

While H.D. employed imagery as an expression of feeling, an element, as Pound observed, that was absent from his own work, Pound himself assigned a more cosmic function to imagery. As we have seen, he thought of the image as impersonal, as giving a "sense of sudden liberation . . . of freedom from time limits and space limits" and generating "that sense of sudden growth which we experience in the presence of the greatest works of art." And he added solemnly, "It is better to present one Image in a lifetime than to produce voluminous works."[46] When he turned to the new movement of Vorticism in 1914, he retained the Image as a central resource for the poet, but described it now as something dynamic, a "vortex" of constantly moving ideas.

H.D.'s images in *Sea Garden* and *The Gods* do not make these pretensions. They recall Hulme's recommendation that the poet limit himself or herself to images that are "small" and "dry" by emphasizing common things seen close at hand, and function with great exactitude to express intimate personal feeling. As H.D.'s Pygmalion says, "I made image upon image for my use."

Many of H.D.'s most sympathetic critics do not accept her claim that her poems are distinct from her own feelings. Robert Duncan, who sensed in H.D.'s supposedly frigid Imagism "ardor for the truth of what is felt and thought," perceived an underlying eroticism in poems of the kind H.D. reluctantly showed Pound in the tearoom. He notes that "Orchard," which reads in part "I fell prostrate / crying: / you have flayed us," originally had the title "Priapus," the name of the phallic god of fertility, when it appeared in *Poetry*. He comments: "the nature poems of H.D. . . . . betray in their troubled ardor processes of psychological and even sexual identification."[47] Janice S. Robinson feels that Pound himself is the subject of H.D.'s tearoom poems. According to Robinson, "Orchard," which mockingly asks, "spare us from loveliness," and seeks to propitiate the god with broken fruits is a reply to the romanticism of Pound's troubadours. She also identifies Pound as the figure in "Hermes of the Ways," a poem in which the god faces three ways and waits patiently.[48] Many of her images, as we have seen, depict violence and destruction, perhaps reflecting the feelings of loss, frustration, and rejection that H.D. suffered during the war years.

There is a strain of H.D.'s production that seems to answer a demand made by Rebecca West in an article titled "Imagisme," which appeared in the *New Freewoman* in 1913: "Poetry should be burned to the bone by austere fires and washed white with rains of affliction: the poet should love nakedness and thought of the skeleton under the flesh."[49] The poems of this period, which established her style, no doubt refer to H.D.'s unhappy relations with Aldington, but it seems likely that some, at least, were generated by Pound's defection. Further evidence that the poems had a personal significance and were connected with Pound is offered by Susan Stanford Friedman's view that their images of fruit and heat are "encoded allusions to ripening sexuality," whose eroticism becomes clear when they reappear in the sexual scenes of H.D.'s autobiographical novel *HERmione*.[50] Since the heroine's lover, George, is a fictional counterpart of Pound, the elusive erotic subtext of these early poems must relate to him. And they were, in fact, written at a time when H.D. still expected that Pound might marry her and seem to reflect her sense of loss at her growing separation from him. This feeling is piercingly expressed in "The Helmsman," whose speaker has wandered far inland but implores the Helmsman to "be swift—/ we have always known you wanted us."[51]

In spite of the different directions in the development of the two poets who wrote under the Imagist aegis, there are underlying parallels that were to emerge more clearly in their later poems, where they tended to exchange poetic modes. In the *Pisan Cantos,* Pound was to turn to the genre of self-revelation and self-exploration, and H.D., in her long works, *Trilogy* and *Helen in Egypt,* would deal with war and other themes that were at least, in part, external to her emotional life.

3

The First War

Into this city from the shining lowlands
Blows a wind that whispers of uncovered skulls . . .
W. H. Auden, "At the Grave of Henry James"

When Great Britain declared war on Germany on 4 August 1914, war inserted itself as a pivotal theme in the lives and works of both poets. Both remained in England throughout the war and underwent profoundly different experiences during wartime.

For more than a year, most English people thought of World War I as a test of honor and courage, and the ranks of the army were filled by volunteers who expected to find glory in battle. The national attitude toward the war changed in 1916, after the disastrous Somme offensive, which produced many casualties, and when conscription was introduced. Recognition of the horrors and destructiveness of war replaced the old idea that it was an opportunity for noble sacrifice, and the new feelings were fully exposed in the classic war poetry of Siegfried Sassoon, Wilfred Owen, and Isaac Rosenberg. Many novels of the postwar period, including Aldington's *Death of a Hero*, expressed profound disillusionment with the war and its results.

The two expatriate American poets did not consider the war to be a noble cause, and when Rupert Brooke, the leading poetic spokesman of the war spirit, died in 1915, Pound's comments about him referred only to his poetry, not to his patriotism. War itself was the subject of a silent disagreement between Pound and H.D. Pound's early poems display no objection to violence. The speaker of "Sestina: Altaforte," published in the 1909 volume called *Exultations*, begins "Damn it all! This our South stinks peace," and Pound displays considerable admiration for the leaders of fifteenth-century Italian wars who appear in the *Cantos* written postwar in the early 1920s. His Vorticism owed a certain debt to the Italian Futurist movement, which openly glorified war, and the Vorticist journal, *Blast*, whose first issue appeared in the summer of 1914, just before the outbreak of hostilities, reflected the aestheticization of violence that characterized both movements. H.D. objected to this attitude, and thought of the war as a point of departure for working toward a future when the value of the poetic calling would be justified.[1]

Perhaps foreseeing what was coming, Pound wrote loftily in 1913, "War is a mess and a bother. It is, between nations of equal civilisation, an anachronism."[2] When the war came, he simply stuck to his last. His literary projects expanded and prospered, perhaps because others were at the front or occupied with matters of national defense. He was able to continue his prodigious literary and editorial activities, and to correspond regularly with America and the Continent, very much as if no war was going on. In January 1915, about six months after the start of hostilities, his contributions to the *New Age* were articles on the Vorticist sculptors and Imagism, and discussions of such aesthetic elements as "rhythm" and "pattern." His 1915 poem "The Coming of War: Actaeon" reduces the idea of war to a group of striking but abstract images.

He had less and less to do with H.D., who was preoccupied with many troubles but continued to write poems that embodied the Imagist principles. He contributed a steady stream of prose and verse to a variety of publications, especially the *Egoist, Poetry, New Age, Blast,* and the *Little Review.* He also recruited writers for these journals, read and revised innumerable manuscript contributions, and cultivated the financial support of John Quinn through letters. He continued his study of Chinese and the Fenollosa papers, wrote the translations of *Cathay,* and published Fenollosa's notes on Japanese drama as *Noh or Accomplishment* and *Certain Noble Plays of Japan.* He carried on his work on the early *Cantos* and published the three preliminary ones in *Poetry,* as well as a volume of verse, *Lustra,* and the collection of writings called *Pavannes and Divisions.* His activities included energetic efforts to publicize the work of numerous new artists and writers, including Iris Barry, T. S. Eliot, Robert Frost, Gaudier-Brzeska, Jacob Epstein, Joyce, and Wyndham Lewis. Early in the wartime years, he began a study of the occult under the guidance of Yeats, and later became acquainted with Major C. H. Douglas and his economic theories, which grew into a lifelong obsession.

All of this and more in the way of miscellaneous essays, introductions, self-education, and editing was done before the Armistice was signed in November 1918. While the war was on, Pound objected to it on the ground that it interfered with cultural exchange ("War is a mess and a bother"), and as late as the summer of 1917, his censure of Germany went no further than criticism of its over-specialized system of education. He had had reason for more serious objection when Gaudier-Brzeska was killed at the front in the summer of 1915. Even that led to something productive, however: an appreciation of Gaudier's work that is also an important Vorticist source, *Gaudier-Brzeska: A Memoir,* published during wartime, in 1916. Hulme met his death in France in 1917, and Pound mentioned the event years later in the *Cantos.*

Pound was so active in encouraging continued interest in poetry and art during the war years that Iris Barry was fully justified in titling her 1936 article on him "The Ezra Pound Period."[3] In it, she described how Pound, in addition to his prolific writing, drew people active in art and literature together in restaurants for weekly dinners in his campaign to keep the pulse of civilization beating.

While the war seems to have stimulated Pound's energies and widened his interests, it affected H.D. in an opposite way, for her life, unlike Pound's, was seriously disrupted by it. After her marriage and the outbreak of hostilities, she was afflicted by a series of emotionally damaging misfortunes. In May 1915, she bore a child who died at birth, and Aldington, after enlisting in the army, was unfaithful to her while she lived at Corfe Castle in Dorsetshire (in order to be near his training camp) and at 44 Mecklenburgh Square in London. As her novel *Bid Me to Live* shows, H.D. herself had a passionate and painful relationship at this time with D. H. Lawrence.

Her emotional life was sufficiently confused. She and Aldington professed to believe in "free love," and she passively accepted an affair Aldington pursued with Dorothy Yorke, an American known as "Arabella," while all three were living at Mecklenburgh Square, just as Aldington was to accept H.D.'s later liaison with Cecil Gray. While he was away at the front, Aldington repeatedly asserted his devotion to H.D., but also acknowledged that he was attached to Dorothy Yorke. "I love you so much that it is an agony, " he wrote. "I love Arabella. This is really madness."[4]

Somehow, during Aldington's absence in France in March 1918, H.D. allowed herself to move into a cottage in Cornwall with the composer, Cecil Gray. The affair quickly cooled into indifference on the part of both, and when H.D. learned that she was pregnant, Gray had already gone to London and did not see her or Perdita, the daughter who was born in March 1919, until many years later.

There were other shocks. H.D.'s brother, Gilbert, was killed in France in 1918, and her father, stricken with grief, died soon after. Aldington, no doubt conscious of his own infidelities, was at first remarkably acquiescent about H.D.'s pregnancy, agreeing, at first, to accept the child as his and to make an arrangement that would allow mother and child to live with him. He continued to encourage her and edit her poetry, for in spite of her personal misfortunes during the war, H.D. managed to remain active creatively, writing poems and translations of Sappho and Euripides, and replacing Aldington for a time as an assistant editor of the *Egoist* when he enlisted in the army. After the war, as "Arabella" pressed him to make arrangements to marry her, Aldington became hostile. He met with H.D. at a French hotel to decide how their family life would proceed, but there was no agreement and they separated permanently. By 1919, therefore, the traumas of the wartime years had wrecked whatever emotional equilibrium H.D. had achieved in the Imagist period.

There was, however, one positive development in the war years. It was while H.D. was living in Cornwall with Gray that Bryher first came to see her, initiating the lifelong relationship between the two women.

Bryher, whose real name was Winifred Ellerman, had taken her pseudonym from one of the Scilly Isles and used it as her official name. She was the daughter of a wealthy industrialist and had a practical interest in business matters herself. One of the first admirers of Imagist poetry, she kept up with the Imagist publications and exchanged letters with Amy Lowell. She memorized the poems in *Sea Garden,* wrote to ask H.D. if she might visit, and came to the Cornwall cottage on 17 July 1918, a date whose anniversary the two celebrated in later years.

Her friendship with Bryher was the most stable and permanent of H.D.'s relationships. A confirmed lesbian who consciously wished she had been a boy, Bryher fell desperately in love with H.D. and planned that they would live together. In 1919 she rescued H.D. from the lodging where she was living, pregnant and dangerously ill, and installed her in the nursing home where Perdita was born. Their lives began to be inseparably entwined as H.D. agreed to allow Bryher to care for her child, as she and the baby visited the Ellerman home, and as she went with Bryher on a holiday to the Scilly Islands.

Bryher and H.D. remained partners until the poet's death. Their relationship, beginning with an attraction in which the two, though differing in temperament, felt a strong identification with each other, survived many separations, attachments to other lovers, and times of disaffection. Bryher despised both Aldington and Pound; she felt that the latter patronized her, and he complained that she had somehow interfered with his projects. In spite of her wealth, she generally lived modestly, but she supported H.D. generously, financed her publications, paid for her sessions with Freud, and in 1940 granted her a large sum that gave her a lifelong income. She was also openhanded with other writers and assisted Jewish refugees in their flight from Nazism during World War II. She published the distinguished literary journal *Life and Letters Today,* where some of H.D.'s work appeared, and pursued a vigorous and independent literary career, producing translations from the Greek, novels, memoirs, and book reviews. When Perdita married and had children, Bryher took an interest in the family as though it was her own.

Both poets were personally sheltered from violence during the war, but there were striking exceptions as the effects of the war reached them indirectly and were reflected in their writing. The autobiographical narrator of H.D.'s novel *Asphodel* feels that daily life in England is completely corrupted by the distant war, that it is a "vast wash of débris and death and filth." The melancholy tone of many of the poems in *Sea Garden* and other poems written at this time may well be attributable to the unsettled conditions of wartime and to H.D.'s relations with Pound and the unfaithful Aldington. One poem, "Loss," while not an antiwar poem, does express a mood of sorrow about the effects of combat, as its speaker, one of the few survivors of a battle, mourns the death of a warrior-lover.

Among the translations H.D. wrote at this time was a passage from Euripides' *Iphigenia in Aulis,* which is significant as her first treatment of the Trojan war, a subject that was to become much more prominent in her later poetry, as well as a theme of the *Cantos.* If the passage had any relation to the contemporary war, its message was a complex one. The chorus of women is moved to admiration by the sight of the Greek heroes and their ships ("This beauty is too much / For any woman"), and the women look forward to the sacrifice of Iphigenia as a way of assuring the defeat of Troy. The chorus is followed by the lamentations of Iphigenia, who is nevertheless proud of her rôle as a sacrificial victim, and it ends as the women celebrate the hope that victory will bring honor to the Greek captain, Agamemnon. Even if H.D. chose this passage as a commentary on contemporary hostilities, the voice that is heard is not that of twentieth-century protest, but that of a fatalist from antiquity who acknowledges the power of the gods.

Only a few of Pound's poems of the time expose his direct response to the war. In the second issue of *Blast*, published in the summer of 1915, a poem denouncing the unofficial censorship practiced by editors unexpectedly closes with what may well be an allusion to the recent death of Gaudier-Brzeska: "the loveliest die, / That is the path of life, that is my forest." Characteristically, Pound regarded the deaths of others as a personal misfortune. "Poem: Abbreviated from the Conversation of Mr. T. E. H." tells us that he learned something about war conditions directly from Hulme. It briefly describes a scene from the front and concludes with "There is nothing to do but keep on," expressing the attitude that Pound, and no doubt Hulme himself, adopted. Pound's awareness of the hardships of war is suggested by his choice of three war poems for his 1915 volume of Chinese translations, *Cathay*. These are spoken by soldiers complaining of hardships and injustice, and frequently seem relevant to the ongoing war:

> Who has brought the army with drums and with kettle-drums?
> Barbarous kings . . .
> And sorrow, sorrow like rain,
> Sorrow to go, and sorrow, sorrow returning.[5]

A more emphatic condemnation of the war appeared in *Hugh Selwyn Mauberley*, where Pound wrote contemptuously that "Daring as never before, wastage as never before" occurred "For two gross of broken statues, / For a few thousand battered books."[6] Pound, always the guardian and interpreter of past civilizations, would nevertheless not accept the defense of culture as a justification for the horrors of the war. However, the note of protest is absent from the *Cantos* written in the early 1920s that deal with the fifteenth-century wars of Sigismundo Malatesta. Here the war theme has become a source of images, colorful "gists and piths," as Pound called significant details, a platform for the glorification of his hero, Sigismundo, and an element in a mosaic of contrasting poetic passages.

The incursion of war into the art and poetry of the Modernist period threatened the dominance of Modernist principles. Pound and H.D., like many of their contemporary artists, strove toward an ideal of abstract form free of temporal influences, an aesthetic perfection achieved without the support of its subject matter. Pound saw in Brancusi's polished ovoids "pure form free from all terrestrial gravitation; form as free in its own life as the form of the analytic geometers."[7] Two mid-century philosophers, E. H. Gombrich and Susanne Langer, later gave strong philosophical support to the Modernist view that the form of an artwork speaks more powerfully than its content. However, neither H.D. nor Pound could achieve quite this level of dissociation, and their poems on the war theme correspond more closely to the situation described by Monroe Spears:

> there are two primary impulses in modern literature, both always present, but one or the other dominating, The first is the drive toward aestheticism, toward the purification of form, its refinement and exploration . . . there is a tendency for the art-world to become separate and independent from life. This is countered by the opposing impulse, to break through art, destroy any possibility of escape to illusion, to insist that the immediate experience, the heightening of life is the important thing.[8]

Spears's example is Joyce's *Ulysses,* and Canto 16 can also be seen as a work in which this conflict occurs. The Canto begins by continuing the theme of the preceding Hell Cantos with a description of a landscape before the mouth of hell based both on Dante's *Inferno* and on Blake's illustrations for it.[9] The scene is one of torment and corruption, a "limbo of chopped ice and sawdust." It includes "a lake of bodies, aqua morta" from whose surface living arms and embryonic forms emerge, side by side with fish and eels. The text then switches without transition to a serene, extravagantly peaceful lakeside scene. The poet enters "the quiet air / the new sky" and sees the heroes of his Pantheon and water nymphs weaving garlands. It is while lying asleep in the grass of this delicious place that he hears voices telling of war, coming as a kind of nightmare reality to interrupt his visit to Paradise — perhaps another dream.

Reportorial impressions of war enter the Canto as these "voices" of witnesses recounting anecdotes of combat are heard.

They include Victor Plarr, an acquaintance of Pound's, who relays information about the Franco-Prussian war, and an anonymous narrator repeating an "old admiral's" account of Byron's funeral during a Greek rebellion against the Turks. Then there is a much closer approach to actual experience as Pound, in his own voice, tells of friends who fought in World War I: Aldington, Gaudier-Brzeska, Hulme, Lewis, Hemingway, and others. Though some of these figures experienced death or suffering, the tone of this passage is far from indignant. It ranges from the matter-of-fact to irony and bawdy humor.

There follows the most remarkable passage of the Canto, the monologue of a French soldier, said to be the painter Fernand Léger, looking back at his war experiences, some horrifying, some ironic. He recalls "Les hommes de 34 ans à quatre pattes / qui criaient 'maman.'" In a convincingly colloquial style that is self-interrupting, staccato, and not entirely coherent, the speaker complains and praises, but his mood, in the end, is one of resignation as he states, without comment: "Liste officielle des morts 5,000,000."

But the war recitals do not end the Canto. They are followed by another slice of life, a voice in the dialect of an illiterate or foreign speaker telling of the reproaches brought against a Bolshevik for Trotsky's rôle in signing a peace treaty with the Germans in the midst of World War I. Another voice then describes Lenin giving a speech and a bloody scene from the Russian revolution. Finally, the Canto turns to rumors about the battlefield that were heard, with exquisite irony, "at the opera."

While the war stories seem to demand direct emotional response, they also participate in the Canto's formal organization, for its incongruous parts do form a kind of thematic design. The hell-mouth scene, with its lake of bodies, and the war stories are parallels, offering two aspects of the same theme. The vision of Paradise can be seen as an ironic prelude to the Utopian promise of the Russian revolution. The two subjects of world war and revolution unite in a condemnation of violence. Further, the tripartite division, in which hell and paradise are followed by a kind of limbo of war and politics, reflects the structure of the *Divine*

Comedy, one of the models for the *Cantos.* Canto 16 is further shaped by being shared out among "voices" that offer a diversity of contrasting tones and feelings. Pound has certainly not allowed aesthetic demands to shield the reader from the horrors of the war, but the war has also become a part of the poem's design, and if the two purposes are not completely integrated with each other, the effect corresponds with the irregularity of the *Cantos* as a whole.

While H.D. did not deal directly with the war, she did refer to it obliquely in poems about war in general. Adopting a method corresponding in some sense to the way in which Pound set the war within a poetic design, she wrote of wars taking place in some period of ancient history. "Loss," for example, deals with the aftermath of a defeat in a setting that must be ancient Greece. The speaker, apparently a woman, recalls details of combat and the noble appearance of her lover, who has now been drowned. She has tried to protect him during the battle, but realizes that "the gods wanted you back."

"The Tribute," written in 1916, is more clearly a protest against war and its debilitating effects on civilization. Though it employs the imagery of an ancient Greek town, it certainly seems to be inspired by wartime conditions in England. The speaker laments the "squalor" of the marketplace, the loss of the city's boys ("the lads who went to slay"), the departure of the happy gods, and the dominance of "one tall god with a spear shaft, / one bright god with a lance." But the speaker asserts that beauty will outlast violence and the viewpoint expands to include a scene that clearly refers to the war front, where "the crowd of the millions meet / to shout and slay." The youths, who have been sent "to strike at each other's strength," will preserve beauty and they are told that "it is you who have kept her alight."[10]

Unlike Canto 16, H.D.'s poetry of protest against World War I is heavily disguised, as if lifted from some Greek myth. Even in the face of modern war, she felt that her late-Greek poetic idiom was appropriate for the Modern age. While this parallels Pound's belief in the relevance of the past, it runs counter to his principle of diversifying and updating poetic resources. On the other hand,

Pound's form-conscious use of the war theme corresponds to some extent to H.D.'s assertion in "The Tribute" that war might be needed to preserve beauty, and that the survival of art is essential to the survival of civilization. The failure of both poets to protest its horrors as openly as did the war poets means not that they were indifferent but rather that they offered the aesthetic qualities of their art as an antidote to aggressive passions. They employed the theme of war for poetic purposes in an effort to demonstrate that art could survive and even conquer its destructiveness.

While war is never entirely absent from the selections of European and Chinese history in the *Cantos* written during the inter-war period, the most significant reversions to the theme by both poets came with World War II. We will return to it with Pound's *Pisan Cantos* and H.D.'s *Trilogy* and *Helen in Egypt*. The first war made only a slight appearance in their poems. But the second, which engulfed their personal lives, dominated the major poems of their mature years.

4

Postwar Years

There is nothing in life except what one thinks of it.
Wallace Stevens, "Adagia"

The Armistice, which was so great a benefaction for the rest of the world, began a time of trouble for both poets. "The years between," wrote H.D. in 1944, as she looked back at this time, "seemed a period of waiting, of marking time. There was a feeling of stagnation, of lethargy, clearly evident among many of my own contemporaries."[1] Pound was undergoing the disillusionment with his prospects in England that is recorded in *Hugh Selwyn Mauberley*. After moving back to London early in 1919, H.D., long troubled by her marital difficulties, was wrung by conflicting emotions caused by the succession of traumatic events that had occurred during and after the war.

While Bryher assumed the dual role of H.D.'s protector and acolyte, Aldington, who continued to work with her on her writing, now withdrew from her, refusing to take responsibility for her or her child, and the relations between the two became painfully rancorous.

H.D.'s relationship with Pound naturally fell into the background at this time. In November 1918, when both Imagism and the war were ending, she wrote to Amy Lowell, "I don't *really* feel friendly with E.P. nor does R.—he just does not matter."[2] But about five months later, when H.D. was about to give birth to Perdita, Pound showed that he had not relinquished his hold on her by coming to the nursing home and declaring that he was sorry that the child was not his.

As H.D. describes this scene in *End to Torment*, Pound appeared at the nursing home at a time of "grave crisis in my life" to declare, "my only real criticism is that this is not my child." She reports that he beat his stick against the wall, an action whose linguistic significance she characteristically emphasized— "pounding, pounding (*Pounding*)"—and which reminded her of his behavior in the taxi when he had taken her away from Frances Gregg and her husband at another time of "grave crisis."[3]

In the spring of 1919 the two poets left London, traveling in different directions. Pound and Dorothy went to France in April and toured sites in southern France connected with the troubadours and the Albigensian heresy, while H.D. went with Bryher to Cornwall and the Scilly Islands. It was a permanent separation and closed a phase of their relationship that had a formative influence on H.D. But her attachment to Pound remained strong.

By September, Pound and H.D. were back in London, and the difficulties of the triangle they formed with Aldington emerged. When H.D. and Aldington tried unsuccessfully to negotiate some solution to their marital difficulties, Aldington begged to have Pound excluded. "Ezra makes me shut up and say nothing and retire behind forty barriers!" he complained.[4] There was a definite parting between H.D. and Aldington in April, when it was agreed that he would stay with Dorothy Yorke. When both Aldington and Pound came later in the year to see H.D. in her Kensington flat, she did not want to see either.

In her unpublished novel, "The Sword Went Out to Sea," H.D. briefly covers her relations with Pound during the postwar years in summary fashion. "Flint," she said, referring to the character based on Pound, urged her to leave England, wanted a new life, went with his wife to Paris, and finally settled in Italy (she makes it Venice rather than Rapallo) in search of "lost beauty." The passage, which closely tracks her real feelings, records her "shock" when he supported Mussolini, attributes it to his need for an income, and says that she stopped writing to him or thinking about him because of his bigotry toward "non-Aryan races."

While H.D. and Pound were no longer in touch with each other, they continued to invent Modern poetry in separate ways, though there were fundamental similarities in their methods. Both wrote in the new free verse forms and adopted severely economical, paratactic styles that continued the Imagist tradition of communicating through images without discursive links. Both employed the method of associating discrete elements to generate meaning through contrast or resemblance, a device that appears as "palimpsest" in H.D.'s works and "superposition" in Pound's.

Both also promoted cultural transmission through translation, though Pound worked with Latin, Chinese, and Provençal and H.D. with Greek. And both moved from the lyrics or dramatic monologues of their early years to epic forms, Pound beginning as early as 1915 with the first Cantos, and H.D. waiting until the 1960s to write *Helen in Egypt*. Both wrote much prose, H.D. in the form of novels, stories, memoirs, and reviews; and Pound in the form of criticism, reviews, and political and economic comment.

In spite of her postwar troubles, H.D. continued to write productively. She and Aldington were in violent disagreement in their personal lives, but they worked together on poetry as if they conducted their writing lives on an entirely different plane. Aldington carefully corrected translations from the *Iphigenia in Aulis* and *Hippolytus* of Euripides that H.D. contributed to the series of pamphlets called the *Poets' Translation Series*, which he had begun to edit for the Egoist Press while he was still serving in the army. These translations are marked both by Imagism and by H.D.'s distinctive style. They are admirably concise, sparing of adjectives, exposing the force of individual words in brief sentences and H.D.'s characteristic short lines.

In the war years, Pound had written translations or near-translations in the first two Cantos — the first from a Latin version of the *Odyssey*, the second from a passage in Ovid's *Metamorphoses* —

and now produced "Homage to Sextus Propertius," a suite of selections translated from the elegies of the Roman poet of the first
century B.C. When he turned to original composition in Canto 3,
he settled upon the method of superposition that was to dominate
the whole of the poem, as he juxtaposed materials from many different sources with each other. He now broke definitively with the
conversational tone of the rejected "Three Cantos," as he reworked his poem, getting as far as Canto 7 before the end of 1919.

The *Cantos*, as they developed in the 1920s, might be seen as a
reply of sorts to H.D.'s conception of Modern poetry. As we have
seen, she thought of her period as "Alexandrine," a time for poets
to refine techniques and seek delicacy and brevity. Her poetry
adopted this model and also maintained the atmosphere of Hellenistic verse, when it did not imitate it or translate it directly, even
in her few poems about war. But the *Cantos* went in an entirely different direction, ebulliently scouring wide ranges of history and
geography, including the present, and exploiting a variety of dialects and languages. Materials from troubadour lore, Catullus,
Ovid, Dante, Italian history, Pound's own experiences, and many
other sources introduce significant thematic patterns, ranging over
a wide variety of emotive effects. The contrasts with the focused,
poised tones of H.D.'s poems and translations are striking. In the
future, H.D. was to stick to ancient Greece as her inspiration, with
a few departures in the direction of such related fields as Egyptian
myth, and, of course, wrote in English nearly exclusively. Pound,
on the other hand, constantly expanded the content of the *Cantos*,
bringing material from American history, Chinese culture, English law, and many other sources into his wandering poem and
salting his text with colorful ventures into a number of other languages. A new phase of the dialogue had begun, as the two poets
turned to different historical sources and proposed entirely different styles for the poetic idiom appropriate to Modern poetry.

H.D. and Pound continued to go their separate ways after 1919, as
they would for the rest of their lives. In that year, H.D. made her

first serious entry into an occult world that she was to visit often, and which appeared prominently in her poetry. While visiting the Scilly Islands with Bryher, she had what she described as a visionary or out-of-body experience. In this state, she felt slightly removed from reality and enclosed by an abnormal state of consciousness she called the "over-mind."

Her proclivity for extrasensory experiences emerged again in an event she later recounted to Freud. In February 1920, while she was on a voyage to Greece with Bryher and Havelock Ellis as companions, she had something between a dream and a vision involving a figure who both did and did not resemble an acquaintance on the ship and who seemed to be associated both with her father and with D. H. Lawrence. Freud was much interested, and thought the event had psychological significance.

While traveling with Bryher, H.D. experienced another vision, the "writing on the wall" episode in Corfu, which she described many years later in *Tribute to Freud*. On the wall of her hotel room she saw mysterious shapes related to her obsession with Greece, and enigmatic lines and dashes. The series of vivid visions, partly shared by Bryher, was a decisive episode in her psychic life. When she told Freud about this experience, which took place in Greece, the country of Helen of Troy, the namesake of H.D.'s mother, he interpreted it as a desire for union with the mother, and therefore a dangerous symptom.

While H.D. was beginning to explore the occult world in this way, Pound and Dorothy, still based in London, went on holiday to Venice and Sirmione. It was at Sirmione, in May of that year, that the famous first meeting between Joyce and Pound took place. After a visit to Paris, Pound was back in London, writing the series of articles called "Island of Paris," which reflected his growing discontent with England and foreshadowed his move to the French capital.

In June 1920, Pound published a more significant expression of his dissatisfaction with his London life in *Hugh Selwyn Mauberley*, a poetic sequence that embodies many of the methods of Modernist poetry. It is discontinuous, made up of sections varied in style, meter, and subject, refers consistently to other texts through imitation or quotations, and can be seen as a unity only if the reader perceives the underlying themes that bring the various poems together. One of these themes, a discontent with "the age," is fairly clear from the beginning of the sequence and reflects Pound's disappointment at his failure to continue impressing the English public.

At the beginning of 1921, Pound had definitely decided to leave London, and he and Dorothy went back to France, apparently in search of a new home. After some months on the Riviera, he moved to Paris, which was to be his base until his departure for Rapallo in 1925. This was the period when many American writers frequented Paris in search of alcohol, adventure, and artistic freedom, mingling with the leaders of France's vigorous cultural life. As usual, Pound made it his business to meet as many resident artists and writers as possible, including Picasso, Gertrude Stein, Ernest Hemingway, Jean Cocteau, Constantine Brancusi, Francis Picabia, James Joyce (who had moved to Paris at his suggestion), and many others.

Against this background, Pound also encountered many of the transient Americans and Englishmen who gravitated to Paris while he was there, including old friends such as William Carlos Williams, Wyndham Lewis, T. S. Eliot, Robert McAlmon, and H.D. Some of the Americans led active and sometimes rowdy social lives in the cafés and restaurants, but they also frequented Sylvia Beach's Shakespeare and Company bookshop, which specialized in English-language books. Pound ventured into musical composition and wrote his opera, *The Testament of Villon*, as well as Cantos 8 to 16, while he lived there. A new phase of his life began about the beginning of 1923, when he met Olga Rudge, a talented American concert violinist. At that time, Pound was thirty-six and had been married for nine years, and Rudge was twenty-seven. A friendship that began with musical activities in which Pound acted as manager, publicist, and a contributor of his own compositions, soon became a love affair and a passionate lifelong relationship. Rudge gave birth to Pound's daughter, Mary, in 1925, and since neither parent felt able to care for the child, she was sent to live with a farm family in the Tyrol, where she was raised. Both Rudge and her daughter were to become significant figures in H.D.'s imaginative life.[5]

During these years, H.D. was traveling widely and visiting sites that were to appear in her writing. The 1920 trip to Greece had been followed by a journey to America with Bryher, where they met Amy Lowell and Marianne Moore in the East, before visiting California. While they were in New York, William Carlos Williams introduced them to Robert McAlmon, a young writer from the Midwest who had published some verses in *Poetry*. Bryher wrote to him from California and arranged a marriage of convenience, which took place on her return in 1921. They were to live on Bryher's money and she could assure her parents that she was not without protection.

When the trio returned to Europe, they lived in Switzerland at the Riant Château, a lodging house in Territet, near Montreux. In 1922 H.D. and Bryher went on a series of tours, through Italy to Greece again and then, in 1923, to Egypt, where they were present at the time King Tut's tomb was opened with much publicity. The Egyptian visit left a deep impression on H.D. She included the Egyptian gods in her pantheon, linked the hieroglyphics she saw to the imagery of poetry and dreams, and used the setting of the great temples at Luxor for her poem, *Helen in Egypt*.

The fact that H.D. continued to evaluate her relationship with Pound is clear from the lyric "Toward the Piraeus," which is clearly addressed to him. It appeared in the 1923 volume, *Heliodora*, but was probably written some years earlier. The title may be seen as a defiant response to Pound's disapproval of her view of Greece, for in heading toward the disorderly seaport that is the entry to Athens, rather than to Athens itself, H.D. seems to be saying that she is determined to depend on her version of Greece for inspiration. Accordingly, some of the poems of *Heliodora* are derived from intensely emotional texts of Sappho, Plato, and Meleager. Its prologue asks to share the strength of a "passionate Greek"; though no gender is indicated, it seems likely that this

Greek is Sappho, whose powers, the poet believes, are capable of prevailing over cowardice and weakness.

That passion is part of the ambiguous and enigmatic attitude the poem adopts toward Pound. Feeling rises to the intensity of pain and violence as it is expressed with such words as "break," "scattered," and "rent with ecstasy." The poem is addressed to one who has played a dubious part in the poet's creative life. The poet feels that he understood and "sheltered" her and made her distinctive, but also took possession of her song: an accusation that, taken literally, seems to refer to Pound's labeling her poems as Imagist and making them a part of his movement. The first section ends with the fragmentary line, "If I escape your evil heart," a resentful, yet inconclusive wish.

The second section begins abruptly, "I loved you." Nevertheless, the poet is afraid to say the word, comparing herself to celebrants waiting in fear as they feel the threatening rumble of the earth under their temple. The first sentence here is in the past tense. But when she associates herself with the imagery of the temple, the poet speaks in the present, as though her feelings are still in suspension and she is still suffering from them. A curious section of painfully short and intermittently rhyming lines then speculates on what joys and inventions might have come about "had you been true," or "If you were great." Deviousness is a part of this subject's character. He was lost in "circumventing" men's tricks, and he caused the poet sorrow by "curious lies."

H.D.'s desire to evade sexual relations with Pound appears as she supposes herself to be a boy who adores his leader and stands aside as he indulges his passion, but comes to him later to give him hands that are "intolerably cold and sweet." In a final section, she declares that she rejected him, not to preserve her chastity but out of fear that her "lesser" power would be "overmatched" by his.

Painful tensions mark this poem. The poet addressed is "evil," "skilled to yield death-blows," yet "I loved you." Declaring that love is ended and rejecting sex, it paradoxically identifies the tree with which H.D., the Dryad, was associated with the woman, "tall like the cypress tree," who takes her place as the subject's lover. There is no suggestion that the poet who is writing owes any part of her art to the poet she addresses. On the contrary, her "weapon" has been "tempered in a different heat." But this image, together with the aggressive language of the prologue suggests that she regards their writing as a kind of contest, if not an actual conflict.

H.D. came to Paris in the spring of 1924 to join Bryher, and no doubt saw Pound casually from time to time, for there are two accounts of actual encounters or near-encounters. Robert McAlmon's memoirs of Paris record an anecdote about a dinner party where Pound embarrassed Harriet Weaver by an awkward joke and where H.D. was among the company. Afterward, according to McAlmon, H.D. said, "I haven't seen dear old Ezra for ages. I'll walk home with him."[6] On another occasion, when Williams, H.D., and some others were dining with Adrienne Monnier in an upstairs flat, Pound called from the street but did not come up. Williams, however, ran down to be reunited with a friend he had not seen for a long time.[7]

In 1925 both poets found homes far from each other. The Pounds, seeking a permanent home, toured Sicily in the early part of the year, but decided on Rapallo, a resort town on the northeast coast of Italy, where they lived until the end of World War II. H.D. took a flat in London at 169 Sloane Street, which she kept until 1932. Pound was to be occupied during these years with his usual enormous range of interests: writing his *Cantos,* translating Confucius, promoting the musical work of George Antheil and Olga Rudge, dabbling in politics, developing his economic theories, and advancing the careers of fellow writers such as Joyce, Eliot, and Louis Zukofsky. He had some contacts with Richard Aldington, who visited him in Rapallo, accompanied by H.D.'s former friend Brigit Patmore, who had succeeded Arabella Yorke as his companion. Aldington reviewed the 1927 edition of *Personae* in the *Times Literary Supplement,* and consulted with Pound about the information to be given to the American academic Glenn Hughes, who was gathering notes for his book on Imagism. At this time, Pound's friendship with Olga Rudge developed into a

sexual liaison, and his life in Italy took a definite shape as he
began to divide his time between her and his wife.

The two poets met again in May 1929, although H.D. was reluctant to see Pound again. In the letters that were now exchanged
frequently, she said that she felt "stunned," "old and tired," and
was ashamed of her changed appearance. Her circle of associates
was also changing. Her visit to Paris in the early 1920s had put her
in touch with the wide creative world of the expatriates gathered
around the Shakespeare and Company bookshop and the Contact
Publishing Company, founded by Robert McAlmon, Bryher's
husband.

McAlmon had been an energizing presence in Paris at the
time. He was incorrigibly gregarious and met many writers and
artists of importance, including Pound. He had some unfriendly
exchanges with Pound, and there was a long initial coolness between them, but McAlmon declared that he admired Pound's
work as a poet and critic. He published a journal and many books
by young Left Bank writers, including H.D.'s *Palimpsest*. The arranged marriage with Bryher was not a success, however, since
McAlmon was a freewheeling, convivial fellow who did a lot of
traveling and spent much of his time in bars, a style of life that
Bryher did not share. He eventually left her, and a divorce took
place in 1927.

There had been another, more serious development in H.D.'s
life in December 1926, when Frances Gregg, who had turned up
living in poverty in London, introduced her to Kenneth Macpherson, a witty, charming twenty-four-year-old whom Gregg
and H.D. found fatally attractive. He quickly became H.D.'s
lover, and after her divorce, Bryher went to join them at Territet.
In an odd sequel, Macpherson and Bryher made a quick trip to
New York in 1927 for a sudden marriage. This was another effort
on Bryher's part to achieve stability in a sexless marriage while
still living with H.D., and the result was a strange triad in which
the husband *pro forma* of one of the women was the lover of the

other, who was in turn the lover of the wife. In the following year, the unconventional family took another shape as Bryher and Macpherson formally adopted Perdita, H.D.'s daughter.

Macpherson turned out to be an even more creative stimulus to Bryher and H.D. than McAlmon had been. In 1927 he began to make movies, and the casual effort developed into a bold venture in the new field of cinema. Working from the Riant Château, he and Bryher set up a company called POOL Productions to make films, one of which featured the prominent black singer Paul Robeson, whom Macpherson had somehow lured to Switzerland. They also published a monthly journal devoted to the art of the film called *Close Up*, edited by Macpherson with Bryher as assistant editor. H.D. was caught up in this exciting work. She performed in two of the films, called *Foothills* and *Borderline*, between 1928 and 1930, and wrote articles for the journal, as did Dorothy Richardson, Marianne Moore, and other friends. A traumatic experience interrupted this work when H.D. discovered that she was pregnant with a child of Macpherson's, and in November 1928 went to Berlin to have an abortion.

This situation no doubt partly accounts for the gloominess of the long and revealing letter she wrote to Pound at about this time, but she said nothing about her pregnancy and instead attributed her disturbed feelings to the state of Aldington's affairs.[8]

The May 1929 meeting took place when Pound planned to stop in Paris en route to London, and H.D. wrote that she would be there at the same time, accompanied by a friend, primarily to see Glenn Hughes. With a precision that betrayed her nervousness, she said that she would meet him at her hotel, at 3:30 on May 1st. Much of her unease was caused by the fact that Aldington and Brigit Patmore were in Paris at the time, and she thought of going to see them with Pound. Another link between the separated poets developed as H.D. arranged for Pound and Olga Rudge, with whom he was now living part of the year, to stay at her flat on Sloane Street while he was in England in the spring of 1929. Writing to Pound that summer, H.D. said she was sure they did "a good thing" to the flat, because "beautiful things" had been taking place since they left.

5

Vision and Sexuality

It is the belief and not the god that counts.
                                        Wallace Stevens, "Adagia"

The two most clearly recognized strands of Modernism are a rationalism connected with rising science and technology, and a sophisticated irrationalism expressed in Dadaism, Surrealism, Freudianism, and scientific theories of indeterminacy. But there is another kind of irrationality characteristic of Modernism, a visionary belief in the occult and supernatural, brought forward from ancient sources. The abstract paintings of Piet Mondrian, for example, may seem coldly intellectual, but they are expressions of the painter's Theosophical views. Vassily Kandinsky, another abstractionist, believed that painting should express certain eternal and primordial feelings, as he explained in his book *Über der Geistige in das Kunst (Concerning the Spiritual in Art)*. A discussion of Kandinsky's book and excerpts from it appeared in Pound's and Wyndham Lewis's *Blast* in 1914, and there are occult elements in T. S. Eliot's poems. But the foremost occultist among the poets was Yeats, who received messages from spirits through his wife's automatic writing, and shaped these into an elaborate spiritual system in *A Vision*.

In every period of English and American poetry, including the later twentieth century, there have been poets who turned to the occult to discover unexpected depths of meaning beyond the visible and tangible world. Like them, the Modern poets and artists shared with religious visionaries an interest in transcending ordinary perception and communicating subtle, unprecedented insights. In invoking occult doctrines, they brought forward neglected mental powers and sought to win rights for imagination, intuition, and other cognitive faculties that poetry shared with the esoteric tradition. By dealing with visionary themes, the poems of Pound and H.D. played a conspicuous part in this effort.

Visionary experiences, usually regarded as the work of imagination, are seen by mystics as evidence of supernatural reality. It may be hard to distinguish between imaginative and supernatural sources of poetry, but, as with the change of night and day, there is no doubt that they are different from each other, even though it may be impossible to fix the exact point of distinction. Blake and Shelley are prominent examples of earlier figures whose poetry embodies an invisible transition between supernatural vision and poetic imagination. Pound seemed to say that vision was a product of imagination when he defined his term "phantastikon" as "a kind of Imagination that involved visions."[1] For both Pound and H.D., the material Image perceived by the senses could easily evolve into a sacred sign such as an ideogram or a hieroglyph. Both made use of the classical myths as a matter of course, and with the encouragement of many contemporaries, extended this imaginary realm into that of the occult.

Robert Duncan's "H.D. Book" is an elaborate, fervent argument, developed through many articles, in support of a mysticism whose chief supporters were H.D. and Pound. He places Pound, together with H.D. (sometimes including Eliot and Lawrence), in an esoteric mystical tradition originating in the Hermetic doctrines of ancient Egypt and changing its form to appear, as Pound argues, in Provençal poetry and in certain modern cults. Duncan justifies the mysticism of Modern poets on both psychological and supernatural grounds: "these poets bring us to see the theosophical and psychoanalytic anew as hints of a primary poetic vision."[2] Noting that the major Modern works, *Ulysses*, *The Waste Land*, and the *Cantos*, overlay the modern world with parallels in the legendary past, he says, "Our work is to arouse in a contemporary consciousness reverberations of old myth." In saying that the Imagists "had sought a new spiritual home among the eternal ones of the European dream, among Troubadours, the Melic poets,"[3] he was accepting some of the forerunners Pound claimed.

Two Canadian scholars, Demetres P. Tryphonopoulos in *The Celestial Tradition* (1992) and Leon Surette in *The Birth of Modernism* (1993), have strongly argued that Pound's work is a structure built on the foundation of occult beliefs. Both maintain that the *Cantos* is a visionary poem, the result of his lifelong devotion to occult doctrines. In fact, says Surette, "the esoteric meaning of *The Cantos* is essentially an occult interpretation of history together with some beatific visions."[4]

The occult principles visible in the pre–World War II writings of Pound and H.D. are among those common to most of the mystic sects. There is a central belief in the continuity of matter and spirit, so that a true knowledge of the material world can lead to knowledge of the transcendental one. This knowledge consists of secret truths open only to a limited circle of believers who gain their status through a ritual of rebirth or metamorphosis, thus becoming initiates with visionary powers. These powers may include such familiar privileges of mystics and spiritualists as access to God, insight into the afterlife, contact with the dead, and knowledge of the future.

The parallels between H.D.'s and Pound's uses of the occult spring from the reading they did together in Pennsylvania, but each developed this interest in different directions under different influences. The two poets agreed in finding an important place in Modern poetry for mystical vision. But both felt that the material world could not be left behind in the poet's search for the transcendental, and that mystical intuition must be accompanied by intellect. Like other artists and poets of the time, both thought art, joined with vision, promised a Utopian deliverance. Visionary passages in the *Cantos* mention ideal cities—Ecbatan, Poitiers, Wagadu—where beauty or enlightenment are preserved. In an extravagant section of her *Notes on Thought and Vision*, H.D. declares that "two or three people" with the right faculties of body and mind could change the world with the power of the intense consciousness she calls the "over-mind," a declaration that echoes the elitist confidence of Pound's view in his "Vorticism" essay that art shares the power of mathematical equations to act as "'lords' over fact."

Visions, spirits, and resuscitations of the past are especially prominent in the later work of the two poets. Their treatments of these themes in the first two decades of the century are only preliminary approaches to areas of occult lore that were to come to new life in such major poems as *Helen in Egypt* and the *Cantos*. Their common interest in these matters began when, as H.D. reported, Pound brought her books about occult themes at the time of their youthful love affair in Pennsylvania, including works by Swedenborg and Blake, Balzac's *Séraphita,* and "a series of Yogi books."[5] The Yogi books were a popular series by a possibly pseudonymous author named Yogi Ramacharaka that offered instruction in Yogi philosophy. Pound's interest in them was not a mere youthful fancy. He and Dorothy were still recommending them to friends in the 1950s when he was in St. Elizabeths. H.D. credited Pound with initiating her interest in the occult by introducing her to these books. In a letter about her psychoanalytic sessions as late as 1957, she wrote: "Amazing that that Theosophist stream-of-consciousness flows into the couch memories & sessions . . . I can not get *over* it & the fact that it was E. who first brought the Yogi etc. to me. I carry the little first book in my hand-bag & read from time to time."[6]

Séraphita, Balzac's fantastic novel, includes a summation of Swedenborgian mysticism, powerful arguments favoring the superiority of intuitive belief over reason, and sweeping visions of the spiritual world. It emphasizes, in particular, the continuity and correspondence of spiritual and material spheres. These ideas seem to have had a considerable effect on the two poets, for *Séraphita* involved androgyny, a theme of later significance to H.D., and the occult interests of the two poets can be seen in germ in such passages as: "man is, in himself sufficient evidence of these two modes of life: Matter and Spirit. In him ends a finite, visible universe; in him begins an infinite and invisible universe — two worlds that do not know each other."[7]

Pound's first poems contain many conventional allusions to the Greek gods and other supernatural entities, and his early critical pronouncements often acknowledge the poetic value of mystical intuition and its possible alliance with the rational faculties. It is clear then, that when he came to England in 1909, he was already prepared to sympathize with the ideas of Yeats, G. R. S. Mead, an associate of the Theosophist Madame Blavatsky, and other believers in occult systems that he met there. In *The Spirit of Romance* (1910), he introduces an idea that motivated many of his early poems and translations: the view that an occult tradition passed from Greek and Latin antiquity to the poems of the medieval troubadours. He calls this "a visionary interpretation" and suggests that the tradition derived from the ancient mysteries is "a cult for the purgation of the soul."

Pound apparently drew this theme from two books by the French Rosicrucian and authority on the mystical tradition, Joséphin Péladan, which he read in 1906 while on a visit to Paris. In these sources he encountered the notion that esoteric doctrines survived from the time of the Eleusinian mysteries and took many forms, including the ideas of Don Quixote, the songs of the troubadours, and the doctrines of the Catholic Church. In an article written at that time, Pound expressed skepticism about the theory that there was a mystical strain in the culture of the troubadours, but in *The Spirit of Romance* he adopted exactly this view. In January 1912, in one of his serial contributions to the *New Age*, he came to a more general mysticism, declaring, "Our life, insofar as it is worth living, is made up in great part of things indefinite, impalpable."[8]

His willingness to accept the supernatural as an element of serious literature appears in his studies of Japanese drama, with its ghosts, spirits, and visions, and in his enthusiasm for the poetry of Rabindranath Tagore, which, he said, gave him the feeling of being a cave man. Like the young T. S. Eliot, who read a seminar paper at Harvard in December 1913 arguing that the modern mind failed to understand the religious ideas motivating prehistoric rituals, Pound saw value in the beliefs of primitive cultures. In a 1914 article, he wrote proudly, "We turn back, we artists, to the powers of the air, to the djinns who were our allies foretime, to the spirits of our ancestors."[9]

The "celestial tradition" that occupied Pound early in his development is not a single unified doctrine, which he sometimes took it to be, but a mingling of varied and sometimes conflicting beliefs, many of them survivals of ancient religions. Influences of Gnosticism, Hermeticism, Swedenborgianism, Theosophy, Neo-Platonism, Masonry, Egyptian religion, and Chinese doctrines can be seen in his work.

Péladan's book may have been Pound's introduction to a mystical tradition whose lore he encountered again in his prewar days in London, where he came into contact with a number of writers on mysticism and a local culture that preserved some of the energies of the nineteenth-century spiritualism that had enthralled Elizabeth Barrett Browning. According to Tryphonopoulos, London was at that time a city "flooded by waves of reincarnationists, palmists, astrologers, and all sorts of groups engaged in arcane activities."[10]

Pound's esoteric sources included a number of figures prominent in occult circles and various books and journals. He was in touch with the Quest Society, a Theosophical group, and with its founder, G. R. S. Mead, and Pound's essay "Psychology and the Troubadours" was first published in the society's journal, *Quest*. He met with Allen Upward, an author whose books he reviewed enthusiastically, and who developed a theory of religion based on the existence of exceptional beings in touch with primordial energies. The three winters between 1913 and 1915 that he spent with Yeats at a cottage in Sussex exposed him to the older poet's mystical interests, which drew upon Rosicrucianism, Theosophy, Celtic legends, medieval demonology, and the concept of the Great Memory detailed in the older poet's *A Vision*.[11]

In *Stone Cottage*, his study of the relationship between Yeats and Pound during the three winters they spent together in the country, James Longenbach has suggested that Pound's Imagism had a secret visionary component, never openly declared, which attributed occult significance to the Image. Although Longenbach does not mention H.D. in this connection, it is possible that Pound told her something about this secret. Longenbach observes that Pound's occultism improved his "visionary powers," placed him in the tradition of the poet with transcendental inspiration, and offered a vocabulary separate from that of ordinary usage.[12] To these might be added a symbolism enriched by visionary suggestion, and identification with historical and mythic figures based on the principle of palingenesis. H.D. also took advantage of these resources; both poets were deeply immersed in esoteric knowledge, and specific ideas drawn from a background of occult lore often rise to the surface of their work.

Many others in Pound's circle of social and literary acquaintances had strong interests in spiritual matters. These included his mother-in-law Olivia Shakespear, the Theosophist and editor of *New Age* and *New English Weekly* A. R. Orage, and Evelyn Underhill, the author of a book on mysticism. He added to his acquaintance with mystical and visionary texts several recommended by Yeats, and commissioned Olivia Shakespear to translate the Cabalistic-Rosicrucian *Comte de Gabalis* for serial publication in the *Egoist*. Although he did not claim to experience visions himself, Pound said that he knew people who had experienced them, and speculated on the way in which such events could be translated into myth and legend.

Pound's statements that the effect of the successful Image, like that of great art, was a sense of "freedom from time limits and space limits" and that it is "the word beyond formulated language" show that he was more than ready to accept the contributions of mystical intuition to his theories of poetry. But for him, as for H.D., mysticism was not in the least incompatible with reason. He called poetic imagination "intellectual vision" (a phrase borrowed from Blake), and described a quality he liked in Richard St. Victor as "a keenly intellectual mysticism." In "The Serious Artist" (1913), an essay that emphasizes the need for clarity and control in poetry, he quoted a passage of verse whose expression of passionate feeling is "beyond the precisions of the intellect," maintained that such poetry has its influence upon the rational mind, and asserted that it was useless to divide intellect from emotion.

While Pound, unlike Yeats and H.D., almost never had visions himself, he was deeply interested in them, and they appear in all of his poetry, from his first volume to the last *Cantos*. For Yeats, the visionary faculty was a supernatural power, but for Pound, to whom a god was "an eternal state of mind," it was primarily a psychological condition. The visions in his poetry tend to be of the sort that recover invisible truths from the visible world. As he says in Canto 81, "First came the seen, then thus the palpable / Elysium, though it were in the halls of hell."

The material of his visionary passages did not come from a kind of telepathy, as they did for Yeats and H.D., but from recollections of his reading in such sources as Ovid, Homer, and John Heydon. His announcement in the first of the rejected "Three Cantos," "Ghosts move about me / Patched with histories," has been proposed as the method of the *Cantos* as a whole, and it is also a good description of his approach to the occult. The elimination of space and time limits attributed to the Image appears when he declares, in the same poem, "I walk Verona. (I am here in England). / I see Can Grande. (Can see whom you will)." These are claims, not of insight into the supernatural, but rather of an imaginative power that brings the dead to life through poetry. James Longenbach considers Pound's claims to visionary experiences dubious and characterizes him, together with Eliot, as "simultaneously profoundly *visionary* and rigorously *skeptical* poet-critics."[13] He reminds us that, in spite of Pound's interest in uncovering transcendental depths in the past, his primary purpose was the writing of poetry.

While Pound learned about vision mainly from his reading, H.D., as we have seen, experienced visions herself. She may have developed this tendency even before her friendship with Pound, since she was brought up in a family of Moravians, a mystical Christian sect with a tradition of secret doctrines. However, H.D. reported that she did not encounter the mystical aspects of the religion as a girl, and learned about them much later, when, during World War II, she wrote the memoir called *The Gift*.

Although she was influenced by Pound, D. H. Lawrence, and possibly by others interested in the fashionable mysticism of the prewar years, H.D.'s visionary power was essentially her own. In a letter written early in her career, she wrote: "You must remember that writing poetry require[s] a clarity, a clairvoyance almost." And although she was often too weak to achieve it, "In the long run, clairvoyance is the only real sanity for me."[14] Her family told her that she had not inherited "the Gift" of wisdom or psychic insight, but she connected the Moravian rituals her grandmother had described with the Hermetic tradition, and believed that she possessed prophetic powers. Her lifelong interest in exploring her psyche through her autobiographical writing and psychoanalytic sessions with a number of analysts, including Freud, seemed to strengthen, rather than to threaten, her confidence in the occult.

It seems that H.D., perhaps especially when she was with Frances Gregg, had had visionary experiences at an early age. A passage in her novel *Asphodel* tells of a visit to the scene of Jeanne d'Arc's martyrdom in Rouen, an episode no doubt based on her 1911 trip to Europe. Hermione, the autobiographical narrator, imagines the saint's fate with a vividness approaching that of an occult vision, and identifies with her, saying, "I don't want to be burnt, to be crucified just because I 'see' things sometimes."

But these first steps in the direction of the occult were cautious, barely anticipating her later immersion in magic, astrology, and spiritualism. She recorded the strange mental state she entered while vacationing with Bryher in the Scilly Islands in 1919 and speculated on the visionary capacity and its relation to art in a series of jottings posthumously published as *Notes on Thought and Vision* (1982). These notes analyze visionary power with the authority of one who actually possessed it, and parallel certain thoughts of Pound.

In them, H.D. describes the state of abnormally sensitive consciousness she calls the "over-mind," which was situated in a cap, "bell-jar," or "jellyfish or anemone" that hung over her head, blurring her vision, and extending tentacles over her body and outward. She attributes visionary powers to the "over-mind," and her ideas about it resemble Pound's linkage of intellect and intuition, for she specifies that the only way of arriving at it is through intellectual effort. This union of intelligence and mysticism emerges in her later poem, *Trilogy*, as an important concept called "spiritual realism."

H.D.'s "world of the over-mind" does not fully correspond with mysticism, for it is directed toward aesthetic satisfaction and "ecstasy," not, as one might expect, toward superior insights or communion with a higher being. She says that she can enter the mystic state by viewing certain works of art, such as the figure of the Charioteer of Delphi, and her examples of those who arrive at it are not the great mystics but Renaissance artists and the Athenians of Socrates' day. Even Christ is characterized as "a great artist, like Da Vinci." In spite of these deviations, the mysticism of the *Notes* does correspond with such doctrines as those of Eleusis and Gnosticism in declaring that the over-mind can only be achieved by a select group of "initiates" with special powers.

If this power possessed by great artists were developed, she says, it could change the world, a declaration that echoes the confidence of Pound's view, in his "Vorticism" essay, that art shares the power of mathematical equations to bring facts under control. H.D.'s mystical capacity seems to be an extension of her extraordinary powers of introspection, supported by an exceptional perceptiveness and an unfailing memory. "We travel far in thought," she wrote, "in imagination or in the realm of memory."[15] Her mysticism transcended Pound's evocations of the past. She was able to recollect vivid dreams based on her childhood during her sessions with Freud in later years, and to describe the "jellyfish" or "bell-jar" state of consciousness that first came to her before the birth of her child. In her later poetry, H.D., perhaps thinking of her relationships with Pound and Aldington, goes on to say that the over-mind can arise from the interchange of ideas between lovers with sympathetic interests.

In writing of the occult tradition, she specified:

Three worlds.

1.World of abstraction: Helios, Athene.

2. Intermediate, or Nature world: Pan, the Naiads.
3. World of the uninitiate men and women.[16]

This tripartite division, a departure from the Platonic division of reality into the two realms of the actual and the ideal, parallels Pound's original plan for the *Cantos*. In this well-known scheme, as he explained it to Yeats, Pound apparently intended to follow the arrangement of the fresco on the walls of the Hall of Months in the Palazzo Schifanoia in Ferrara. The mural has three levels, the top one showing gods, the middle one showing the sign of the zodiac for each month, together with human figures, and the bottom one showing activities from contemporary life. Yeats's account of Pound's idea is not entirely clear, but he concluded that the *Cantos* were to emulate the fresco by mingling archetypes, transformations of the cosmic into the earthly, and modern events. These three levels of reality are perfectly visible in the *Cantos*, although as Guy Davenport has observed, other organizational plans were added.[17]

The correspondences with H.D.'s three worlds are not perfect, but they suggest that his poem would embrace all levels of spiritual and physical experience. H.D.'s world of Helios and Athene corresponds to Pound's archetypes. Her intermediate world of Nature is like Pound's level of transformation or metamorphosis, where the divine and human come together. And her world of the uninitiates, those ignorant of the visionary tradition, is Pound's (and the fresco's) world of daily life. H.D. would not introduce all three realms of consciousness into her poetry until she wrote *Trilogy* during World War II, but they appear in the *Cantos* almost from the beginning.

Perhaps the most significant level of experience recognized by the two poets is the middle one, where the abstract and the concrete, the transcendental and the earthly, come together. This meeting between two realms considered separate informs the concept of imagery the two poets had in common: the use of the material world as a key to the spiritual, so that the image becomes the site of a metamorphosis that transforms the earthly into the numinous.

H.D.'s effects of this kind are generally subtle and suggestive. In "Pygmalion" she asks, "is this fire a god / that seeks me in the dark?" And in "The Pool," noting that the water seems alive, she asks, "What are you—banded one?" Similarly, throughout the *Cantos*, but more often in the later sections, visionary glimpses may spring out of mundane contexts. In Canto 83, a poetic treatment of the prison camp's environment suddenly rises to a transcendental level as the poet observes insects:

> And now the ants seem to stagger
>   as the dawn sun has trapped their shadows
> this breath wholly covers the mountains
>   it shines and divides
> it nourishes by its rectitude
> does no injury
> overstanding the earth it fills the nine fields
>   to heaven [18]

The fact that these lines are derived from a text of the Chinese sage, Mencius, does not compromise their visionary force. On the contrary, Pound's persistent use of visionary traditions strengthens and confirms his expressions of divine exaltation. A superb example is the invocation of Canto 90:

>   Sibylla,
> from under the rubble heap
>   m'elevasti
> from under the dulled edge beyond pain,
>   m'elevasti
> out of Erebus, the deep-lying
>   from the wind under the earth.
>   m'elevasti
> from the dulled air and the dust,
>   m'elevasti
> in the great flight,
>   m'elevasti,
>   Isis Kuanon
> from the cusp of the moon,
>   m'elevasti [19]

"M'elevasti," a word derived from a speech of Dante to Beatrice in the *Paradiso,* is used to address Greek, Egyptian, and Chinese deities. This eclecticism characterizes the entire Canto, where rituals and texts from Christian, pagan, and modern sources are interwoven with each other. The theme of the Canto is love. The many religious traditions embedded in it testify that love has the power to lift the mind from mundane experiences to the world of heavenly vision. H.D. reported that she felt a healing power in the passage, perhaps because it mentions Isis, the goddess with whom she identified herself, perhaps because it returns, on another level, to the idealizing love of "Hilda's Book," written for her so many years before. (However, the object of Pound's love at this time is thought to be Sheri Martinelli, a young woman who visited him in St. Elizabeths.)

As we have seen, H.D. had a confusing dream or vision during her voyage to Greece in 1920. But the vision she experienced at a later point on this trip, in April, in a hotel room in Corfu, was far more positive than her earlier ones. She was able to describe this vision, which she called "the writing on the wall," in great detail when she wrote *Tribute to Freud* about twenty-five years later. It began with the appearance of three luminous shapes in a space on the wall, a man's head and shoulders, then a form like a goblet, then a lampstand that she associated with the tripod where the Priestess of Delphi sat. When she told Bryher what she was seeing, a new phase began as small black midge-like figures appeared. She felt able to withdraw from the vision, but Bryher encouraged her to continue, and she felt the need to concentrate: "This has never happened to me before, it may never happen again." The original shapes were now joined by a series of dots and lines that gradually formed a ladder, and finally a figure like an angel or a Greek Victory slowly appeared, followed by a series of curved lines. Bryher did not see any of this, but strangely, when H.D. stopped looking, she did see a disk enclosing the figure of a man, which H.D. considered the final symbol of the vision.[20]

She herself could not decide whether it was generated internally, from the subconscious, or externally, as a supernatural phenomenon, and thought it could be seen either as an expression of the suppressed wishes of a mind filled with Greek and biblical lore, or as a manifestation of imaginative power. Recalling it after some years, H.D. said she considered it as belonging to a state midway between the psychological and the supernatural, a phase of the "supernormal, abnormal (or subnormal) states of mind."[21] She experienced similar states later in life, and a remarkable passage in *Asphodel* describes a visionary experience attributed to the heroine, Hermione, when she finds she is unexpectedly pregnant, as H.D. did. Hermione senses the world as a unity of intricately interwoven particulars in which she is imprisoned, able to escape only through union with God. This vision seems to belong to the author writing in the 1920s rather than to the troubled, pregnant woman H.D. was in 1919.

Her conviction that she had the gift of clairvoyance was confirmed by her experiences during World War II. As she recalled these events in the "Hirslanden Journal" begun in 1957, she plunged into studies of mysticism and joined the Society for Psychical Research, where she met the medium Arthur Bhaduri, who became her adviser. Bhaduri and his mother came to her flat, where they guided H.D. in conducting séances using the small, round three-legged table built by William Morris and once owned by Violet Hunt that Bryher had bought at auction. H.D. contacted the spirits through this table, keeping her left hand on it while recording the messages delivered through the tapping of one of its legs on the floor.

Bhaduri gave her a ticket to a lecture by Sir Hugh Dowding, a retired chief air marshal who had commanded the RAF during the Battle of Britain. He had become an advocate of spiritualism, claiming that he communicated with dead pilots. When she heard his lecture, H.D.'s clairvoyance took a new turn. Only later did she recognize that its source was her early friendship with Pound. "Ezra," she wrote in later years, "was the first person to introduce me to Yogi philosophy." But she says that she did not make much progress until Dowding's lecture linked up with her memories of the books on occultism Pound had given her. [22]

She exchanged letters with Dowding and made "psychic contact" with him when Bhaduri read a letter from him in the dark, and transmitted messages involving a Viking ship and the air marshal. The power of this experience remained with her many years later. In 1957 she wrote in her "Hirslanden Journal": "The over-whelming excitement & intensity of this contact with the ship is shared with the Air Marshall. It is the abstract of Plato, absolute beauty, absolute truth, strength, valour—all the Abstracts, whatever they were, of ancient Greece & of eternity."[23] Although her spiritual guides forbade it, she did meet with Dowding, and he made so strong an impression on her that she considered herself "engaged" to him in connection with the Viking ship. In the journal, she scrupulously recalled the seven meetings she had with him.[24]

"The Sword Went Out to Sea" gives further details about her encounter with Dowding. Through the Morris table she received messages from the dead pilots that were to be passed on to him. When she met with him in 1945 and told him about this, he was infuriated, implied that the messages were false, and told her she must stop communicating. He told her that within the general pattern of reincarnation, "You yourself, for instance, do not matter." She felt this rejection as a repetition of the wound she had suffered in childhood when she had separated from "Allen"—the character based on Pound. Eventually, according to the novel, she freed herself from the "work" of clairvoyance. And, in fact, it is possible that she was being victimized by Bhaduri, her intermediary in her communications with the spirits.

But "The Sword Went Out to Sea" recalls another curious episode of spiritualism that occurred, if it occurred at all, in Paris in 1912, soon after the death of Margaret Cravens. The narrator and a character based on Aldington are on the Pont Neuf, watching the boats on the Seine, and he suddenly says, "My God, Astraea, she's here." Then, "Don't leave me—Like that poor girl." She knew then, says the narrator, that he was thinking of "Dorothy"—

Margaret Cravens. "She's been here," adds the man, "since the boat turned." "I had no idea," says the author, "that he was what they call 'psychic.'" In 1933, we recall, H.D. described a similar scene with Pound in her contribution to *The Cantos of Ezra Pound: Some Testimonies*. While it is barely possible that she shared thoughts of Margaret Cravens with both Pound and Aldington on Seine bridges, it seems far more likely that she fictionalized her moment with Pound.

Trilogy reflects the clairvoyance H.D. was experiencing at the time it was written. Like the *Pisan Cantos*, it turns to the "secret tradition" inherited from pagan antiquity, not only as a remedy for wartime suffering but as an appropriate context for poetry. Both poems depend on mystical vision for gaining access to a state of mind that regards war as a prelude to a utopian deliverance. The theme is far more prominent in *Trilogy*, which merges it with Christianity, than it is in the *Pisan Cantos*, where it appears only intermittently.

Immediately after the opening of *Trilogy*, H.D. adopts the voice of the prophetess she thought she might become, turning to a defense of the "old values," the occult tradition inhabited by the gods of Egypt and Greece. In language reminiscent of *Notes on Thought and Vision*, she defends those who preserve esoteric wisdom. Before long, however, moving tones of doubt and suffering enter the atmosphere of prayer and ritual. The grain of salvation is not easy to accept in a time of war:

> how imperceptibly the grain fell
> between a heart-beat of pleasure
>
> and a heart-beat of pain;[25]

Section 30 of "The Walls Do Not Fall" interrogates some of H.D.'s mystical values, including some that she shared with Pound. Statements we would be justified in attributing to the clairvoyant H.D. herself are followed with such denials as "oneness lost, madness." In the following sections surprising warnings about the unrestricted power of occult insight appear, as the poet develops her principle of "spiritual realism," the balance of visionary intuition and intelligence that Pound also valued. She does not abandon mystic insight, but warns that the "over-soul," the state of heightened consciousness described in *Notes on Thought and Vision,* may be offered in "a cup / too brittle, a jar too circumscribed." She treats imagery connected with "the new dimension" and "the alchemist's key" with the same skepticism. Section 33 might be the practical, economist-minded Pound challenging his pretentious prophetic side:

> Let us measure defeat
> in terms of bread and meat.
>
> and continents
> in relative extent of wheat
>
> fields; let us not teach
> what we have learned badly
>
> and not profited by;
> let us not concoct
>
> healing potions for the dead,
> nor invent
>
> new colours
> for blind eyes.[26]

These injunctions do not counsel the abandonment of either Hermeticism or prophecy, but lead to a call for "spiritual realism" that employs intelligence as well as intuition, and for the "true magic" drawn from ancient gods. Still, she feels unable to match the myth of the past with the reality of the present, and turns to the realm of the occult by asking an astrological figure, the dog-star Sirius, "what mystery is this?" This spiritual path is followed unswervingly through the rest of *Trilogy,* where the theme of transcendence is intensified by accounts of actual visions, until "The Flowering of the Rod" takes up its biblical story.

Both the *Pisan Cantos* and *Trilogy* enter the transcendental realm through visions that offer spiritual deliverance from the psychological afflictions of war. In *Trilogy,* H.D. mentions a

"Presence" appearing in a "mystery" observed by "companions / of the flame." In a later section, she tells how she came upon a burned tree still blossoming in the ruins of the city, a symbol of survival amid destruction, and felt that it was a sacred presence. Although the place was perfectly ordinary, even squalid, H.D. is moved to ask: "Invisible, indivisible Spirit, / how is it that you come so near?" The scene has both physical existence and spiritual significance, for while "my eyes saw . . . yet it was a vision, / it was a sign." The experience is one of transition from material to spiritual reality, for she feels the intercession of God and the Holy Spirit, and acknowledges "transubstantiation." By calling this vision "the flowering of the rood," subtly varying her "rod" formula, H.D. identifies the pattern of suffering and salvation that is one of her main themes with the crucifixion.

This vision is soon followed by another, more elaborate one: the vision of the Lady. H.D. had told Freud of a related dream in which a "Princess" who seems to be both natural and supernatural is about to find a child hidden, like Moses, among reeds. The poem develops at length the concept that this is a generic female figure, a counterpart of women seen in paintings and sculpture. While some of these are Raphael Madonnas — "Our Lady of the Goldfinch / . . . Our Lady of the Chair" — H.D. denies that her Lady should be associated with Christianity, declaring that she represents the occult religion of pagan times:

> she is the Vestal
> from the day of Numa,
>
> she carries over the cult
> of the *Bona Dea* [27]

This universalized feminine principle is an antidote to the sufferings of the present, for "she is not-fear, she is not-war."

Both H.D.'s visions and those mentioned in the *Cantos* are dominated by female figures, most of them goddesses of the celestial tradition. While both poems frame the feminine principle in a variety of forms, Pound groups mortal women with his deities, while H.D., never mentioning actual people, develops a series of idealized figures derived from artistic representations. She explicitly separates her Lady from conventional religious values and images, linking her instead to a still unrealized future.

The climactic vision of "The Walls Do Not Fall," however, is experienced by a man, although its inspiration is a woman. In his encounter with Mary in "The Flowering of the Rod," the Mage Kaspar stoops to pick up her scarf, and he has a vision of a lady's head circled with jewels. One of these jewels opens like a flower, and "it would go on opening / he knew, to infinity" so that

> he, in that half-second, saw
> the whole scope and plan
>
> of our and his civilization on this,
> his and our earth, before Adam.[28]

In this way, H.D. viewed material objects, especially beautiful ones like flowers and jewels, as embodiments of the cosmos, as though she were echoing Blake's aspiration "To see a World in a Grain of Sand . . . And Eternity in an Hour."

In spite of the many imagined scenes and magical transformations described in the *Cantos*, there is no record, as we have seen, that Pound actually shared H.D.'s visionary capacity. But there is one possible exception, occurring many years later, toward the end of World War II, for a well-known passage in Canto 81 seems to report a mystical or hallucinatory experience he had in the prison camp at Pisa. In his study of Pound's drafts, Ronald Bush has found that the lines describing this vision were written before Pound's imprisonment and transplanted to the setting of his tent in the DTC.[29] Written before the *Pisan Cantos,* they continue a visionary theme found throughout the *Cantos.* Having declared, in the preliminary "Three Cantos" that "ghosts move about me," Pound continued to exploit the possibilities of the supernatural throughout his long poem. It opens by retelling magical episodes from the classics, the visit of Odysseus to the underworld in

Canto 1, and the transformation of the sailors from Ovid's *Metamorphoses* in Canto 2. In Canto 3, as Pound recalls his visit to Venice, "Gods float in the azure air," and the gods, together with the visionary world they inhabit, often return in later Cantos.

Canto 17 consists nearly entirely of mythic visions, and a fragmentary passage in Canto 76 describing a grassy cliff inhabited by goddesses and sacred cats echoes the dream or vision of the earlier Canto: "The green slope with white hounds . . . cliff green-gray in the far." Canto 17's treatment of a group of mythical and historical female figures noted for heroism mirrors a visionary scene in a manuscript draft of material for the *Pisan Cantos*, a meeting at a triple crossroads, or "triedro" of three women, one of whom is Cunizza da Romano.[30] In the *Paradiso* Cunizza, a thirteenth-century lady whom Dante praised for freeing her slaves, is introduced by Beatrice in the sphere of love and speaks from within a sacred radiance. Pound refers to her from time to time in his prose and in earlier Cantos as a figure of aristocratic beauty and the bearer of traditions that he associated with the troubadours. There are allusions to this scene in the final text, but they hardly convey the visionary quality of the rejected draft. In Canto 74, the line "Io son la luna', Cunizza" is one of these echoes of the lines Pound had prepared for what was apparently to be a new phase of his poem that would include the idealization of women and the radiance of vision.

Thus, the mysticism of the *Pisan Cantos* is a continuation of the mysticism of earlier Cantos. In the vision of Canto 81, the imprisoned Pound sees the eyes of a masked face inside his tent:

Ed ascoltando al leggier mormorio
        there came new subtlety of eyes into my tent,
whether of spirit or hypostasis,
        but what the blindfold hides
or at carneval
           nor any pair showed anger
        Saw but the eyes and stance between the eyes,
colour, diastasis
        careless or unaware it had not the
      whole tent's room

nor was place for the full (Eιδὼς)
interpass, penetrate
>casting but shade beyond the other lights
>>sky's clear
>>night's sea
>>green of the mountain pool
>>shone from the unmasked eyes in half-mask's space.[31]

The power of these eyes is affirmed by the refrain of a Chau-
cerian love lyric quoted just before the vision appears: "Your eyen
two wol sleye me sodenly / I may the beauté of hem not sustain."
The poet is unable to decide whether what he is seeing is supernatural or substantial—"spirit or hypostasis"—but it seems transparent—"interpass, penetrate"—and as the last lines say, these
eyes seem to project a beauty like nature's.

The significance of this vision as a transcendental insight is
clarified by other passages in the *Pisan Cantos*. Pound originally
intended to begin with these eyes, for as Ronald Bush has shown,
the lines about Mussolini's death that open the *Pisan Cantos* were
inserted later. Without them, Canto 74 would begin:

The suave eyes, quiet, not scornful,
>rain also is of the process.
What you depart from is not the way . . .
The wind also is of the process . . .[32]

The third line of the quotation and "the process," a concept central to Pound's thinking, are borrowed from his translation of a
Confucian text where "the process" is defined as the working of
the divine will through earthly phenomena. "What heaven has
disposed and sealed is called the inborn nature. The realization of
this nature is called the process." Further, "You do not depart from
the process for an instant; what you depart from is not the process." Also, "The celestial and earthly process pervades and is substantial; it is on high and gives light, it comprehends the light and
is lucent, it extends without bound, and endures."[33] In a passage
in Canto 83 celebrating the beauty of the world, the spirit of the
universe is "Boon companion to equity / it joins with the process."

The association of the eyes with rain and wind as part of "the process" is not fixed until Canto 83 where the eyes appear among peaceful images of nature: "in the drenched tent there is quiet / sered eyes are at rest" and "A fat moon rises lop-sided over the mountain / The eyes, this time my world." The eyes in Canto 83 that shine with natural scenes—"sky's clear / night's sea / green of the mountain pool / shone from the unmasked eyes in half-mask's space"—are the same eyes, seen in a vision embodying "the process."

The original opening of the *Pisan Cantos*—"The suave eyes, quiet"—with its link to the vision, would have established a mystical register for the Canto as a whole, briefly foreshadowing Pound's allusions to his belief in a divinity of order and tranquillity, or, as he calls it, "equity." But Pound has seen this harmonious universal order destroyed by war and defeat, and the *Pisan Cantos* is a desperate effort to survive that destruction. In what were to have been the opening lines of his poem, the poet linked two things the war has not destroyed—visionary experience and nature—as parts of the heavenly and earthly "process."

There is a striking counterpart to the appearance of Pound's masked deity in "The Walls Do Not Fall," where H.D. dreams of an Egyptian deity appearing in an incongruous setting, "a bare meeting-house," and, waking, asks, "whose eyes are those eyes? / for the eyes . . . / were all one texture." The eyes of H.D.'s god play a part in imagery calling for destruction of the old world and for progress toward renewal. The eyes of Pound's figure, on the other hand, when they are related to the eyes at the beginning of Canto 74, are parts of the harmonious order of the celestial and earthly realms.

Pound's sense that celestial power shines through the natural world as part of the universal "process" and H.D.'s tendency to involve material objects in "transubstantiation" link *Trilogy* and the *Pisan Cantos* with each other. Both poets, beginning with the Imagist response to the significance of material objects, cross over into the supernatural, seeing in such objects not only meaning but transcendental meaning. They use poetic resources to move in the same direction, toward some reordering of the worlds that they know will survive the destruction of war. Their utopian aspirations are embodied in Venice, which infiltrates both *Trilogy* and the *Cantos*, and Pound revisits the theme with his references to the cities of Ecbatan and Wagadu. Ultimately, however, the two poets are driven by the afflictions of wartime to seek strength within themselves, as Pound says, "what thou lovest well remains," and H.D. declares, "I go to the things I love."

In spite of these parallels, occult elements enter their poetry in contrasting ways. Nearly all of Pound's visions, as we have seen, are derivative, brief intertextual borrowings reworked from his many sources. They are primarily literary effects operating under conscious control and they are often juxtaposed with passages that return abruptly to the material world. H.D., on the other hand, possessed a genuine clairvoyant power and declared that it was essential to her poetry. According to her accounts, visions came to her spontaneously, and while she does not seem to have transferred any of these recorded experiences directly into her poetry, the occultism of her poems is clearly derived from them. In her poems, material reality is usually subordinated to imaginary or visionary experience. Her immersion in table-tapping, astrology, angelology, palingenesis, Tarot cards, and mystical prophecy took her into esoteric fields that Pound did not penetrate. Although he was able to exploit some of these mysteries for poetic purposes, his insistence on anchoring the *Cantos* in the material world establishes a sharp demarcation between his work and H.D.'s. Their similar, yet differentiated use of occult lore is an important aspect of their poetic dialogue.

The early century was a time when frankness about sexual matters was emerging as a part of the literary reaction to the repressiveness of Victorianism, and both poets linked sexual energy to artistic creativity. At a time when the potentialities of electricity were also being recognized, they both equated sexual energy with this new, invisible power. In his 1912 essay "Psychology and Troubadours," Pound proposed to deal with sex "as sub-species of electricity," and in her *Notes,* H.D. attributed "electric force" to the aesthetic effects she considered partly sexual in origin.

More significantly, both poets attributed a sacred quality to sex, noting that sexual images played a part in the Eleusinian mysteries. H.D. reported that the "jellyfish" consciousness seemed to have sources both in the head, and like a fetus, in "the love-region of the body." She declared: "The brain and the womb are both centres of consciousness, equally important."[34]

Pound (who probably did not see H.D.'s *Notes*) in a postscript to *The Natural Philosophy of Love,* a translation of Remy de Gourmont's *Physique de l'Amour,* produced a wildly imaginative masculine counterpart to H.D.'s idea that womb-vision and brain-vision must work together. He began with the strange idea that the brain was "a sort of great clot of genital fluid," on the ground that brain and semen both have the power to create forms and to generate the vigorous inventive energy associated with the male rôle. He speculated, as H.D. did, on the relation between intellectual and sexual activity, but the two neatly divide the field, as Pound took the sperm as the image for this, while H.D. took the womb.[35] This bond between the mystic and the erotic has ample support in other views of the two poets. For example, H.D. thought that the over-mind could be approached through pornographic literature, and Pound believed that the poetry of the troubadours identified love and religious devotion with each other.

In her study, "Visions in the Crystal Ball: Ezra Pound, H.D., and the Form of the Mystical," Kendra Langeteig brings H.D.'s and Pound's themes of sex and mysticism together to demonstrate their connections.[36] Thus, she argues, the image of the acorn that recurs in the *Cantos* is phallic, even when it culminates in the "great acorn of light" in Canto 116, while H.D.'s vision involving the "jellyfish," a reversion to the idea of the fetus on the part of a woman who had recently been pregnant, is "womb-centered." Both poets refer to the mysteries of Eleusis as a basis for their mysticism, but Pound emphasizes the sexual act that was supposed to be part of the ceremony, while H.D. dwells on its Earth Mother aspect and on the relation between Demeter and her lost daughter, Persephone. In this way, Langeteig develops at length the contrast between "Pound's phallic vision" and H.D.'s "vision of the womb."

While detailing these contrasts, Langeteig mentions numerous parallels in the occultism of the two poets. She recognizes that both looked forward to retrieving from ancient sources a lost spiritual tradition that would overcome the deficiencies of contemporary life. Both employed images of seed as an embodiment of fertility, and of a crystal ball as a mystical solidification of light denoting absolute spiritual illumination. Langeteig feels that references to crystal in Pound's early poems and in Cantos 74 and 76 show that he and H.D. "are on the same wave length" as they see fluid substance becoming a stable and structured form: "Pound's vision of the ultimate light as a consolidation . . . is very parallel to H.D.'s vision of the ultimate light as a formal conversion." Hence, Langeteig's study shows that while each poet colored occultism with a strong consciousness of his or her own gender, they shared a general aim and used similar imagery to convey their sense of the transcendental.

Both poets thought romantic love, as distinguished from sex, was intimately linked to the poetic faculty. Pound shared the belief, traditional among poets, that the capacity for love offered an entry into a higher spiritual life. The love of women was a central element in his theories of troubadour poetry, for he considered it an aspect of the energy that pervades both the material universe and the world of such mystics and quasi-mystics as the troubadours. He praised love as the motivation for his favorite works of art, such as Dante's *Vita Nuova*, Cavalcanti's "Donna Mi Prega," and the Tempio in Rimini built by Sigismundo Malatesta as a monument to his wife. The figure of H.D. is in the background of Pound's imagination here, for his first poems in "Hilda's Book" were mainly love poems addressed to her as a sacred figure.

But the *Cantos* speaks more directly of sexuality and its association with fertility and creation. Canto 39 presents a series of fragments suggesting a ritual celebration of the coming of spring that culminates in the declaration: "His rod had made god in my belly." After passages on the irresistible forces of nature ("Moth is called over mountain") and a paraphrase from Hesiod's *Works and Days* on the proper time and method of plowing, Canto 47 addresses someone, probably Odysseus, asking questions that transpose the agricultural theme into images of copulation as a power parallel to that of nature's fertility:

> Hast thou found a nest softer than cunnus
> Or hast thou found better rest
> Hast'ou a deeper planting, doth thy death year
> Bring swifter shoot?
> Hast thou entered more deeply the mountain?[37]

After this comes the answer: "By prong have I entered these hills, / That the grass grow from my body." The complaint, in Canto 45—"They have brought whores for Eleusis"—is a metaphor for the abuses of "usura." But behind it is Pound's belief that the Eleusis ritual centered on a sacred sexual union symbolizing fertility. Pound's robust praise of male sexuality is naturally quite different in tone from H.D.'s erotic themes, which tend to focus on the complex feelings connected with love.

H.D.'s *Notes* also emphasize the creative power of love. She says flatly that "There is no great art period without great lovers" and that the "love-mind" must collaborate with the intensified consciousness of the "over-mind" if one is to attain vision. Physical love has a subordinate place here, but it is not rejected. H.D. characterizes the attachment of Christ and the Chinese poet Lo Fu to material things as a kind of love nearly indistinguishable from sexual love, and suggests that spirit arises from the bodily heat that also generates physical love: "Perhaps we cannot have spirit without body."[38]

Christ has an important place in H.D.'s *Notes* as an exemplar of love, but her observations about him reveal an eclectic view of religion much like that of Pound. Pound did not reject Christianity, but saw it as one aspect of mankind's general religious consciousness. Since he defined a god as "an eternal state of mind," it followed that the persistent human tendency to worship transcendental beings was itself divine. In concluding the *Notes*, H.D.

aligns the idea of Christ's divinity with the theme of the Eleusinian mysteries, and obliterates the idea of a special Christian revelation by declaring that Christ is present in flowers, shells, and birds. It is clear that she shared with Pound the conviction that religious belief is based in nature — that it is, in its origins, a celebration of nature's fertility.

6

Between the Wars

Every human talent, like every tree, has properties and
results which are entirely peculiar to it.

La Rochefoucauld

In the late 1920s and throughout the 1930s, both the lives and the
work of H.D. and Pound continued to lie apart, although the two
poets maintained an intermittent correspondence with each other.
During that period, H.D. lived at the Riant Château and her London flat at 169 Sloane Street, traveled to Venice and the United
States, and sometimes came to rest at Kenwin, the Bauhaus-style
house that Bryher had built at Territet in 1930–31. At this time,
Pound steadily wrote and published Cantos that ventured into
many historical periods, moving from Renaissance Italy to early
American history and the post–World War I period, but often reverting to classical antiquity. He was extending his field of interests voraciously, as usual, and incorporating these new materials
into his *Cantos*.

Very little of this had any meaning for H.D. She was indifferent or hostile to Pound's growing obsession with the Social Credit
theories of Major C. H. Douglas, his enthusiasm for Fascism, and
his interest in the anthropological theories of Leo Frobenius, and
disapproved of his anti-Semitism, for Bryher, after all, was of
Jewish descent. H.D. had moved to new scenes and cultivated

new interests, such as the cinema, remote from those of Pound, as she lived with Bryher and her successive husbands, McAlmon and Macpherson, in Paris, London, and Switzerland.

The Kenwin house provided H.D. with a quasi-permanent home after 1931. Her writing during this interwar period followed two distinct strands: poems that were either Greek translations or Greek-originated free verse, and prose novels and stories closely based on her own history. Both were sharp diversions from what Pound was doing and from what he had thought she ought to do. He showed little interest in her fiction and no interest in her film work, though she wrote to him about it.

The letters the two exchanged in this period are now in the Beinecke Library at Yale University. Much of Pound's side of the correspondence is lost, for H.D. wrote that "I don't file your letters or keep them as a rule." In these letters, the two childhood friends exchange birthday greetings, dwell on the personal relations of very old friends, and occasionally discuss matters of business and publishing. H.D. dealt mainly with such personal topics as her anguish at Aldington's new love affairs and his negotiations for a divorce, her travels, and common friends, with frequent expressions of affection. There are only a few references in the letters to what they were writing at the time. H.D. once wrote, apparently in reply to an inquiry from Pound, "I have no good poems by the way," but later sent what she called a sample of her "new incarnation," modestly suggesting that it showed that she had learned "to fly a little with my own wings."[1] This sample was probably something from her translation of Euripides' *Ion*, a project she had worked on for many years and was now taking up again. She did not preserve Pound's comment on it.

The letters from Pound that survive are mainly in the same vein, containing Christmas greetings and similar sentiments, with occasional blasts at Pound's usual targets—banks, America, England—and such news as the arrival of James Laughlin in Europe. H.D. and Pound apparently continued to write to each other while their writing and their travels took independent courses, but a letter of 27 August 1928 from H.D. in reply to one from Pound sounds as if there has been no serious communication for some time. It also suggests that she felt distance growing between them. She says she has not written because she did not know what to say, and speaks uneasily of finding some common basis for continuing their friendship. The natural thing, she says, would be to go back to "the very far past," by which she apparently means their Pennsylvania days. But she warns Pound of her sense of alienation by adding, "I have no real tie at all with that . . . everything is different and I am different."[2] Her statement that she has no tie should be taken with some skepticism. She had just completed writing *HERmione*, which involved a long immersion in memories of "the very far past."

It is easy to believe that she was now "different," but the past still mattered, as we see from the very different letter she wrote to Pound in 1929, at a time of deep emotional disturbance.[3] Her failed marriage, her travels, and her painful experiences with lovers of both sexes during the intervening years must have affected her profoundly, for she remained vulnerable and indecisive in everything that did not pertain to her writing. She told Pound that she had built a wall between her two selves and kept away from her old friends, but that the wall had collapsed when she learned that Aldington and Dorothy Yorke had parted. Aldington's new effort to secure a long-overdue divorce in order to marry Brigit Patmore made H.D. realize that she still loved him, and reminded her painfully of the episodes connected with Perdita's birth and Aldington's hostility. "I put down a lot of myself," she wrote, "after Perdita's birth." She was emotionally attached both to Bryher and to Macpherson, but wrote that she still loved Aldington It is not surprising, considering the whirlpool of emotions in which she was living, that she should admit to feelings of confusion: "Well . . . I don't understand anything," she wrote, adding an expression of gratitude for the kindness of Pound's letter.

H.D.'s sense of her own identity appears to have been an issue with her since childhood. In her letter, she reported: "One side of me is rich and creative, the other has not yet had time to let the Sun get to it." She yielded easily to domination by others at first, but then struggled to overcome this submersion and to assert her independence and self-confidence, a pattern we see repeated in her relations with Pound, Frances Gregg, Bryher, Freud, and others. She had explained her feelings of insecurity years before, in a 1916 letter to John Cournos: "I have faith in my work," she wrote. "What I want at times is to feel faith in myself, in my mere physical presence in the world."[4] H.D. now said that the intended divorce from Aldington promised to give her this sense of "physical presence." She wrote: "I had no place in the air and no place on earth. Now maybe I have a place in the air and a place on the earth."

As for the past that had seemed so distant in her letter of 1928, she said, in a sentence beginning "I love you Ezra," that it was not forgotten, as she had thought, but still "there." While she was now living quietly with Bryher and Macpherson, she said, she sometimes felt lonely: "they just ARE not of that cycle, and I was made by that pre-war London atmosphere and cycle, you, Bgt. some, Rummel, all the in and out and mellow strength one got in those days, from London."[5] Perhaps because she felt the loss of those times, she asked Pound to give her "fair warning" if they were to meet. While assuring him that his letters were valuable to her, she wrote, "I couldn't bear to see you . . . I should cry and cry." Nevertheless, she suggested, in a scrawl in the margin of the typed letter, that she might borrow Bryher's car and meet Pound at some halfway point between Territet and Rapallo. She closed by suggesting that she and Pound might do something experimental in cinema work, and wrote: "Anyhow Ezra whatever I do . . . and decide to do, it won't be for lack of affection and of loyalty to everything you managed to do for me." Pound, still displaying interest in H.D.'s writing, had apparently asked her to send poems she had written. She said she would try to find some, adding, with her continued tactful deference to his critical powers, that she hopes he will not mind if they are "not suitable."

In 1925 Pound published his *Draft of XVI Cantos* and H.D. her *Collected Poems,* and the latter sections of the two books of verse offer a fair indication of their relation as poets at this time. H.D. is immersed in ancient Greece, concerned primarily with sacred and erotic themes, the relations of gods and mortals, and her settings are the beaches and shrines of the Greek islands. Pound, on the other hand, had been writing the Cantos dealing with the wars of fifteenth-century Italy, the "Hell Cantos," and verses condemning modern warfare and lamenting its victims. The personal elements in the two bodies of poetry contrast with each other. There is much intensely emotional first-person verse in H.D.'s lyrics, while Pound refers to his own experiences only rarely, in matter-of-fact tones: "I sat on the Dogana's steps / For the gondolas cost too much that year," or, in an allusion to a Paris hotel revisited after some years, "The Elysée carries a name on / And the bus behind me gives me a date for a peg."[6]

However, the styles of both are still strongly shaped by Imagism, or, more generally, by the Modernism both had introduced into poetry. The lines of free verse are clipped and economical, establishing variable rhythms; there is much dependence on sensuous imagery; and the syntax and vocabulary are free of archaism, approaching natural speech. The two poets have in common a fascination with their respective historical periods, and much of the vitality of their work is owed to their colorful historical or legendary sources. H.D. introduces one stylistic feature completely foreign to Pound's practice: a subtle interplay of rhyme, near-rhyme, and other phonic effects that frequently appears in her later free verse. An example appears in "Thetis," where the goddess speculates on what an unsuspecting fisherman would have thought of her as she emerged from the sea:

> Little he would have guessed,
> (had such a one
> watched by his nets,)
> that a goddess flung from the crest
> of the wave the blue of its own
> bright tress of hair,
> the blue of the painted stuff
> it wore for dress.[7]

There is no evidence that Pound gave much thought to H.D. during this time, though he seems to have initiated a 1928 exchange of letters. However, as the chapter on H.D.'s autobiographical novels will show, she remained intensely aware of him, and if he no longer entered her creative life as a guide, he played a significant part in it as a subject. For years after they had parted, memories of Pound and his influence continued to occupy her thoughts and to find places in her writing.

The events of 1933 show how far the interests of the two poets were diverging. It was on 30 January that Pound, now a full-fledged admirer of Italian Fascism, had the meeting with Mussolini recorded in Canto 41. H.D., on the other hand, now turned more seriously to psychoanalysis. She moved to Vienna in March to begin sessions with Freud, which lasted until July 1934, when Freud became ill and H.D. went to Kenwin. She returned for further sessions in 1934, and later continued psychoanalysis with other analysts. Pound considered Freudian theory to be nonsense, and H.D., of course, had no sympathy with Fascism or Mussolini.

In a letter of 24 March 1933, H.D., announcing that she had come to Vienna to study with Freud, adopted an almost apologetic tone. She feels it necessary to admit that Freud is "of course of the house of Israel and the seed of David," expecting that Pound will be sarcastic about her venture into psychoanalysis, but tries to mollify him by assuring him that Freud has seen his periodical contributions. She reports that at this time she is "somewhat caught in the old war-vibration, and don't in all ways like it," an enigmatic comment that seems to refer to the mixture of emotional stimulation and marital troubles of her war years. It is an affectionate letter, proposing a meeting in Paris, and signed to "dear Ezra" as "Dryad."[8]

Her regard for Freud no doubt increased H.D.'s distance from Pound. At this time, some years before the Anschluss, Nazis were already agitating in Vienna. H.D. reported that swastikas were chalked on the pavement outside Freud's door, and that he felt threatened and considered it dangerous for her to come to see him. These developments must have made H.D. more impatient with Pound's anti-Semitism, which no doubt was one component of his persistent hostility to Freudianism. As late as May 1954, he wrote to H.D.: "Have felt yr / vile Freud all bunk . . . You got into the wrong pig stye, ma chere. But not too late to climb out."[9]

The two records of her sessions with Freud in 1933 and 1934, *Advent*, written (against the doctor's advice) while she was being treated, and "Writing on the Wall," written in London in the fall of 1944, while the city was under siege, mention Pound only incidentally.

H.D. found in psychoanalysis a confirmation and extension of Imagist poetics. It has long been recognized that the dreamwork's devices of condensation, displacement, and visual imagery, as Freud described them, resemble the tropes employed in poetry. Her sessions with Freud convinced H.D. that the dream mechanisms were important, and they appear prominently in such late poems as *Helen in Egypt* and *Sagesse*, where characters, places, and events undergo the effects of the dreamwork. Pound, on his part, did not miss the affinity between poetry and mental process. He said in the early days of psychoanalysis that the image was a psychological "complex." He reported that one of his Imagist poems was based directly on a dream, and such images as those in "The Return," with their occult suggestiveness, resemble dream imagery.

As a perception whose significance is inexhaustible, the Image of H.D.'s poems conforms to Pound's idea that the Image should produce a sense of freedom from the limits of space and time, and that it is better to produce a single Image than many books. In her work with Freud, H.D. learned that the enigmatic visual images that disguised unconscious emotions were like this, that they harbored unsuspected treasures of personal meaning when they were interpreted. In calling them "hieroglyphs of the unconscious," as she did in *Tribute to Freud*, she took the hieroglyphs she had seen in Egypt to possess not only the immortal prophetic capacity mentioned in "The Walls Do Not Fall" but also the latent psychological significance that psychoanalysis attributed to the imagery of dreams. As we have seen, H.D.'s idea of the hieroglyph parallels Pound's ideas about the ideogram. Both use visual form to suggest covert meaning, and these other forms of writing led both to extend the Image into imagery that was more enigmatic and packed with unexpressed mythic significance of the kind Fenollosa saw in the Chinese characters. Thus, in *Helen in Egypt,* hieroglyphics appear to Helen to tell her own story, but they also conceal it, as dream images do, and are understood only intuitively. Pound's use of the Chinese characters in the *Cantos* is perhaps the ultimate extension of the Image, as they create an impressive visual effect that, to the Western eye, is at once indecipherable and suggestive of rich and remote meaning.

While their letters continued, the two poets now suspended their poetic dialogue, as neither was writing poems with the other in mind. Pound did continue to acknowledge H.D.'s importance. In a review of the women poets of his generation published in the Rapallo paper *Il Mare* in 1933, he put H.D. at the head of the list, and credited her with a "profound and true mytho-poetic sense." He noted that, as an Imagist, she had adhered to the principles of the first manifesto by never using a superfluous word. On the other hand, she had displayed no development in twenty years, and had written novels of "incredible silliness." This suggests that Pound had read at least some of the novels in which characters obviously patterned on himself appeared, but there is no record of his reaction to them. He did not claim that he had influenced H.D., but instead said that while she was not a "disciple" of William Carlos Williams, her work could be related to his.[10] Pound sent a copy of the paper to H.D., and in spite of the mixed evaluation, she thanked him for remembering her.

H.D. had psychological counseling for many years as a consequence of her occasional breakdowns. Havelock Ellis's equivocal relation with her had been something of that nature; she had consulted Mary Chadwick, a London practitioner, and Hanns Sachs before Freud, and was later treated by Walter Schmideberg and Erich Heydt. Her two sequences of sessions with Freud convinced her, in opposition to Freud's own strictly scientific views, that the rational and the occult were parallel paths to truth. Although she said she "adored" him and thought of him as a "great artist," she nevertheless felt that while they never openly disagreed, "there was an argument implicit in our very bones." She recognized that Freud refused to believe in the afterlife or in occult phenomena, but limited his work to analyzing human relationships.

Her account of her sessions with Freud, *Tribute to Freud*, written about ten years later in 1944, and *Advent*, a rewritten version of a journal she kept in 1933 while the sessions were in progress, are continuous with the persistently autobiographical mode of her fiction and much of her poetry. One of the discoveries she made about the subconscious has a bearing on the apparent discontinuities of both her own later poems and Pound's *Cantos*. As she and Freud worked together, "My imagination wandered at will . . . Fragmentary ideas, apparently unrelated, were often found to be part of a special layer or stratum of thought and memory, therefore to belong together . . . The dead were living in so far as they lived in memory or were recalled in dreams." Then, speaking of "memories, visions, dreams," she says "there are priceless broken fragments that are meaningless until we find the other broken bits to match them."[11]

Such voyages into her mind and memory brought H.D. into the realm of the rhetoric that governs the *Cantos*, and reveals an underlying correspondence between her approach to the long poem and Pound's. Unrelated, fragmentary thoughts and recollections, randomly gathered, fall together when they are recalled within the arena of imagination. Past events resurrected in visions or recollections, set side by side without extraneous connective comment, acquire meaning that lies beyond mere articulation. Unity and coherence were less important than striking isolated passages, and these could be even more effective if they protruded sharply from the body of the poem because of discontinuities of subject or style.

Her sessions with Freud naturally took H.D. back to recollections of her early life, but there are only passing references to Pound in *Tribute to Freud* and *Advent,* including one that connects him with her clairvoyant powers. When she was eighteen or nineteen, H.D. had a curious vision of a stone divided into two panels, one showing a snake, the other a thistle. The young Pound consulted some reference books and announced that the vision was "a flashback in time or a vision of some future event" having to do with Aesculapius, the god of healing. He proved to be right, at least with regard to the future, for a few years later, H.D. came across the design on a ring displayed in the Louvre, the only instance of it she ever saw. The experience of course confirmed her belief in her visionary gift.

When she felt a sense of separation from her own poems, she attributed this, speculatively, to the loss of "the early companions of my first writing-period in London." But the companions she mentioned in this connection are Aldington and Lawrence, not Pound. Pound did appear, however, in her dreams. In one, he is associated with both Frances Gregg and D. H. Lawrence, and seems to object to H.D.'s consultations with Freud. In another, she seems to be recollecting dancing with him at school. Freud was told about their courtship and the opposition of her parents to Pound—"my first serious love-conflict." After noting this, H.D. added a brief lyrical passage—"Ezra and I took long walks"—recording their pleasure at finding early spring flowers. Freud seems to have completely missed the part that H.D.'s passionate and ambivalent feelings about Pound played in the disturbances of her psyche, attributing her problem to a fixation on her mother. However, her association with Pound emerged as a major theme in her later sessions with Dr. Heydt in Switzerland.

Tribute to Freud was written in London in the fall and winter of 1944, during the fifth year of World War II, and it is natural that H.D. should revert at that time to the thoughts of war's destructiveness that she and Pound had shared in the World War I period. She says that she wanted to discuss her psychological reactions to that war with Freud, but the approach of the new war prevented it. She succeeded, she reports, in taming her "personal little Dragon of war-terror" until the outbreak of World War II, which released a new tide of suffering and fear. Her *Advent* notes of 1933 mention an enigmatic fantasy of a tiger that will threaten Freud, but what the tiger represents is soon made clear as she says she recalls the "mob scene" before Buckingham Palace in August 1914, when she and Aldington were there to hear the king declare war on Germany.

Freud's influence on H.D.'s thoughts and poetry was permanent. When she broke her hip in 1956 and was bedridden in the Hirslanden Clinic for many months, the journal she kept was largely devoted to recording and analyzing her dreams in accordance with the principles she had learned from him.

A new phase of the Pound-H.D. relationship opened during a visit H.D. made to New York in 1937 to be interviewed by Norman Holmes Pearson, who was then a Yale graduate student co-editing the *Oxford Anthology of American Literature*. H.D. and Pearson quickly became friends, and the friendship deepened during World War II, when Pearson was stationed as an intelligence agent in London. The bond between the two was characterized by an enduring affection, but they were not lovers. Pearson came to know Pound through H.D. and ultimately became a third partner in their relationship, as he passed communications between them and took part in Pound's affairs, as well as H.D.'s. He was enthusiastic about H.D.'s poetry and became her most important supporter, reading her work in manuscript, advising and encouraging her, and handling such business matters as relations with publishers. In time, he grew nearly as close to Pound and did much to publicize his work. Unlike Pound, he consistently helped H.D. with praise and advice.[12] He set up an archive of her work at the Yale University Library and, after her death, acted as her literary executor.

One of the services Pearson performed for H.D. was attentiveness to Pound. He went to see Pound when he was confined at St. Elizabeths, sending H.D. accounts of his visits. Also, during a time when H.D. was alienated by Pound's Fascist opinions and unfriendly letters, Pearson urged her to renew the friendship. He became an indispensable intermediary when H.D. was reviewing her relationship with Pound and was so immersed in their exchanges that he felt himself to be part of a mystic triangle.

H.D. quite consciously identified herself with any woman who might be close to Pound. Over the years, Olga Rudge had become a fixed aspect of Pound's life. He frequently met her in the places in France and Italy where her musical activities took her, and spent summers with her and their small daughter in her house in Venice while Dorothy was in England visiting their son, Omar, and her mother. The strong-willed Rudge regarded herself as Pound's true partner and moved closer to him when, in 1929, he found a house for her in the village on the hill above Rapallo and began to divide his time regularly between his wife at 12 via Marsala in Rapallo and his lover at Casa 60 in Sant'Ambrogio. H.D., far from being jealous at this attachment, tried to help Pound secure a Guggenheim grant for Rudge to aid in her musical work.

In October 1938, Olivia Shakespear, Dorothy Pound's mother, died. Pound had first met his future wife when he had been invited to tea by Olivia; she had befriended both him and H.D. during their years in London and had raised the Pounds' son, Omar, from the time of his birth. Since Dorothy was too ill to travel, H.D., at Pound's request, came to London to help him clear out Mrs. Shakespear's flat. They had not met since their rendezvous nearly ten years before at H.D.'s Paris hotel in May 1929.

According to H.D.'s report to Bryher, during this meeting Pound gave her the facts about Maria's birth and spoke of recent times, no doubt describing the double life he was leading with Dorothy and Olga and the two children, who were being cared for by others. H.D. felt that Pound had shown a callous indifference to those whose lives he affected, and his revelations led her to feel grateful that she had not been involved with him. "It did upset me because I might have been landed in just such a mess if I had not broken with that past."[13] However, she did not break with him completely. Before leaving London, she told him that her new address would be the Villa Kenwin. Although they continued to correspond, and each remained a figure in the imagination and poetry of the other, the poets never met again.

In 1937 Pound had commented in some way on H.D.'s translation of *Ion*, and she defended the Hellenistic period, no doubt in response to his disapproval of her immersion in it. Perhaps as a sequel to their meeting in London, or in response to the writing she had sent him as evidence of her "new incarnation," Pound, writing in 1939, tried to regain his authority over her work. "Now time to go back to an effort of 1912," he wrote, "to get down into meaning and leave off the school room hellenism." He asked, in hectoring tones, whether she had read or understood anything since their association ("for the past 25 years"), and whether she had learned anything from her translations. But the letter is signed "love, ever perdurable."[14] H.D. meekly replied by admitting that she was not doing anything noteworthy, reporting on her current reading, and inviting Pound to tell her whom he had met during his recent visit to America.

Pound had spent from April to June 1939 in the United States, and had met a variety of people, including old friends such as E. E. Cummings, William Carlos Williams, and Louis Zukofsky, and new ones such as Marianne Moore and H. L. Mencken. He had also been able to see a number of members of Congress and officials of the Roosevelt administration while wandering around Washington. Much of his writing in recent years had been concerned with his eccentric political and economic theories, and he wanted to bring them to bear on American policies through contacts with the politicians. But he had wildly mistaken the value of his authority, and his offers of service were rejected. He visited various universities and received an honorary degree at his alma mater, Hamilton College, but if he intended to make some entry into politics, he was disappointed.

In June 1938, after long and painful negotiations, H.D., at Aldington's urgent request, secured a divorce from him. Aldington's companion was now Brigit Patmore's daughter-in-law,

Netta, and the timing of the divorce was critical, for Netta was pregnant, and Aldington wanted to be free to marry her so that the child could be declared legitimate. This definitive uprooting of the past caused H.D. much anguish, and soon afterward she turned to memories of her wartime life with Aldington in her novel, *Madrigal,* which was published as *Bid Me to Live.* This was in some respects a retelling of events mentioned in her novels of the 1920s, of her life in wartime London, and of the unhappy marriages and love affairs in the flat on Mecklenburgh Square. However, it differs from the early novels in one significant respect: there is no figure representing Pound in it. The major male character is based on D. H. Lawrence.

Pound, on his part, had little time for H.D. in the years between the wars. He was steadily working on and publishing his *Cantos,* which were written in a variety of poetic styles, with some still recalling the Imagist principles. However, one of the finest of these Cantos shows Pound reverting to themes neighboring those of H.D.'s classical world. Canto 47 begins with an impressive paraphrase of Circe's advice to Odysseus, and soon moves to one of the few uses in the *Cantos* of non-Homeric Greek poetry, a quotation from Bion's "Lament for Adonis."

By this time, both poets had moved away from their early concepts of romantic love, and H.D.'s love poetry had acquired a tone of anguish no doubt connected with the rejections she had suffered from Aldington and Pound. She chose to translate such passages from Sappho as:

> Ah, love is bitter and sweet,
> but which is more sweet,
> the sweetness or the bitterness?
> none has spoken it.[15]

And, in spite of her claim that her poetry did not reflect her "personal self," as her novels did, there is a deeply personal note in such lines as these from "Epigrams":

> O ruthless, perilous, imperious hate,
> you cannot thwart

the promptings of my soul,
You can not weaken nay nor dominate
Love that is mateless . . .[16]

Also by this time, the two poets had found different uses for the themes of love and sexuality in their work. Pound connected human congress with the general idea of the earth's fertility, while for H.D. the paradoxes of passion and affection offered a field for exploring the psyche.

However, some stylistic resemblances persist in these interwar years. Both speak of love through imagery that is often similar, depending heavily on nature, as in H.D.'s garden or seashore poems and Pound's passages on farming. And more fundamentally, their love poetry of this period springs from the same conviction, apparent in the earlier writing of both poets, that the libido is allied to spiritual insight and is an important source of creativity.

The last poems Pound wrote before the outbreak of World War II, Cantos 52–71, published in January 1940, took him even farther from the stylistic and thematic ground he had once shared with H.D. These are the so-called Chinese and John Adams Cantos, drawn from Chinese and American historical sources. While carrying forward his epic, Pound also involved himself, as usual, in a wide variety of other activities. He wrote the critical books, *ABC of Reading* and *Guide to Kulchur,* agitated energetically about politics and the state of learning and publishing, and continued his study of Chinese and Japanese ideograms. His musical activities continued. He assisted Olga Rudge in recovering the lost compositions of Antonio Vivaldi, and collaborated with her in presenting a series of concerts in Rapallo. In addition, torrents of letters continued to stream out of Rapallo in many directions. Much of this correspondence has to do with recommending authors to editors and publishers, but H.D. is never mentioned in this connection.

When England and France declared war against Germany in early September 1939, neither Pound nor H.D. was at first greatly affected. But when Italy entered the war in 1940, Pound could no longer write to most of his usual correspondents. This, of course, included H.D., and their occasional exchanges of letters, which had become less frequent, now ceased altogether. However, the war was to provide a setting for their best poetry, and to raise their poetic relationship to new levels.

7

Pound in H.D.'s Fiction

Ezra was no more than a gesture out of the infinite hu-
mour of space.

Frances Gregg to John Cowper Powys, 21 April 1929

H.D. was altogether too elusive for me. I puzzled over
her mystique.

Perdita Schaffner (daughter)

Throughout her life, H.D. wrote a considerable body of autobiographical fiction, some of it unpublished or published posthumously. She is one of the most self-revelatory of novelists. She
said, in later years, that her motive in writing these was to create
her "legend," her search for an ideal, Eternal Lover based on
Isis's quest for the scattered fragments of the body of Osiris.
Pound had used the Egyptian myth in his own way by calling
the series of articles that he wrote for the *New Age* in 1912 "I
Gather the Limbs of Osiris." Critics are accustomed to differen-
tiating between the authorial voice and the actual writer, but in
H.D.'s persistently autobiographical novels, the two are nearly
indistinguishable.

H.D. herself explained why this is so. In a letter written to
John Cournos in 1918, she said she was beginning to work on a
novel because she did not want to put her "personal self" into her
poems, since this "personal self" had come between "me" and "my

real self, my real artist personality." She was writing the novel, therefore, she said, not as a work of art but as a way of purging her mind of the "personal self" that somehow interfered with the poet she felt to be her "real self."[1]

As H.D. acknowledged, many of the heroines of these novels are "the same woman," whose lives reflect her own "legend." She said in a letter to Pearson that she wrote one of her novels under a pseudonym, Delia Alton, because it was "too near and too intimate for H.D." It is fairly safe, therefore, to read the feelings of the autobiographical characters as a record of her own emotions. Many recognizable figures from her life appear in these novels, and Pound is among them.

However, the novels are certainly intended as works of art. Often rewritten and produced with great care, they make skillful use of the psychology-based styles that came into vogue after Joyce's *Ulysses*, display much originality, and have strong aesthetic qualities. Since she considered their author to be an identity separate from the H.D. of her poetry, she experimented with a number of pseudonyms, ultimately settling on "Delia Alton" as the name of this author.

These romans-à-clef are exceptionally candid. Many of them follow the events of H.D.'s life closely, exposing her passionate and confused feelings about Pound as well as her attitudes toward other people. The prominent place Pound occupies in some of them shows that she continued to be occupied with memories of their relationship for years after they had parted.

As we have seen, considerable light is shed on the youthful love between the young Ezra and Hilda in *HERmione,* which was completed in 1927 but not published until 1981, twenty years after her death. When she wrote it, H.D. was forty years of age, had been married and separated, and was recalling events that had occurred about twenty years before, when she was between nineteen and twenty-two, and Pound was writing the love poems addressed to her that appear in "Hilda's Book." The character of the heroine's young lover, George Lowndes, is unmistakably based on Pound, as is immediately clear when she receives a letter from Venice exactly in Pound's style, consisting of "huge scrawled-over handwriting taking up, in one sentence, the whole of a wide square of distinguished thin sea-grey paper."[2]

The setting is the Philadelphia suburbs of H.D.'s youth, and many of the details, such as her family situation, her failure at Bryn Mawr, and Pound's fame as a writer in England correspond to the facts. It is therefore reasonable to suppose that the relations between Hermione and George represent H.D.'s recollections of her love affair with Pound and her feelings about him. However, the chronology of the novel is not that of the actual events, and allowances must be made for the tension that exists between autobiography and the demands of fiction, and for the reflexive views of the mature woman looking back at her past.

HERmione is focused on the emotions of the heroine, the counterpart of the young H.D., and deals with family and other concerns, yet her obsession with "George" occupies a large part of her inner life. When George returns from a visit to Venice, the two enact scenes of virginal passion that were fairly serious in those puritanical times. Hermione hopes that George will take her away from her unhappy life and clarify her vision of herself, but her attitude toward him is confused and ambivalent. He is an overpowering presence, and she admires him and finds him beautiful, almost able to transform the woods where they are kissing into the Forest of Arden. But she is also strongly resistant, thinks of him as a "harlequin," believes he is incapable of true love, unreliable, artificial, even nonexistent — "Is there a George at all?"

Worse, she senses that he obliterates her identity, for she feels "smudged out" when he is kissing her, and is most aware, not of his ardor, but of the feeling that her head resting on the moss where she is lying is turning to marble and that she is becoming "dehumanized." In her tangled thoughts, rendered with masterly sensitivity and detail, she feels that George does not understand her, yet she admires him because he has traveled, is widely read, and possesses a powerful charisma. While she does not respond to him erotically, she wishes she did. Resting on her bed on a hot day, she reflects:

George was like a great tawny beast, a sort of sub-lion pawing at her, pawing with great hand at her tousled garments. George had been like a great lion but if he had simply bared teeth, torn away her garments with bared fangs, she would have understood, would have put narrow arms about great shoulders, would have yielded to him. George was neither beast nor man . . .[3]

These impressions perhaps tell us more about H.D. than about Pound. If they exaggerate the young Hilda's actual thoughts, the fact is that her expectations of him lasted for some time after the period reflected in the novel, for she followed him to England and suffered a shock when she learned of his engagement to Dorothy Shakespear. In the novel, Hermione's ambivalence about George continues up to the point where she tells her parents that she intends to marry him, although she has felt all along that it is impossible, and tells George so when he assumes that they will be married.

Literature is an important aspect of the love relations between the two. The way in which the young lovers of the novel speak in a literary idiom, with allusions to Shakespeare, Swinburne, and Longfellow, reflects the conversations between Ezra and Hilda. Poetry and passion blend as George forces Hermione down to kiss her violently, repeating the lines from Swinburne's "Atalanta in Calydon" beginning "The hounds of spring are on winter's traces," lines whose rhythms often recur in her mind afterward. It is as if he has impregnated her with poetry. Hermione identifies herself with her namesake from *The Winter's Tale*, and H.D. herself entered into this merging of life and literature in later years by naming her daughter Perdita, after the daughter of Hermione in Shakespeare's play.

In a scene that seems to recall an actual conversation, Hermione shows George some of her writing: "Pages fluttered in the hands of George Lowndes . . . What George holds in his hands is my life's beginning. What George flutters is my life's ending." After expressing doubt that she could have done the writing without help, he unexpectedly responds to it with animation, saying,

"I tell you *this is writing*" with an emphasis H.D. conveys by spacing and italicizing the words. She often repeats to herself his rather confused words of praise: "it's like the choriambics of a forgotten Melic."

However, this harmonious moment is accompanied by an exchange that, even if it is fictional, represents the different approaches to poetry the two were to take for large parts of their careers. When Hermione displays a picture painted by her mother, George speaks of it with contempt, and she defends it by saying that her mother loved it. George replies that "Love doesn't make good art." Hermione silently contradicts by thinking, "Love is writing."[4] Pound, always striving for objectivity, wrote, as he said, through a series of masks, and used historical documents and other texts as sources. H.D., on the other hand, exploited her capacity for strong emotion, using her writing to elaborate a personal legend centered on passionate attachments. In a fascinating reversal, the two were to exchange these perspectives as they renewed their poetic voices in old age.

The text of *HERmione*, like most of H.D.'s fictions, reflects a freedom and variety of style characteristic of the Modernism in which she and Pound participated. The paratactic passages of interior monologue recording the heroine's jumbled thoughts create the impression of discontinuity seen in Pound's mature style. The heroine often thinks about the difficulties of language: "Words were her plague and words were her redemption." While this consciousness of language is not remarkable in a Modern author, these passages may reveal underlying responses to Pound's doctrines of the word in such essays as "How to Read," where exact reference and "the loose use of words" are prominent themes. When Hermione is lying ill she says, in reply to comments about science, "abstractions are so frightening," which perhaps recalls Pound's injunction, "Go in fear of abstractions," from the 1913 statement "A Few Don'ts by an Imagiste." There is a clear echo of former times when H.D. has Hermione say, in trying to explain the elusive nature of their friendship to Fayne Rabb, "Images form, we can't talk in mere words."[5] Other responses, however, are clearly challenges to Pound's influence. In acknowledging that

"Writing had somehow got connected up with George Lowndes," Hermione seems to mean that he is an impediment, for she thinks he is unable to connect "writing" with real things.

In the second part of *HERmione*, the heroine draws away from George, turning from the heterosexual lover, with his suffocating amorousness, to a more fulfilling lesbian attachment to Fayne Rabb. Susan Stanford Friedman, in her reading of *HERmione*, characterizes the novel as an instance of "birth and rebirth," in which H.D. overcomes her earlier self, the young woman in love, by writing her story through another, more mature identity. As she puts it, the narrator knows what her heroine does not know, that her struggle with convention is a way of winning freedom as a woman artist. Friedman observes that the novel shows the experience of passion and the escape from it to be essential to the artist—a pattern, she points out, seen in Lawrence's *Sons and Lovers* and Joyce's *Portrait of the Artist as a Young Man*—and she regards Hermione's move from heterosexual to lesbian love as an essential step in her development.[6]

George, who is unacceptable as a lover and inconsistent in his appraisal of her writing, does stimulate Hermione's interest in literature, but Fayne Rabb, while offering her emotional satisfaction, does not. George leads her to write, while Fayne, who values her for herself, tells her, "Your writing is nothing really."[7] Ultimately, Hermione's two friends deceive her by becoming lovers, and she contracts a serious illness that ultimately releases her from her dependence on both—developments that correspond to the actual events of H.D.'s life, and to the brief love affair between Pound and Frances Gregg.

Friedman illuminates H.D.'s complex relation to Pound's work within the framework of her view that the borrowings from the writings of men that appear in many of her texts—as in *HERmione*—constitute an "appropriation" of masculine power to feminine, and often specifically lesbian, energies that free her from the domination of men and promote her personal liberation and empowerment as a writer. Identifying the younger Hermione with the H.D. of the Imagist period, she also characterizes the style of the novel as a repudiation of Imagism. She calls allusions to other texts, including Pound's and her own, "rescriptions" that transform their meaning. Among Friedman's examples are echoes from H.D.'s *Sea Garden* poems, whose imagery, widely admired for its cold precision and objectivity, reappears in *HERmione* in contexts that expose its erotic subtext.

The poems of "Hilda's Book" use such imagery as "My Lady is tall and fair to see / She swayeth as the poplar tree," and "She hath some tree-born spirit of the wood / About her . . . ," an identification Pound pursued by dubbing H.D. "Dryad." Friedman shows that H.D. borrows this imagery in *HERmione* to frame a codified reply to Pound's depiction of her as a passive love object by having her heroine use the tree imagery to express her rejection of this rôle.[8] Hermione applies the tree image to herself, frequently repeating the formula "I am tree" or some variation of it, such as, "I am in the word . . . TREE. I am TREE exactly." Tracing the recurrences of this image and others from "Hilda's Book" in Hermione's developing thoughts, Friedman finds that she uses them to liberate herself from George's dominance, for while she first feels imprisoned by them, she soon realizes that "George would never love a tree" and ultimately declares, "I am free of George."[9]

At a moment when she is about to turn away from George, Hermione thinks, "TREE. I am the Tree of life. Tree. I am a tree planted by the rivers of water." The source of her idea appears when she thinks, "I am a tree. TREE is my new name out of the Revelations,"[10] an allusion to Revelation 2:7, "To him that overcometh will I give to eat of the tree of life." This radical displacement of Pound's imagery is a decisive claim of independence. The tree is no longer a surrogate for the trite chivalric view of woman found in "Hilda's Book" but a symbol of independent spiritual fulfillment.

Friedman shows that while George challenges Hermione's sense of independence, she nevertheless uses Pound's metaphor to assert her autonomy and to see his power as negligible. As the tree image becomes the vessel of Hermione's transformation, she thinks, "*I am the word Aum* and I am Tree and I shall have a new name and I am the word tree."[11] She is now "tree," in a different, mystical sense, even if the metaphor enabling this shift originated in Pound's early poems.

Friedman has also pointed out what is perhaps a more fundamental verbal link between H.D.'s novel and Pound's early verses. The name that H.D. chose for her heroine is derived, of course, from Shakespeare's *Winter's Tale*, but she was also strongly influenced by a converging vocable from one of Pound's "Hilda's Book" poems, "Shadow." It tells a lover that the speaker has seen another who is more desirable, saying, "I saw HER yesterday." By incorporating the capitalized pronoun into the name of the heroine who is her surrogate, H.D. casts herself as the preferred lover. She usually employs the shortened version of the name, "Her," in grammatically subjective positions, constantly creating jarring effects, as Friedman observes. Friedman regards this borrowing as further evidence of H.D.'s effort to counter Pound's dominance, but her heroine accepts the label, thinking, "I am . . . I am . . . HER exactly" and even preserves Pound's sense that it refers generically to a lover, for she expresses her self-regard and her love for Fayne by thinking, "Her. I am Her. She is Her. Knowing her I know Her."[12]

H.D., we recall, was first introduced to Swinburne and the other late Victorians by Pound within the framework of their erotic relationship in Pennsylvania. In her novel, she transfers the poetry that accompanied their lovemaking from a heterosexual register to a lesbian one. Hermione's relationship with Fayne Rabb is punctuated by quotations from Swinburne. She repeats such lines as "O sister my sister O fleet sweet swallow" from Swinburne's "Itylus," and seems to experience her life with Fayne in the world of his poetry, actually calling her "Itylus." Recollections she had shared with Pound of Swinburne and the Victorian poets occur in H.D.'s other novels as well.[13] By including echoes of poems written by Pound or associated with him as features of her own work, H.D. was continuing her dialogue with him, using such references to declare her independence, but also acknowledging his enduring influence.

♪

Paint It Today, written in 1921 but not published until 1992, overlaps and follows *HERmione*, since it is based on events occurring between 1909 and 1912, set first in Pennsylvania and then in England. It deals mainly with H.D.'s lesbian relationships, but there are a few allusions to a figure called Raymond (recalling that Pound's childhood name was "Ra") who appears as "the fiancé" of the heroine, Midget, and later as a lover and poet. At first, this character is called a "hectic, blundering, untried, mischievous, and irreverent male youth," who has somehow rifled the heroine's sacred feelings and left them "exposed by the roadside, reft from the shelter of their holy setting."[14] This no doubt refers to the time when Pound betrayed the nineteen-year-old Hilda with other girls, and she turned to her friendship with Frances Gregg.

Later comments on Raymond are less absolute and more confused. He had shown Midget "the shadow of an understanding" rather than understanding itself, but the narrator also feels that, although this shadow was something even weaker—"the very small and watered shadow of a shadow"—nevertheless, such a shadow, on reflection, becomes "a glorious color, not a glorious color, but the heart of a glorious color, like the innermost heart of the intense anemone, or like the fervor of dark eyes."[15] The ambiguities of Midget's feelings are compounded when, after a quarrel with her mother, she recalls that she would not have accepted Raymond's attentions if she had not "cared for" him. It is hard to know what to make of these uncertain comments, but if they reflect H.D.'s 1921 thoughts about Pound, they suggest that she thought their relationship might have matured into passionate love.

Paint It Today offers the fullest account (perhaps partly fictionalized) of the time when Pound showed his possessive attitude toward H.D. by preventing her from accompanying Frances Gregg and her husband to the Continent. Pound also seems to have a part in Midget's account of a lover with whom she shares a house in the woods. This idealized figure seems to be based mainly on Cecil Gray, but since he is described as "a great poet," and writes poems better than Midget, H.D. seems to have Pound in mind as well.

H.D.'s recollections of Pound appear again in one of the sections of *Palimpsest,* a triptych fiction which was begun soon after her return from her trip to Egypt with Bryher in 1923. This work consists of three narratives or novellas—"Hipparchia," "Murex," and "Secret Name"—with very different settings and actions. The heroine of the first is a young Greek woman living in second-century Rome; the second portrays a woman who talks to a friend in her London flat in the early 1920s about the woman with whom her husband has been unfaithful; the third is about an American woman visitor to the Egyptian tombs and temples of Luxor. The protagonists of these stories are clearly based on H.D. herself, for each one does writing of some kind and has difficult relations with a lover or husband. The stories are sensitive and introspective, and their complex thought processes are followed in extremely resourceful and varying styles that range between the intricacy of Henry James and the interior monologue of Joyce. Only one, "Hipparchia," contains a Pound-like character. However, the name of the woman in "Murex," who seems to be a self-portrait, is "Raymonde," which recalls that of the "fiancé" based on Pound in *Paint It Today,* suggesting, however deviously, a process of identification.

The relations between the facts of H.D.'s wartime life and "Hipparchia," the story set in ancient Rome, are close and intriguing. Hipparchia's lover, Marius, is clearly Aldington; Olivia, her rival, is Dorothy Yorke; Hipparchia's second lover, Verrus, is Cecil Gray (he calls Hipparchia "Person," Gray's way of addressing H.D.); and Julia Augusta, the admirer who comes to see Hipparchia after she has disposed of her lovers, is a counterpart of Bryher.[16]

The character who occupies a place in Hipparchia's life, corresponding in many respects to the one Pound occupied in H.D.'s, is a minor one, her father's younger brother, Philip. It is a much kinder treatment of Pound (if it is, in fact, based on him) than the one in *Paint It Today.* Philip and Hipparchia had wandered in the mountains together during her youth, and he had urged her to work harder at her writing. However, he is now only a memory, for he fell in the wars against Mithridates before the time of the story. While she is in a state of perplexity about her love affairs, Hipparchia longs for "intimacy without intercourse," such as she enjoyed with him. It is dangerous, of course, to extrapolate from fiction to real life, but Hipparchia's memories of Philip seem to be convincing echoes of some of H.D.'s feelings toward Pound.

Hipparchia is preoccupied with preserving the refinement of Greek culture in the dominant but coarse cultural environment of Rome, and Philip represents the Greek spirit to her, for he has left an unfinished compilation of Greek works for her to complete. (In this respect, he does not resemble Pound, who differed with H.D. on Greek matters.) As she prepares to leave Rome for the country, she seems to see him everywhere, even in her own reflection: "It was herself (yet Philip) facing her from a pure goblet."[17] When, in Tusculum, she turns to her writing, her feelings are aroused by memories of Philip: "He goaded her fine tempered intellect with his precision, with his flaming subtlety. Philip was her passion, her intellect, her mind which none had broken . . . Would I know this intellectual ecstacy [*sic*] when body and brain are merged like a sword and its very victim? I am the victim of the sword my spirit. This is true marriage. Philip shows me true enlightenment."[18] One wonders, can these be feelings that Pound once inspired in H.D.?

However, these emotions are not without their ambiguities, for she identifies Philip with Verrus, the lover who does not appreciate her literary work and whom she comes to hate: "She had loved Verrus because he was like young Philip," and, "It was Philip she left when she left Verrus."[19] This apparently contradictory identification corresponds with what H.D. often said about her own ideas. She tended to blend her various lovers together in her mind in an effort to configure the ideal lover she regarded as the object of her life-quest.

H.D. also assigns to her heroine her own tendency to idealize masculine figures, but Philip, in a feminizing pattern that occurs in her poetry, is gradually transformed into a female deity in her thoughts. "Philip was a sword, Philip was her mind but mind was

pure god, mind was a goddess with ember violets and no san-
dals."[20] Hipparchia herself becomes a kind of prophetess with
powers matching those of her mentor.

But, after she recovers from a fever, Hipparchia feels that the
world of immediate experience is of more significance than literature, and she is ready to give up her effort to preserve Greek culture, conceding that "Greece is now lost." As she hears the pierc-
ing song of a bird, she asks herself, "Of what use was poetry and
inspiration?"[21] With this insight, she moves beyond Philip's influence. Recalling that she identified herself with him through the
reflection in the silver goblet, she feels that although "Philip was
herself yet magnified," still, "She did not love herself however
magnified."[22] This is a change, for she realizes that in earlier times
she did love herself, and valued her lovers because they loved her;
the change is the root of her change toward the memory of Philip.
These intricate shifts seem to retrace H.D.'s view, at the time of
their engagement, that Pound was a suffering soul, and the better
knowledge of him she acquired soon afterward.

There is a final reversal in Hipparchia's mind, however, as Julia
Augusta, a young girl who admires her work on Greek poetry, visits and asks her to leave retirement and come with her as a teacher.
In a final burst of confused thought, Hipparchia declares that
"Greece is a spirit. Greece is not lost," and agrees to go.[23] The episode is an obvious parallel to the appearance of Bryher, which is,
however, treated in a far less joyous tone in *Asphodel*.

It seems fair to say that in the passages about Philip, H.D. was
making use of the mixed feelings she recalled from her complex
friendship with Pound. "Intimacy without intercourse" defines
their relationship accurately, and Pound, as we have seen, did in-
struct the youthful Hilda and intermittently encouraged her when
she wrote poetry and translations. Two elements in Hipparchia's
attitude toward Philip may reflect the mature H.D.'s estimate of
Pound's influence. First, the recollection that "Philip was her passion, her intellect, her mind which none had broken," suggests
that she thought Pound had, at one time at least, helped her to
maintain her independence of mind. In the early poem "Ortus,"
presumably addressed to H.D., Pound wrote, "I beseech you learn

to say 'I.'" Second, it is of major importance that Philip is dead. His spirit motivates Hipparchia only until the time of her fever, the arrival of her new friend, and her conviction that Greece can survive without him. This seems to frame a declaration that H.D. herself was now free of Pound's influence.

Rereading "Hipparchia" more than twenty years after it had been written, H.D. reported that she felt that it was "hallucinated," and Pound in at least one instance offered a similar explanation for a disordered passage of the *Cantos*. In a letter to his father, Pound explained the merging of several separate stories in Canto 20 by saying that the passage consisted of Nicolo d'Este's confusion of the death of Roland with the Cid's attack on the city of Toro, with fragments from the Trojan war: "The whole reminiscence jumbled or 'candied' in Nicolo's delirium."[24] Nicolo's delirium, Pound explained, was related to drug-induced states like that of the lotus-eaters who are the main subject of the Canto. Both authors were adopting styles that abandoned conventional mimesis in order to present the realities of psychological processes. They found new technical possibilities in the vivid and agonizing adventures of mental derangement, a prominent topic in the post-Freudian years that also produced the Night-town scene of Joyce's *Ulysses*.

Palimpsest, which was published as a volume of three novellas in 1926, exhibits a fundamental parallel with Imagist doctrines. H.D.'s definition of her title, "a parchment from which one writing has been erased to make room for another," seems to correspond to the layers of experience or memories in the lives of the heroines. These appear to be irrelevant to the experiences of the present, but there is an underlying identity between them. Raymonde, the heroine of "Murex," speaking of Botticelli's *Primavera*, says, "Back of the Botticelli there is another Botticelli," and she has the same feeling about London and about her own identity. Each of the heroines is disturbed by her consciousness of past experiences that have been overlaid by later ones which seem contradictory or unconnected, but nevertheless recall the earlier ones. This psychological "palimpsest" effect, employed as a stylistic device, parallels the principle of "superposition" that Pound used to explain the juxtaposition of apparently unrelated elements in an Imagist poem. It is also an interesting foreshadowing of the dream imagery H.D. was to analyze under Freud's guidance, for it described a structure consisting of manifest and latent contents that are apparently dissociated from each other. The principle of palimpsest corresponds to many effects characteristic of Modernist styles, such as repetition and parataxis. It appears, for example, in "Murex": "Feet, feet, feet, feet, feet. There was no use going on. Everything in life was blighted, still-born—that was the crux of the matter. Feet, feet, feet, feet, feet. They were a still-born generation."[25]

It is not hard to share Raymonde's apparently disordered ideas here, for their sources have already been mentioned. She is connecting the noise of the passers-by in the street outside with her feeling that her significant life is behind her, and this feeling has some relation, in turn, with the place at the end of the street, Victoria Station, where years before, she had said good-bye to her husband as he left for service in World War I.

Asphodel, written in 1921 and 1922 with later revisions, but not published until 1992, many years after H.D.'s death, is another continuation of *HERmione.* In it, H.D. bases the story of her surrogate, Hermione Gart, on the events in her own life between 1911 and 1919, beginning with her journey to France with Frances Gregg and her mother, then moving to her time in London with Pound and a circle of English friends, and ending with her pregnancy and her parting with Aldington. H.D. apparently tried to suppress this novel and marked her manuscript "DESTROY," perhaps because it betrayed intimate thoughts and painful scenes she was unwilling to reveal. Employing interior monologue with exceptional freedom and imagination, it depicts the heroine's character with great success, and gives perhaps the fullest exposure of the relations between H.D. and Pound through the characters of Hermione and George Lowndes. Written as fiction, it nevertheless expresses the narrator's feelings in its many poetic passages in a thoroughly convincing manner, and most of the episodes correspond with what is independently known about the events of H.D.'s life.

The relation between George Lowndes and Hermione is thoroughly ambiguous in a variety of ways. When she joins George in London, Hermione's already mixed feelings about him are complicated by his critical attitude. She feels that he is repressing and suffocating her. Claiming that he is her "nearest male relative," he objects to her clothes, the friends she has made, the neighborhood she lives in, and her general style. Reproaching her for not completing her sentences, George tells her, "You are an oracle manqué." The recollection of his remark, "All a matter of technique your verses," follows a paragraph of perplexing thoughts about marriage, suggesting that George's disapproval extended to her poems. It seems that he is trying to "damp her ardour," and that he is "purposely, wilful, purposely dragging her up, away." At first, she is concerned that he no longer "likes" her, but after a time she relies on what others say about her.

There is every reason to believe that this accurately reflects the tone of the H.D.-Pound friendship in their London days and the beginning of her new friendship with Aldington. The conversations in the novel are the frank exchanges of two old friends. Hermione objects to George's possessiveness, but is also unwilling to give up her hold on him, an attitude that resembles the young H.D.'s thoroughly indecisive feelings about Pound. It also anticipates the lifelong relation between the two poets; each claimed a certain amount of affectionate authority over the other, but neither was ready to marry or, apparently, to engage in sexual relations.

An account of George reading poetry to piano accompaniment at a London event gives a vivid impression of the exhibitionist Pound, and expresses H.D.'s admiration:

> The two candles flared in exact symmetry and George (as Hermione twisted on the pouffe to watch him) stood in amazing radiance like some pre quattro-cento saint before an altar . . . George brought to mind these perfect compositions though he himself was rough, a little, a little too rough, something powerful and strong in old George though people had a way of sniggering "decadent." What was decadent? Not George. Facing them with his head flung back, with his excellent throat emerging from his loose collar, George tossed back a petulant lock.[26]

The question of their engagement is still troubling to Hermione. A stray recollection, "George said there needn't be any children," seems to imply that marriage is intended. However, when she is asked whether the engagement, broken several times earlier, is still in force, she says she doesn't know and will ask George. His reply is "Gawd forbid." She still loves Fayne Rabb passionately, but she also loves George, and wishes he too loved Fayne. (In real life, of course, there had been a serious flirtation between Pound and Frances Gregg.) Although it now seems clear that George will not marry her, when she sees him with another woman, "Hermione felt for the first time in some time, a little gasp of terror. Really terror. Did she still love George Lowndes?"

When she feels attracted to "Darrington" (Aldington, of course), warnings against marrying George turn up in her thoughts, but she also recalls: "After all, George had kissed and kissed her. Famished kisses, like a desert wind full of sand, the wrong flowers, hybiscus, scarlet line of his really beautiful mouth." And when she thinks of "Kisses arid but not here (in London) quite so full of desert heat and blinding, wilted sand, met hers," H.D. is recalling the occasion in the late fall or winter of 1912 when she and Pound spent a long evening alone in May Sinclair's studio for an affectionate interlude of kisses and hyacinths (not hibiscus). In the novel, Hermione recalls their engagement, acknowledges that "according to ordinary standards I shouldn't do this," but nevertheless, "Famished and forgetting she lifted hyacinths to George's kisses."

At this time, Pound and Dorothy Shakespear were seriously contemplating marriage, and that may explain why H.D.'s character, Hermione, found George's kisses less ardent than they had been. Hermione, on the other hand, seems to have been hungry for love, "famished." Afterward, she tells George she is happy, and feels that she has risen from the underworld, like Persephone, and that "Pain had vanished." *End to Torment* adds another detail to this event. Pound had begun by warning H.D. against the books on Sinclair's table, and high-handedly flung them up to an inaccessible shelf.

There are sequels that follow the scene in the studio. Hermione's confusion emerges when she learns of George's engagement to someone else. She feels "forgotten" and "lost," since she "had been under a vague half-impression that it was she herself who was vaguely half-engaged to George Lowndes." When George persists in his advances, she asks him if it was right to kiss her when he was engaged. She repels him and envisions the scene as an ugly one. George is merely roguish, teasing, and unapologetic, perhaps an accurate reflection of Pound's philandering rôle. As for Hermione, "she wasn't any longer interested in George."

With that, the character based on Pound is dropped, although he does enter the story in a transparent recapitulation of H.D.'s involvement in the Gregg-Wilkinson marriage. Hermione occasionally thinks of him as the story follows the lines of H.D.'s marriage to Aldington and succeeding events.

After completing "The Sword Went Out to Sea," one of the unpublished novels H.D. wrote in the 1940s, she wrote to Pound that he appeared in it under the name of "Allen Flint," and said that she hoped he would not mind.[27] The novel is dominated by H.D.'s wartime experiments with clairvoyance and Lord Dowding, and appears to record many actual events of the time, in addition to the earlier episodes connected with Pound. In the reminiscences of the Pennsylvania flirtation, the young Flint appears at a school dance, but the narrator's attention is fixed on another boy; he reads William Morris's poems to her and "I was both Iseults." He brings her books and appears among a chorus of maidens in a Greek play.[28]

At a much later point, after an account of her rejection by the father-figure based on Lord Dowding, the narrator writes: "Perhaps the blow went back to childhood. I was only seventeen when I separated from Allen. My father was right. That did not mitigate the force of the blow. I lost Allen. I lost my father."[29] This reminiscence records H.D.'s painful emotional trap. She has by now realized that her father was right to prevent her from marrying Pound, but also feels the separation as a loss. The novel covers the late period of the war when V-2 rockets were falling on London, and the terror stirred up memories. Somehow, friends rose out of the war ruins, including "Allen Flint from a sunken marble city and my own childhood," a recollection of Pound in Venice and Pennsylvania.[30]

As we have seen, H.D.'s tendency to merge figures in her search for her ideal lover is reflected in her novels. In "Hipparchia," the heroine combines in her mind figures corresponding to Cecil Gray and Pound, and her heroine in "The Sword Went Out to Sea" does something similar, with significant results: "I had superimposed Geoffrey [Aldington]—a hero in a small way—on Allen Flint [Pound], a traitor." This changed her, she says, and she was "no longer a Greek."[31] This change was followed by a crisis that was apparently a mental breakdown, whereas, in "Hipparchia," the corresponding trauma is a fever.

If we accept their convincing autobiographical dimensions, this series of novels seems to show that H.D., after extricating herself with considerable pain from the sexual relation to Pound that had begun in their Pennsylvania days, still felt the need, throughout the 1920s, and even later, to reprocess her feelings about him through her fiction. More significant, perhaps, is the separation they suggest between her shifting personal relation to Pound and the indebtedness she continued to feel to his influence on her writing. The distinction is clear in Hipparchia's relation to Philip, and in Hermione's acceptance of George's teaching and comments about her writing, even though she ultimately finds him too cerebral and insensitive as a lover.

While H.D.'s feminist critics tend to regard her lesbianism as a correlate of her liberation as a woman and her key to artistic freedom, there is considerable evidence that calls for some modification of this view, and of the gender-centric interpretation of H.D.'s poetic development.[32] H.D. herself characterized the autobiographical *Madrigal* as the "eternal story" of a woman's search for fragments of the perfect lover, a story whose prototype is the myth of Isis and Osiris.[33] As both H.D.'s love affairs and the novels show, and as the Egyptian myth determines, this is a search for a male archetype, not a female one. For example, H.D.'s name for this ideal in "The Sword Went Out to Sea" is "Le Prince Lointain."

Pearson, in characterizing this search, did mention a female figure among the metaphors H.D. employed—"the lover, the father, the mother, the brother, the hero"—but the males certainly dominate his list. Pearson added that she took men as symbols of what she was seeking, and that she thought of Pound in her quest for the lover "in a very indirect way."[34] It seems clear that Pound was the first bearer of the fragments H.D. spent her life trying to assemble.

Although Freud told her she was a perfect bisexual, it seems unlikely that H.D. ever really welcomed sexual relations with men. Her marriage and liaisons did not last, and if we are to rely on evidence from her novels, she found Pound's lovemaking oppressive and thought Aldington's wartime demands on her made him "over-sexed." Her attitude toward men was a rather helpless admiration, on other than sexual grounds, of powerful masculine figures. Men, on their part, seemed to value her for her talent rather than her sexual attractiveness. Pound supported her literary work for a time after both were married to other people, and Aldington continued to work with her after their separation, to correspond with her, and even to visit her in Switzerland in later years.

The pattern seen in her relation to Pound seems to have replicated itself often in H.D.'s life. Her most lasting relations were those with women, but she persistently sought relations with men, and her literary achievements sprang mainly from these influences. In the unpublished "Compassionate Friendship," which is in the form of a journal recording her 1955 sessions with her analyst, Erich Heydt, she lists as her "initiators": Pound, Aldington, Cournos, Gray, Macpherson, Schmideberg, and Heydt. "Ezra," she said, "was the first of these initiators," and she added that Lawrence also "counts."[35] The one clear female influence on her poetry is that of her mother, whose Moravian background entered her work, and whose place in her unconscious life was revealed to her by Freud.

This is not to say that she imitated the male writers she knew. On the contrary, as we have seen, she made use of what she found in their work to strike out in her own way. Her early relationship with Pound established a pattern vital to H.D.'s poetic life, and one repeated with nearly all of her "initiators." Suffering rejection or emotional trauma, often at the hands of a man, she descended to depression or actual breakdown, but soon recovered and seemed to find within herself a new poetic power as a result of the experience.

These experiences have been well defined by Rachel Blau Du-Plessis, who finds that H.D.'s frequent infatuations involved a kind of subordination on gender grounds, which DuPlessis calls "romantic thralldom."[36] But she finds that "the pain of thralldom seemed to fire H.D.'s creativity," although it also wounded and handicapped her. Pound enters DuPlessis's discussion when she observes that H.D.'s use and misuse of his early poems in *HERmione* "suggests . . . some resistant, stubborn matter which will not be captured." This strength appeared early. "A number of H.D.'s early poems," says DuPlessis, "concern the sort of hard-edged beauty created by resistance to devastating force." She does not find that a conflict of the genders is prominent in H.D.'s poetry. Instead of challenging male domination, DuPlessis says, she tried to bypass it by cultivating a genderless consciousness that claimed equality. Since the men she knew did nothing to help her escape male domination, she asserted her independence by turning to the love of women.

Much of the evidence for these unhappy experiences comes from H.D.'s novel, *Bid Me to Live,* which deals with her experiences during World War I (and does not include a Pound figure), but DuPlessis sees many themes of spiritual recovery in *Trilogy,* even though it continues to acknowledge the fact of "thralldom." Consequently, she sums up this part of H.D.'s emotional life by stating, "the first war was death, the second was rebirth."

DuPlessis's analysis makes it possible to see the theme of gender difference so prominent in H.D.'s work as a kind of collaboration, in which the division is less important than the emergence of aesthetic literary values accessible to all. Friedman, throughout her vital and extensive studies of H.D., is insistent upon her independence as a woman writer and a lesbian. Nevertheless, Friedman says that H.D.'s novels display the pattern of "textual revisions of authoritative men whom she revered, even loved," but whom she "had to remake in her own image so that their power intensified instead of overwhelming her own . . . H.D. marks out a dialectical interaction, one that stresses the active power of the creative woman to reinterpret, reclaim and reconstitute these men whom she loved into a source of her own validation."[37] These comments suggest the conflicts and contradictions that accompanied the process of reclamation, and are relevant to her relationship with Pound.

H.D.'s fiction, like much of her work after the Imagist period, richly embodies the legacy of the Modernism led by Pound, even if it shows her turning to a form, the novel, that he had little interest in. The wild, extravagant imagery and unconventional language forms generated by the psychological disturbances of the characters constitute an approach to style that H.D. shared with Pound and other Modernists, particularly those in the Futurist, Surrealist, and Dadaist groups. Her novels repudiate Pound as a lover, and take a different literary path from the one he followed, but they nevertheless manifest his continuing presence in her imagination. In spite of their occasional alienation from each other, she continued to use "Dryad," his name for her, throughout her life in writing to him.

8

The Second War

Nothing is given: we must find our law.

Auden, "In Time of War"

World War II and its sequels shattered the lives of both poets, but
it also drove them to new feats of introspection that led them to
write their best and most mature works. Both suffered the hardships of wartime Europe, and a comparison of the poems written
from different sides of the conflict offers a flickering pattern of significant similarities and dissensions. H.D.'s *Trilogy* and Pound's
Pisan Cantos were written under wartime conditions, during or
immediately after the hostilities. H.D.'s *Helen in Egypt,* completed
some six years later, deals with the aftermath of another conflict,
the Trojan War, but echoes her wartime experiences.

The two poets had exchanged letters regularly until 1939, but
they were, of course, not in touch with each other during the war,
although H.D. heard about Pound's broadcasts, read about him in
the newspapers, and was curious about her old friend's state of
mind. Bryher joined H.D. in her small apartment at 49 Lowndes
Square in September 1940, and the two, motivated to share the
wartime dangers and deprivations of the Londoners by a surely
misguided sense of patriotism, lived there throughout the war.

H.D. should have known better. She recognized that the first
war had caused her to suffer from "my own personal Phobia, my

own personal little Dragon of war-terror," and thus undertook her sessions with Freud in 1933, she said, in order to guard against the shocks of another possible war.[1] But the Dragon broke loose a few years later, and "terrors too dreadful to be thought of" led to another postwar breakdown, even though, as Bryher said, this second war was "easier to bear" than the first because the people were more united. She and H.D. were supported by Pearson and a circle of literary friends including the three writers of the Sitwell family, which Bryher dubbed the "Lowndes Group." In spite of the daily dangers and deprivations of wartime, they led an active social life and continued their writing.

H.D.'s troubles in this second war were different from those she had experienced during World War I. In that war, she had gone through tension and anxiety because of her strained relations with Aldington, but now, while surrounded by friends, she suffered from ill health, the deprivations of rationing, and, of course, the terror of the Blitz, as the German bombers came over London night after night.

The profound fear she experienced during one of these attacks oddly awakened her visionary faculty, as it led her to recall pleasant childhood memories and thoughts of the ritualistic meeting of her Moravian ancestors with the Indians. She feared that the mystical tradition connected with her Moravian heritage would be lost with her death, but when she survived, the recollection of this tradition produced a surge of joy. She felt that "we have crossed the chasm that divides time from time-out-of-time or from what they call eternity."[2] Even when German bombers were attacking London in nightly raids, causing her a terror akin to panic, she felt a paradoxical sense of liberation, saying she was happier than she had ever been. The weird wartime conditions made her feel that:

> we know no rule
> of procedure,
>
> we are voyagers, discoverers
> of the not-known,
>
> the unrecorded;[3]

There was a general sense in the country that the arts should be kept up in wartime. H.D. continued with her poetry while the bombs were falling around her, and in April 1944 she took part in a poetry reading at the Aeolian Hall organized by Osbert Sitwell. T. S. Eliot, Edith Sitwell, and John Masefield were on the program, and the event was attended by the Queen and the royal princesses. Pearson joined her and Bryher in the spring of 1943 and was a frequent visitor. Although the two friends rarely left London, H.D. did make two visits to Stratford-on-Avon during and after the war.

At this time also, she became obsessed with Sir Hugh Dowding, and with his spiritualism and his belief that he received messages from dead airmen. As we have seen, Dowding's occultism energized H.D.'s growing interest in spiritualism, and she began to engage in various spiritualist activities with the guidance of Arthur Bhaduri. Because of the Blitz, she later wrote, "the past is literally blasted into consciousness," leading her to regret that she had been unable to marry Pound, and to realize that "with my loss of him" she had forgotten the poems he had written for her and the books he given her. She identified Arthur Bhaduri with the Yogi Ramacharaka, the author of the "Yogi books" Pound had brought her, and was glad that she could now share the "Yogi philosophy" with another person, as she had "in the beginning."[4]

In the years before the war, Pound was more alert to the gathering clouds than was H.D. Like many others, he sensed that the Munich agreement and Hitler's annexation of Austria and Czechoslovakia were preludes to conflict, although he thought the adversaries might be Germany and the Soviet Union. The threat of war did not interfere with his numerous activities for a time. After Italy entered the war in 1940, he apparently made some efforts to leave, but finally decided to stay in Rapallo.

He urged the Italian government to allow him to speak to an American audience on the radio, and when permission was given, recorded the first of his infamous broadcasts in January 1941. The attack on Pearl Harbor in December of that year and the subsequent entrance of the United States into the war did not change his plans, for in the following month he secured official permission to stay in Italy and was allowed to continue his broadcasts on behalf of the Fascist régime. He naïvely believed that he could support the Axis powers and attack the United States government without compromising his loyalty to his native country.[5]

At this time he was working on Chinese translations and other projects remote from the war, but he aspired to an active part in the Italian war effort. His support of Mussolini and Fascism seemed to harden, for he continued to broadcast and to write for Italian periodicals. Even when Mussolini had fallen from power and been arrested, Pound, after desperate and aimless journeys to Rome and to his daughter's home in the Tyrol, linked himself with the puppet Salo Republic the Germans had set up in the north of Italy with the defeated Mussolini at its head, and continued his broadcasts under its sponsorship.

As the Allies engulfed Italy, however, the fragile refuge he had built for himself was completely shattered. In the spring of 1944, the Germans forced the Pounds to leave Rapallo, and they could find no better place than Olga Rudge's apartment, where the three lived together in a cramped and extremely uncomfortable situation for about a year. This ménage ended when, in May 1945, Pound was taken into custody, first by Italian partisans, and then by American authorities. He maintained that he was simply expressing his independent views in his broadcasts, and was surprised to learn that he had been indicted for treason in the United States. He was turned over to the American army, and transferred to the army prison known as he Disciplinary Training Center (DTC) near Pisa in May 1945, where the period of intense hardship recorded in the *Pisan Cantos* took place.

He was unable to write to H.D. until some years later, after he was removed to the United States for trial as a war criminal. Since it was nearly certain that he would be convicted for treason, a sentence that carried the death penalty, his lawyers succeeded in having him judged insane and unfit for trial, and in December 1945, he was transferred to St. Elizabeths Federal Hospital in Washington, D.C., where he remained as a patient for twelve years.

ℱ

As we have seen, the two poets dealt with the problem of reconciling war with the aesthetic demands of poetry at the time of the first war: Pound by making the war an aspect of Hell and a support of the *Cantos*'s structure, H.D. by enclosing war and the survival of beauty in Greek settings. But with the outbreak of World War II, and because of their personal involvement in its chaos and horror, they faced the problem far more directly.

H.D. began *Trilogy* in 1942 while sharing the Lowndes Square flat with Bryher in a bombed-out London suffering from a state of siege after three years of war. Most of the *Pisan Cantos* were written between June and October 1945, when Pound, as a prisoner at the Disciplinary Training Center, was allowed to use the typewriter in the center's office. In these poems, the two poets unwittingly continued into their later years the dialogue about the mission of Modern poetry that had been going on throughout their lives, a dialogue that became overt when H.D. wrote *Helen in Egypt* as a reply to the *Pisan Cantos*.[6]

This dialogue turns on a number of prominent themes. Both poems are quests for peace and personal serenity in a setting of physical and psychological ruin. Both pursue this quest through visions that transcend material reality. Both find encouragement in the details of threatening environments. The two poems have certain symbols in common, notably the figure of a female divinity and the related images of crystal and gems as symbols of perfection and fulfillment. And both employ, in differing ways, ideas of poetic form descended from Imagism.

The doctrinaire objectivity of Imagism and Eliot's influential statement that poetry is an escape from personality had made direct self-expression difficult for Modern poets. But it was impossible to assume a stance of detachment in the presence of war. Under the stress of wartime crisis, the poets explore and expose feelings in *Trilogy* and the *Pisan Cantos* that are their own, and not those of imagined personae. These passages anticipate by some years the emergence of the American group of "confessional" poets. After the mid-century, a genuinely personal mode that acknowledged weakness or failure became fashionable among American poets as varied as Robert Lowell, Allen Ginsberg, and

Anne Sexton. *Trilogy* and the *Pisan Cantos* speak from moods of that kind.

While both poems were occasioned by the war, they are re-moved from the horrors of the battlefield, as if the poets agreed that the answer to war is an introspective quest for personal re-demption. Pound found support through memory, and much of the *Pisan Cantos* consists of brief allusions to his experiences in better times. H.D. also values memory, but her chief resource is the belief that the occult tradition surviving from ancient times will ultimately prevail. Numerous correspondences emerge against the background of these differences. Both poems turn to exotic grounds of conviction— *Trilogy* to Ra, Venus, and other gods of the Egyptians and Greeks, and the *Pisan Cantos* to similar pagan sources and Confucian tradition. There are similarities in style dating from the Imagist period, and a relatively free concept of form. Both poems report mystic visions. Both are dialectic, incor-porating conflicting points of view; both employ varying levels of language; and both use the structural effect of bringing apparently unrelated elements together that H.D. called palimpsest and Pound called superposition.

H.D. moves close to Pound's doctrines in writing:

> grape, knife, cup, wheat
>
> are symbols in eternity,
> and every concrete object
>
> has abstract value, is timeless
> in the dream parallel . . .[7]

The passage recalls the quasi-mystical statement from "A Few Don'ts by an Imagist" that the Image gives a sense of freedom from the limits of space and time. The point about "abstract value" recalls Pound's further elaboration of the image in his essay "Vorticism," where he argues that art refers to life in the way that an algebraic equation refers to the general concept of the circle, to a "symbol in eternity" rather than to a specific circle.

ℐ

Pound's first response to the war was a series of Cantos with occult passages composed in the winter of 1944 after the fall of Mussolini and before Pound's arrest. Written in Italian, they expressed
his defiant loyalty to the defeated Italian cause. Cantos 72 and 73
were originally published in the Italian naval journal, *La Marina
Repubblica*, where they served a propagandistic purpose, but they
were omitted from succeeding editions of the *Cantos* until the
edition of 1987, where they appeared in the original Italian.[8] In
these preliminary war Cantos, which narrate conversations with
ghostly visitors in an atmosphere recalling Dante's *Paradiso*,
Pound laid down some of the visionary themes of the *Pisan Cantos*. These excursions into the occult were, of course, a continuation of those that had appeared in previous Cantos. To explain his
communication with the dead, he quoted, in the first of the *Pisan
Cantos*, the claim that first appeared nearly thirty years earlier in
the drafts called "Three Cantos": "Ghosts move about me /
Patched with histories."

In the two Italian Cantos, Pound, consulting his ghosts, looks
to the past, as he continued to do in the *Pisan Cantos*, while H.D.
in *Trilogy* looks to the future, when the war will be over. Pound,
with his usual indifference to facts, calls for the shattered Italian
cause to continue the war with an utterly hollow call to arms,
while H.D. writes of using tradition to fashion a new spirituality.
Their common reliance on the occult appears, as Pound calls upon
his ghosts and H.D. invokes the gods of past civilizations. Pound
himself hardly appears in these Cantos, though his voice is heard
in his denunciations of Allied politicians. But much of "The Walls
Do Not Fall" is concerned with personal responses, and has many
lyrical expressions of feeling: "I sense my own limit, / my shell-
jaws snap shut / at invasion of the limitless, / ocean-weight."[9]

H.D.'s poem embodies some of the principles carried forward
from the Modernist revolution led by Pound, which Pound's Italian Cantos ignore, occupied as they are with the immediacies of
the war. The two poetic responses to war mark a time of severe

disagreement between the two poets. *Trilogy* speaks of patient endurance and the blessings of peace, while Pound's two Cantos praise the nobility of wartime sacrifice and belligerently call for Fascist victory. In declaring that "the stylus, / the palette, the pen, the quill endure," and that "Word" is prior to "Sword," H.D. confirms the centrality of language emphasized in Pound's critical essays, while Pound's Italian Cantos ignore "Word" and recommend only "Sword." It is interesting that *Trilogy* should continue with a condemnation of "the burning of the books," a reference to an outrage perpetrated by Pound's side of the war that he never mentioned.

Although *Trilogy* and the *Pisan Cantos* have the war as their contexts, they make surprisingly few direct allusions to it. The poets of World War I, Wilfred Owen, Siegfried Sassoon, and Isaac Rosenberg, had dealt vividly with the horrors of the front, but the two civilian poets of the second war seem to agree that poetry, even in wartime, is best occupied with thought and feeling. Even when there is no open protest, however, both poems implicitly condemn the waste and injustice of war. This subtext is visible in two lyrics H.D. wrote at about the time she was composing *Trilogy*. In "R.A.F.," the poet feels a mystic identity with the wounded pilot who comes to see her, and during a train trip with the same man, thinks of the injustice of the war that has victimized him. "May, 1943" takes place in a London setting. It shifts from thoughts about a war-damaged palace to a seedy wartime crowd, and then to a newspaper report about a young woman ambulance driver killed during an air raid. Unlike *Trilogy*, these poems report contemporary events in a diary-like fashion (resembling the mode of the *Pisan Cantos* in this respect), anchoring themselves to reality by specifying place and time. Significantly, in most of *Trilogy*, H.D. dealt with the war in an entirely different way, turning from external affairs and retreating into her own thoughts.

"The Walls Do Not Fall," the first section of *Trilogy*, was written in 1942 as a defiant reply to the Blitz in which German bombers were devastating London. H.D. described her poem as "runic, divinatory," and said that it was written as a deliberate departure from the style of her early poems. She said that she had grown tired of having these poems described as "crystalline," and asked dismissively: "For what is crystal or any gem but the concentrated essence of the rough matrix, or the energy, either of over-intense heat or over-intense cold that projects it?"[10] She felt that *Trilogy* was so different from her early style that she was tempted to drop her distinctive "H.D." signature, and sign the poem "Delia Alton." The discursive mysticism and extended narrative of *Trilogy* can be taken, therefore, as something of a rejoinder to Pound and Imagism. Seen face to face with the *Pisan Cantos,* it marks a significant stage in the poetic dialogue.

It opens and closes with tentative assertions that a new spiritual revelation will arise from the ruins of war. Its forty-three sections may claim a kind of thematic unity, but they reject uniformity, as most Modern long poems do. Questions about her feelings and about the mission of poetry lead H.D. to declare that a mystical tradition, persisting through Egyptian and Greek religion and hermeticism, will triumph over the destructiveness of the war. The structure of the sequence is not linear. It deviates into debates and reversals about the integrity of the self, the value of the pagan gods, and the merits of the author's poetry. But it leads the poet to find salvation by escaping her old self and accepting Christ and a mystic but all-embracing "Presence" that is felt even among the ruins of London.

There is an anticipation of this visionary response to war in H.D.'s story "Kora," written in 1930. The plot, which bears some resemblance to the effects of World War I on H.D.'s family, concerns the guilt that its narrator, John Helforth, feels about the loss of his brothers in the war. The story is told in a narrative idiom that blends psychological analysis and mythic parallels. In this environment, the tormented Helforth at first resents the sacrifice of his brothers because it has exposed his own passivity. He thinks of one slain brother as Dionysus, sacrificed in the name of atonement, and when he overcomes his resentment, casts himself and the woman who is either his mother or his lover as mythic figures, ending his story by saying, "Now we are Kore and the slain God . . . risen." This sacramental and redemptive view of war is taken up again in *Trilogy.*

"The Walls Do Not Fall" begins with a scene of the war's destruction that imposes the ruins of Luxor and Pompeii upon the bomb-shattered ruins of London, and finds a paradoxical salvation in it. The final section returns to this theme, as the assertion that the walls still stand leads to a sense of liberation and the conclusion that "possibly we will reach haven, / heaven." Section 5 of *Trilogy*'s second part, "Tribute to the Angels," puts war on a lower level of importance than the inevitable contingencies of life, asking: "what is War / to Birth, to Change, to Death?" The question is part of a series where "the flowering of the rod" symbolizes the emergence of life out of the ruin of war, and the phrase becomes the title of the final, devotional part of *Trilogy*.[11]

Like *Trilogy*, Pound's poem begins with an episode of violence: the murder of Mussolini. It leaves behind the martial spirit of the two Italian Cantos to focus on the destructiveness of war in a sharp reversal that now parallels the spirit of *Trilogy*. It soon looks beyond immediate catastrophe, as *Trilogy* does. The immediate consequences of war for Pound are not ruins and a paradoxical freedom, but the remembered deaths of friends in the first war, the failure of his political cause, and, of course, his own isolation and imprisonment. The prison environment brought him such new imagery as the soldiers, birds, and insects of the DTC. In rare direct protests, Pound foresees "woe to them that conquer with armies," and declares at the close of Canto 78 that "there are no righteous wars," giving his message extraordinary emphasis by centering the sentence, one word to a line, in the middle of the page. In brief and tentative comments, Pound, like H.D., sees hope coming after the war. He imagines "the stillness outlasting all wars," where the sound of waves will still be heard, and, responding to the cloudscape over Pisa, feels that "out of all this beauty something must come." The *Pisan Cantos* and "Tribute to the Angels" end with expressions of gratitude that foresee spiritual recovery. Pound ends his poem: "If the hoar frost grip thy tent / Thou wilt give thanks when night is spent." H.D. ends "Tribute" by repeating from an earlier section, "we pause to give / thanks that we rise from death and live."

In *Trilogy* and the *Pisan Cantos,* the two poets seem to be saying that the correct response to the horrors of war is to resist the passions and ambitions of the conflict and to live in the virtual reality of poetry: a theme first suggested, as we have seen, in H.D.'s World War I poems and in Pound's Canto 16. The later poems are offered as realms of feeling where the reader is called upon to respond to form, technique, and method as well as to the topics that furnish material for them. The personal self-scrutiny that occupies them is a counterpart of the way in which the poems call attention to their methods. Imagism, we recall, began in the time of Cubism and owes something to Clive Bell's "significant form." The Modernist principles that shape the self-reflexive work of art are still present in the later poems of the two Imagists. As with Cubist or Fauvist painting, the relation of the work to external reality is complex and indirect, the deviations from convention and realism being its major means of expression. *Trilogy* and the *Pisan Cantos,* while sharing these tendencies, also share the special task of defining the rôle of poetry in time of war.

When *Trilogy* as a whole and the *Pisan Cantos* are compared within the perspective of the long relationship between Pound and H.D., each acquires new meaning. The poets had different views of the place of personal expression in poetry, but the two texts contain significant similarities in style and manner stemming from the ideas that H.D. and Pound shared. In both poems, ancient tradition is juxtaposed with current realities, as Pound calls up figures from contemporary life, and H.D.'s first triplet reports "rails gone (for guns) / from your (and my) old town square" before turning to the ruins of Egypt and Pompeii. Both poets use the occult to gain access to the past. Pound's colloquies with the ghosts of the dead are imitations of Dante, but H.D.'s reversions to "Ra, Osiris, *Amen,*" to Thoth and Hermes and a swarm of ancient deities refer to the general occult tradition.

Pound is present in *Trilogy* only as the theorist of Imagism and as a silent partner in H.D.'s mysticism. However, it is easy to imagine that H.D. is addressing Pound or someone who shares his views when she wearily admits that the "search for historical parallels . . . has been done to death before" and adds "my mind (yours) / has its peculiar ego-centric / personal approach / to the eternal realities." First and second persons are easily substituted for each other in this framework as the poet acknowledges that she shares this tendency to see history from a private point of view with the person she is addressing. If this person is Pound, there is a sense of identity with him in spite of disagreement, for the poetry of both leans heavily on the past, but not in identical ways. Later in this passage, H.D. accepts the search for parallels on the ground that different opinions about history are possible. Her approach was to find counterparts to her own feelings and experiences in the Greek myths she employed. For Pound, on the other hand, individual episodes acquired their significance as details of the larger patterns he brought to his view of history.

We cannot be sure that H.D. had Pound in mind in the "historical parallels" passage, but there is a clear and significant reference to H.D. in the *Pisan Cantos*. In Canto 83, Pound addresses her, speaking from the "death cells" in what is unquestionably his own voice to review a series of images confirming the beauty and harmony of the world. In the first part of this lyrical passage, H.D. is lovingly associated with these things through her nickname — "your eyes are like the clouds over Taishan . . . Dryad, thy peace is like water."[12] This address to H.D. leads into a remarkably tranquil passage about the "rectitude" and "equity" seen in nature.

H.D. understood another passage in the *Pisan Cantos* as a reference to her relationship with Pound. In *End to Torment*, recalling the time when her father had found them curled up in an armchair, the aged H.D. wrote: "Mr. Pound . . . you turn into a Satyr, a Lynx, and the girl in your arms (Dryad, you called her), for all her fragile, not yet lost virginity, is *Maenad, bassarid.* God keep us from Canto LXXIX, one of the Pisan Cantos."[13] H.D. is referring to the passage in Canto 79 that addresses "my lovely lynx" as a deity who has the power to protect and preserve the speaker's crops and home: "Keep watch over my wine-pot . . . O

Lynx, guard this orchard." The prayers for merely material bene-
fits extend, however, into imagery of intense religious feeling:
"This fruit has fire within it . . . No glass is clearer than are the
globes of this flame." A lush landscape thronged with lynxes and
divinities emerges, and other sacred cats join the lynx in a sweeping vision of pagan deities.

H.D. may have had a good reason for thinking that the lynx
passage was addressed to her, and that Pound was taking up a
poetic exchange with her, following her early poem, "Orchard."
This poem, addressed to the "rough-hewn / god of the orchard"
and originally titled "Priapus," was thought to be meant for
Pound, and was one of the group he sent to *Poetry* for publication.
Because Pound's lynx prayer asks for protection for his orchard,
H.D. may have felt the invocation, "O Lynx, guard this orchard,"
was a reply to her poem.[14]

However, she was wrong to believe that the passage referred to
her. It does not depict a scene of erotic passion, but celebrates fertility. Pound's word is not "maenad" but "maelid," a divinity associated with fruitfulness. Further, the history of the lyric's composition shows that it was directed to a different person. Pound
wrote Canto 79 in the fall of 1947 at the DTC, and meant to send
it to Dorothy on 14 September as a birthday present, but it was
delayed in the mail and did not arrive in Rapallo until the end of
October. Pound referred to it as Dorothy's birthday Canto, and
she wrote that she had sent a copy to Bride Scratton, adding that
"I think she'll 'see' it," meaning perhaps that Bride would realize
it was addressed to herself.

H.D. began as a nonconforming poet of Greek paganism, but
Trilogy is a pious poem, suffused with the spirit of the New Testament, although it continues to invoke the gods of many religions.
As the poem reconfigures the traditional materials it uses, it reflects the subconscious desire exposed in her sessions with Freud:
the desire to be the founder of a new religion. It calls for the blessings of angels, and its final section, "The Flowering of the Rod,"
closes with an elaboration of the story about the woman who
brings myrrh to Jesus, a totally fictional extension of the few brief
sentences in the gospels of Matthew and John.

The subject matter of *Trilogy* is varied and the free verse form is original, but it is generally consistent in tone, employing a voice that is rarely very far from the conversational. After the triplets of the first section, the scrupulously complete and grammatical sentences are shaped into unrhymed couplets. The rhetorical discipline of Imagism is still present, although it is interrupted by narrative or discursive passages that address the reader or some other figure directly. Precise imagery remains H.D.'s main resource, but some of her tropes exhibit a warmth that lay far below the surface of the *Sea Garden* poems. In her desire to reach the reader, she even uses conventional clichés as in "the plowshare for the sword" and "the heart's alabaster / is broken."

The *Pisan Cantos*, on the other hand, turns to the ancient gods in a spirit of rampant paganism, finding sacred sources far from conventional Christianity. Pound's verse forms, tone, chronological sequences, and other structural features are widely disparate, in the eclectic style of the foregoing *Cantos*. Much of the text consists of fragments that lack predication, so that it begins to resemble an inventory of recollections; thus when complete and extended sentences appear, they convey great emphasis. *Trilogy* is by no means linear, yet it seems smoothly continuous in contrast to the sharp and jarring juxtapositions of Pound's poem. Behind this feature are Pound's early theory of "superposition" and his conviction that Paradise is "jagged," that it is "spezzato apparently / it exists only in fragments."

Various interpretive strategies have been suggested for such apparently enigmatic couplings as:

> But Mr. Joyce requested sample menus from the leading hotels
> and Kitson had tinkered with lights on the Vetta[15]

If research into Pound's often obscure references does not produce an obvious connection, the two terms may be regarded as a sort of musical chord, producing a third effect without being identified with each other. As we have seen, the Fenollosa essay on the Chinese written character declared that metaphor is "the use of material images to produce immaterial relations" and that "Relations are more real and more important than the things which they relate."[16] Accordingly, Pound uses superpositions to suggest relations that weave the fabric of his ideas about the world. In the *Pisan Cantos,* his context of ideas is enlarged and partially transformed by his war experiences, and the juxtapositions acquire new material and a sharper cutting edge. In Canto 77, for example, "Das Bankgeschäft / '. . . of the Wabash cannon ball'" juxtaposes the German term for the banking community and the words of an American folk song about a train, perhaps heard in the DTC. If the combination implies that there is a link between banks and the existence of prison camps or American railroads, the lines are Pound's bitter and ironic commentary on his favorite target of usury.

But other interpretations are possible, and enigmatic juxtapositions of this kind as well as the potential relevance of various parts of the text to each other open the poem to the reader's imagination. This multiplicity or indeterminacy affects the *Cantos* as a whole, for the reader is free to make or omit relationships, and to accept or reject Pound's judgments as he surveys the very wide range of the poem. This effect, Jerome McGann has suggested, is intentional. Pound wants to "enter a dialogue" with the reader, and "calls out for reciprocal acts of thought," opening itself to unforeseen readings.[17]

Trilogy, in contrast, adopts forms that court consensus. It controls the suggestions between fragments quite firmly within conventional grammatical forms. When section 39 of "The Walls Do Not Fall" declares that words are "boxes . . . conditioned / to hatch butterflies," the linkage is explained in the following verse paragraph that shows anagrams producing new words out of old ones. The three sections of *Trilogy* are only loosely related to each other, but the relations are nevertheless clear enough. The second section, "Tribute to the Angels," follows the theme of "The Walls Do Not Fall" by asserting that the spiritual tradition will survive the war, adopting the new context of angelology, and introducing the radiant figure of the "Lady" as a source of spiritual deliverance. The third section, "Flowering of the Rod," continues the theme by devoting its first eleven parts to expressions of joy at Christ's assurance of resurrection. This "ecstasy" is beautifully developed with images conveying the suffering and pleasures of earthly life as preludes to resurrection. However, a sharp break that compromises the effect of continuity occurs at number 12, with the anecdote about Kaspar and Mary.

Pound was enthusiastic about Joyce's *Ulysses,* whose composition he had followed closely, and the style of the *Pisan Cantos,* with their apparently random and transitionless forays into myth, memories of London, the events of the DTC, and nearly everything else, resembles the interior monologues of Stephen Dedalus and Leopold Bloom. In planning the *Cantos,* Pound said that it was to be a poem from which nothing could be excluded. While his method was certainly not automatic writing or spontanous composition, the material of his text appears to consist of thoughts that came to his retentive mind just before and during his internment in the DTC, so that he veers energetically from Confucius to John Adams and an early Rothschild on a single page. Unlike H.D., he avoids familiar phraseology, but nevertheless employs numerous quotations from scattered sources, sometimes in the original languages, which intensifies the "jagged" quality of his text.

While the contrast cannot apply uniformly to such varied texts as these long poems, the general difference between them recalls the distinction between classical language and the language of modern poetry Roland Barthes made in *Writing Degree Zero (Le Degré Zéro de l'Écriture).*[18] Barthes, speaking from within the French literary tradition, characterizes classical language as social, conventional, uninventive, braiding words into chains of expression rather than using them as individual vessels of meaning. He finds that in modern poetry, on the other hand, the word is independent, freed from preordained limits, capable of bearing any number of meanings assigned to it, but lifeless in itself. This is the "zero degree" of his title. Each style, according to Barthes, implies a social view. The classical mode is euphoric, collaborative, lending itself to conversational situations. Modern poetry, on the other hand, disrupts relationships, transforming the world into discontinuities and isolated objects.

These contrasts seem to bring forward an essential difference between the war poems of H.D. and Pound. *Trilogy* is hardly "classical" in the French or any other sense, yet it fits many of Barthes's specifications, and corresponds with his view that the classical use of language implies an optimistic, receptive attitude toward Nature and society. The *Pisan Cantos,* however, like the Cantos that preceded them, seem to be very much what Barthes means by Modern poetry. Pound foregrounds the word, a practice made particularly obvious by his Chinese quotations. As exegesis has shown, so many significations can be assigned to the language of the *Cantos* that its words seem to float freely in a current of possibilities.

A general comparison between *Trilogy* and the *Pisan Cantos* exposes a partial reversal forced on the two poets by the war. H.D., whose past work was prevailingly personal and autobiographical, now felt that the "crystalline" style of her early career was inappropriate in wartime. She briefly permitted the external realities of the war to enter her poem and supported her conviction that "The Walls Do Not Fall" with the doctrines of a mystic, quasi-Christian tradition. Pound, whose prewar Cantos dealt with a wide variety of topics that had little to do with the poet himself, now inserted personal experience and occasional feelings of remorse and doubt into the masses of recollection, historical events, and contemporary fact that had been the method of the *Cantos*. The result, as Michael Alexander has observed, is that Pound's method now included "a subjective mode," so that external material "appears, not as epic data, but primarily as personal memory, reflection and reading—as contingent phenomena of the shocked and distractable mind of Ezra Pound."[19] Thus, H.D.'s source of strength in her wartime poem is a generalized one, capable of being shared with others, while Pound's is the memory of what he loves, things peculiar to himself and his experiences. The change of places is not complete by any means, but it shows each of the poets acknowledging the value of a conception of poetry held by the other.

9

After World War II

> Bodily decrepitude is wisdom; young
> We loved each other and were ignorant.
> Yeats, "Speech after Long Silence"

When the two poets resumed their correspondence in 1946, they wrote to each other from mental hospitals, though their situations were, of course, entirely different from each other. Pound had been committed to St. Elizabeths Federal Hospital for the Insane in Washington since December 1945, after surviving the American army's prison camp and a trial for treason that led to his being declared mentally incompetent. Just two months later, H.D.'s wartime "Dragon" overcame her. She suffered a psychological breakdown as a result of wartime tensions, and in February 1946 she was sent to a rest home in Switzerland, Dr. Brunner's Nervenklinik at Küsnacht, near Zürich, a luxurious place where she stayed until December.

When she recovered, she moved back to her Lowndes Square flat for a short time, then took up residence in Switzerland, normally spending most of the year at the Hôtel de la Paix in Lausanne and the summers at various hotels in Lugano. She followed this routine until July 1953, when, weakened by two operations to correct an intestinal disorder, she returned, at the age of sixty-seven, to Dr. Brunner's sanatorium, where she lived, with interruptions, until its closure in 1961, shortly before her death.

H.D. was very comfortable at the Nervenklinik, where she could discuss Pound's work with some "alarmingly cultivated" friends. She wrote several of her prose works at this time, and in 1952 began her most ambitious poem, *Helen in Egypt,* sending it, part by part as it progressed, not to Pound but to Pearson, who usually responded appreciatively. Her work was delayed by surgeries and subsequent hospitalization, but the poem was completed by the fall of 1954, with additions in 1955.

Her residence at the Nervenklinik was interrupted again in early November 1956, when a rug on a waxed floor slipped from under her, and she fell and broke her hip. (Pound's sympathetic comment was "I am sorry yu bust yr / bone.") She was transferred for treatment to the Klinik Hirslanden, where she stayed for sixteen weeks before returning to Dr. Brunner's sanatorium. Thus, for much of this period, the letters between Pound in St. Elizabeths and H.D. at the Nervenklinik and the hospital continued to be an exchange between places of confinement. While she was at Hirslanden, and for some years afterward, H.D. kept the journal devoted mainly to her dreams and the recollections they called up. Pound is occasionally mentioned in it, and at one point, possibly in preparation for the writing of *End to Torment,* H.D. went over the notebooks, and made the notation "Ezra" on the blank pages opposite these references.

Pound's stay at St. Elizabeths offered a remarkable spectacle. He was able to gain a certain degree of privacy and comfort among the insane people who were his fellow patients, and, after an initial period of mental confusion, continued many of his usual activities. In the summer of 1946, Dorothy left Italy, took a room in Washington, and thereafter stayed with her husband throughout the hospital's visiting hours, helping him with his Chinese studies and his correspondence. There were many other visitors, including Charles Olson, H. L. Mencken, James Laughlin, Ronald Duncan, Norman Holmes Pearson, Kenneth Clark, and young acolytes who came to study with him on a regular schedule. Olga Rudge, who suffered intensely at being separated from Pound, made plans to come to Washington to see him, although there was some feeling that her appearance might arouse additional prejudice against him. After much delay, she did make the trip, and spent a few hours with him at the hospital while Dorothy stayed away.

Pound wrote and received an enormous number of letters, and took up his interrupted correspondence with H.D., which continued through the time of his release from St. Elizabeths in May 1958, and his return to Italy. He also exchanged letters with Aldington, who was often thoroughly impatient with him. He worked on his court case, had access to books, kept up with the world through newspapers and magazines, and even supervised the publication of a series of booklets.

In the postwar period, the two poets sometimes exchanged letters as often as once a month, but at one point, H.D. told Pearson that she found it hard to reply to Pound's "flighty, disconnected little notes." Another time, she complained that she was getting too many letters from him filled with "blind prejudice" and commands to undertake literary projects. She was so disturbed by his situation and by the eccentricity of his letters that she found it hard to read them or answer them. "I should write to him," she once said in a letter to Pearson, "it is all so heart-breaking and impossible."[1] His letters were, in fact, sometimes patronizing and overbearing and sometimes incoherent. Throughout the first months of 1950, she kept in touch with him mainly by sending picture postcards from Greece, while Pound regularly sent brief airmail letters.

After they had been corresponding for years, she complained that "you always seem to turn on me at a moment of *rapprochement*."[2] Nevertheless, she felt great pity for him, despite the revulsion she and all his old friends felt for his political opinions. Her letters are always signed with her old nickname, "Dryad," and an affectionate closing word or two.

In spite of her discomfort, she did write, and the correspondence became fairly regular in 1948, although H.D. sometimes asked Pearson to write for her. The dialogue between the two poets was now largely confined to their letters, since Pound's only writing was a translation of Sophocles' *Trachiniae* (*Women of Trachis*). H.D. was working mainly on prose narratives embodying her occult interests. Some of these, as we have seen, reflect H.D.'s continuing effort to understand the rôle Pound played in her life. She offered to send him books, told him that she had acquired the table once owned by William Morris, a poet Pound had introduced her to, and reported that she was rereading Morris's poems. (She did not, however, reveal that she had used the table for her communications with spirits.)

The two exchanged birthday greetings in 1948, when H.D. was sixty-two and Pound was sixty-three, and they continued to remember Christmas and birthdays, often referred to old times and friends in their letters, and sometimes mentioned literary matters. Pearson sent H.D. the issue of the *Hudson Review* containing Pound's translation of the *Trachiniae*, and H.D. wrote to Pound that she found it "very exciting and stimulating." She told Pound what she had been writing, mentioning *By Avon River*, a book on Elizabethan themes, "The Red Rose and the White," a novel about the Rossetti circle, and an autobiographical novel that seems to be the unpublished "Majic Mirror." Of these, only *By Avon River* was published, and she had a copy sent to Pound. She wrote that she had seen some reviews of the *Cantos* and was rereading the *Pisan Cantos* herself.[3] Pound's replies from St. Elizabeths said little about writing, but asked about the people they had known and discussed pictures H.D. had sent him.

H.D. wrote frequently to Dorothy, and expressed her concern about Pound's situation: "I myself have been haunted by E and by you too, wondering what might be done."[4] She also heard from Olga Rudge and her daughter, Mary, and found these relationships with Pound and his family comforting. In 1950 she wrote: "What a long time it has been! . . . but just keeping in touch makes a sort of ring of memories and in a small way, blessings."[5]

Pearson's services to the two poets were indispensable. When communication between them failed, Pearson often filled the gap, keeping each informed of the other's situation. Pound at first found Pearson deficient and uncongenial, but after the services he performed for both poets over the years, Pound wrote, on his return to Italy in 1958, "Bless N.H.P. for existing."[6] During the St. Elizabeths years, a three-cornered correspondence flourished, as the two poets and the Yale professor exchanged letters. On occasion, Pearson sent books each poet had published to the other. As we have seen, he had entered the scene as an advocate of H.D., but he was of even greater service to Pound. He sent letters to St. Elizabeths frequently, supplied Pound with needed material, taught the *Cantos* in his Yale seminars, compiled notes about it for his students, worked on proofs of the ongoing *Cantos,* wrote an introduction for an early study of Pound, read from the *Cantos* on television, advised Pound on the sale of his manuscripts, and shared news about the literary figures he met. Pearson also did much to publicize the two poets and preserve their reputations, setting up archives of their works at Yale, and promoting exhibits at the university.

He was able to pass on to H.D. information about Pound's situation at St. Elizabeths from a follower who spent an afternoon a week with him. In 1952 he visited the hospital himself, and sent her detailed accounts of Pound's life there.

Pearson assured Pound that H.D. valued his letters, and he often reported on her health. In April 1954, he told Pound that she was working on the series of poems that became *Helen in Egypt,* and in 1956 he told him about the approaching publication of her *Selected Poems* and *Tribute to Freud.* Pearson was sensitive to the fact that the two were not in perfect harmony with each other. In offering to send a copy of the Freud book, he acknowledged, "[I] know Freud is not your cup of tea." When he sent Pound H.D.'s *Selected Poems,* he added, "No comments required," and said there was no reason to write to her about it, as if he feared Pound's usual thunderous disapproval of her new work.

In spite of their bitter past relations, Aldington and H.D. remained in touch with each other through frequent letters, and concern about Pound was a frequent topic of their correspondence. Aldington, after reading Pound's *Guide to Kulchur,* told H.D. that "His mind is like a mirror broken into fragments," and advised her not to become involved in the efforts to free him.[7] Although H.D. visited America twice during Pound's confinement, she could not bring herself to see him. Pound, regretting that she could not come during her 1951 visit, sent the addresses of some friends in New York that he thought she might like to meet.

During H.D.'s visit to the States in September 1956, Pearson drove her to her old neighborhood in Pennsylvania. "Hilda's visit," he complained to Pound, "is a full time job." He also reported: "She is much torn between past and present and even considers coming back to the States in a year or two." She went to New York, New Haven, and Pennsylvania, but still did not feel able to see Pound in St. Elizabeths. Perhaps that was why Pearson wrote, toward the end of her visit, "Dryad full of jumping beans, but exhausted."[8]

When Pound sent H.D. a copy of the *Pisan Cantos* in the fall of 1948, the new poem made a strong impression on her. In thanking him for sending it, she wrote: "I find the canto sequence full of suggestion and glimpses of old-time," and "I will be looking forward to the other canto sequences."[9] The poem renewed her interest in her old friend's work, for in an undated letter apparently written in that year, she wrote: "I am going over the Cantos again . . . it goes on giving out new patterns and catching fresh lights; especially, I find the corn-flower, morning-glory, wasps, leopard, peach-blossom sections or 'beads,' translucent."[10] She singled out the nostalgic passages and sensuous particulars, an odd response to a poem concerned with much larger themes, but thoroughly consistent with H.D.'s poetic taste. In a later letter, after a recent move to her Lausanne hotel, she wrote: "I am re-reading your Pisan again as soon as my books are re-assembled," and said that she was gathering his other books. When Pound sent her a reprint of *The Chinese Written Character as a Medium for Poetry*, she wrote that she had begun to "de-cipher or de-code the wonderful pages," and suggested others to whom the book should be sent.

The "glimpses of old-time" in the *Pisan Cantos* led H.D. to ask about Walter Rummel, and to recall a concert "at your summer house, outside Philadelphia . . . Frances was with us."[11] She says that she had not heard from Frances for ten years, unaware that Gregg, together with her mother, had been killed in an air raid on Plymouth in 1941.

When Aldington wrote in 1948 to complain that he could not understand the *Cantos*, H.D. expressed her honest confusion about it in vigorous and imaginative language that reflected the lasting ambiguity of her feelings about Pound:

> I was surprised to find that it carried me along; I was leafing it over to get "some idea" when I found myself caught up in it; I felt, almost for the first time, that E. had really genius . . . I got the idea of some grand Elizabethan writing ABOUT a mad poet; a sort of King-Lear-cum-Fool-in-Lear; as if someone were writing lines for someone in a play; as if there were genius back of it; as if E. were not controlled but uncontrolled by this genius or daemon. I was actually very upset, as I had not bothered to analyze E. at all and my early impressions were mixed.[12]

She thought that Aldington's comparison of the *Cantos* with *Finnegans Wake* suggested a parallel between Pound and Joyce, and, in contrasting Pound with Lawrence, said:

> E. is the more rugged, a sort of post-49er, blasting up rocks, giving up his gold-field in a mad rush on; sifting stones and pebbles for a gleam of gold (and the gleam is there), not properly "panning" the gold-sand when sifted, dangerous, undecorous, no dulce et decorum. potentially magnifico, disguised in harlequin rags? Or harlequin disguised as Magnifico?[13]

Disturbed by the undertone of insanity she detected and by Pound's "dangerous" but "magnifico" challenges to convention, H.D. said she had "better get the book out of the way." She sent it to Bryher, who reported that she had reread all of Pound's poems, and found both genius and a narcissistic desire for fame in them.

When the Bollingen Foundation of Yale University awarded its poetry prize to the *Pisan Cantos* in February 1949, H.D. wrote to Pound that she learned about it from the Lausanne newspaper and sent him a clipping of the article. In the United States, an enormous controversy erupted as the award was challenged on the grounds of Pound's anti-Semitism, disloyalty, and questionable sanity, and Pearson sent H.D. a newspaper clipping about it. In a letter to Dorothy, H.D. repeated her congratulations, wrote that she was "deeply impressed" with the *Pisan Cantos*, and hoped that Pound would continue to write. But it is clear that the new Cantos made her feel, as she always had, that Pound's genius somehow threatened her originality. Nevertheless, she continued to study the *Cantos* for years and to gather critical articles and books on Pound's works.

As Pound's release from St. Elizabeths in April 1958 approached, Pearson and H.D. exchanged letters about him, beginning with Pearson's letter of 30 March in which he described a visit to the lively and garrulous old poet.[14] A few days later, he sent her some newspaper clippings about the news that Pound might soon be released, and reported that Dorothy thought he would want to see H.D. when he returned to Italy. As the final decision approached, he assured her that the Pounds would not need the financial assistance she had offered.

At last, in a letter of 19 April, Pearson could write that "Ezra is free!" and the faithful Pearson regarded the event as a birthday present for himself. Pound, after making nostalgic visits to his youthful home in Pennsylvania and to New Jersey for a brief reunion with William Carlos Williams, left for Italy, accompanied by Dorothy and Marcella Spann, a young woman who had become his assistant. When she heard from Pearson that Pound was returning to Italy, H.D. sent Pound a brief, affectionate letter in longhand as a "welcome home," saying she had followed events concerning his case by radio and newspaper, and closing with "don't forget your old Dryad."[15]

The Pound party landed at Genoa in July 1958 and was taken to Schloss Brunnenburg, a castle in the Tyrolean Alps, the home

of Pound's daughter, Mary, and her husband, Boris de Rachewiltz. Pound was physically frail and the castle was uncomfortable, so the old poet, reluctant to stay there, made visits to Venice,
Rapallo, and Rome. A letter written to H.D. from Rapallo some
time in the first part of 1959 was strangely unkind, perhaps because Pound was suffering from various ailments. He blamed her
for frequenting "the murderer's daughter," by whom he meant
Bryher, who, he said, "sabotaged my work for 40 years." He also
said that he had found a letter of H.D.'s "full of more idiotic reports than might have been expected."[16] But he also offered to be
of service to her in Rome, if he went there, and H.D.'s reply was
placid, even mentioning the "wild idea" of coming to Rapallo to
see him. When he returned to Brunnenburg, he wrote about the
possibility of a Christmas visit to Küsnacht, but nothing came of
this or other plans to meet.

These exchanges suggest that, in spite of Pound's prickliness,
the two poets were drawing together again. A number of factors
were leading H.D. to reflect on her feelings toward Pound, and to
review them in the notes that became *End to Torment: A Memoir
of Ezra Pound,* which was written at the Nervenklinik between
7 March and 13 July 1958.

A complication arose as Bryher, after seeing Pearson's letters to
H.D., wrote to Pearson, bitterly criticizing his participation in
Pound's affairs and objecting to the idea that Pound should see
H.D. The grounds of Bryher's protest are, of course, perfectly
clear. Like most of the general public, she viewed Pound as a traitor, a Fascist, and an anti-Semite. She and Pound had always
been at odds with each other in their personal relations, and their
political views were directly opposed. She had, of course, been a
loyal supporter of the Allied side during the war, and had been active in helping Jewish victims of Nazi persecution, in contrast to
Pound's wartime conduct. She told Pearson that she doubted his
sanity, repeated her view that his poetry depended on translation,
and objected to Pearson's mediation between Pound and H.D.

H.D. felt the need to defend Pound, and there was a painful
scene at the Nervenklinik when Bryher and Sylvia Beach came to
visit. As H.D.'s confused and anguished letter to Pearson describes

it, the two women "turned violently on me about poor Ezra." But the result of this, she said, was to thrust her back to another time when Pound had suffered ostracism, after he had been fired at Wabash College. She now realized that her "deep love for Ezra" was a part of her psyche that had been hidden during her sessions with Erich Heydt, her analyst. "I *did* have a life in US," she wrote, "before Fido [Bryher]—& I feel so violently American, in the pro-Ezra sense, though it has gone so badly with him."[17] The letter suggests that she had never relinquished her love for Pound, in spite of objections from family and friends, Pound's betrayal and marriage to another woman, and his reputation as a traitor. This split centered on Pound—"my *inner* schism," she calls it—and is a key to the indecision and division she often suffered and recorded in her fiction.

In the year after he left St. Elizabeths, Pound complained that his friends were uncooperative and asked H.D. if she could tell "why my friends don't get on with each other." He looked back to the Imagist period as a time when he had last enjoyed a Confucian peace. "Not since Brigit, Richard, the four of us, has there been any harmony about me."[18] In this observation, Pound put himself at the center of the group, and it is amazing that he could not see that he was also the center of the disagreements. It is easy to understand that his literary supporters like Aldington and Pearson would have little interest in such "friends" as the quasi-Fascist characters whom he had welcomed at St. Elizabeths or the Italian Fascists he frequented after his return to Italy.

Two phrases from this letter help to fix Pound's attitude toward H.D. at this time, the summer of 1959, about a year after he had left the hospital. He felt that he could ask her opinion about his friends due to her "Having known me longer than any surviver [*sic*] save old Bull Wms . . . having also criticl [*sic*] eye if not much connected with utterance." He was confirming the fifty-year-old link between them, but also expressing doubt about her literary judgment ("utterance") while crediting her with satisfactory sense about other things. He had not changed his mind about her critical ability since 1917 when he wrote to Margaret Anderson, "H.D. is all right, but shouldn't write criticism." H.D. was not offended by this casual slight, but continued to write about a television program on Pound produced by Pearson, her new grandchild, and similar neutral matters.

The immediate stimulus that led H.D. to write *End to Torment,* her fullest comment on her relationship with Pound, was the record of a visit to St. Elizabeths titled "Weekend with Ezra Pound" by David Rattray published in *The Nation* on 16 November 1957. It was a long piece of about six thousand words that did not set a very pleasant scene. Rattray described a sturdy and talkative Pound who lived in camping-out style in a room littered with miscellaneous scraps of food, derelict papers, pencils, and books. Tea was served and guests were received in an adjoining alcove. Dorothy, a young Bohemian named Sheri Martinelli who had befriended Pound, and Jean–Marie Chatel, whom he described as a novelist, were present at Rattray's first visit.

Aldington sent a clipping of the article to H.D., probably intending this report to cool H.D.'s attachment to Pound, but it had the opposite effect, for she felt that it described a "personal" Pound and that the "actual Ezra" came through in it. She said it had motivated her to begin to make the notes of her own recollections of Pound that became *End to Torment.* When she was planning it, she wrote to Pearson: "I have been infinitely distressed, & only now, after 12 years, have been able to face the *Pisan* legend."[19] However, there is nothing about the Pisan imprisonment in *End to Torment.* The sources of "distress" it mentions are mainly the conflicts of the early Pennsylvania love affair. But the memoir does show that H.D. had read the *Cantos* with care.

Another influence was that of Dr. Erich Heydt, the clinic's resident psychiatrist between 1953 and 1961. When she returned to the Nervenklinik, H.D. saw him frequently in a relationship that included, but also in time transcended, psychiatric treatment. He told her that he had spent some time at St. Elizabeths, where he had seen Pound and observed his sessions with his "students." Heydt impressed her as a widely cultured man with a great interest in the arts, including H.D.'s work and that of "The Poet in the Iron Cage," as he called Pound, referring to the poet's imprisonment in an open-air cell at the DTC near Pisa.

When he first began treating H.D., he asked her whether she had known Pound while giving her an injection, and five years later, H.D. felt that "Dr. Heydt injected me with Ezra," since he continued to explore their relationship. He realized that her feelings about Pound were a source of her disturbance, and compelled her to review them in detail. She usually showed him Pound's letters, and he made her relationship with Pound an important theme in her analysis. She wrote to Pearson: "I have made a few *very simple* notes on my reactions. It is Erich's interest & concern that are responsible. He always said, 'You are hiding something.' It seems yes, my deepest depth did hide the real Ezra relationship cum family—you know! Then so much, so much after!"[20] These notes would be developed into *End to Torment,* where H.D. attempted to explore those "deepest depths."

End to Torment is a rambling, digressive journal that mingles memories of fifty years earlier with events of the present. Its entries are dated from 7 March to 13 July 1958, a period that straddles Pound's release from St. Elizabeths in April 1958, and they record H.D.'s mixed reactions to it. It shows that Pound was a central figure in the "legend" that H.D. was fashioning of her life, both in her fantasies and in her writings. It opens with an impression of the nineteen-year-old Pound in the Pennsylvania snow, and moves on to recall some of the scenes of their erotic friendship, the kisses in the woods, the treehouse, the books Pound lent her, and the poems he recited. H.D. recalls the young Pound's physical presence, which reminds her of Paderewski and Swinburne, also redhaired, and recollects such later events as their encounters in Kensington and the scene with the Wilkinsons at Victoria Station. These recollections show that the elderly H.D. cannot shake off her identification with the young, attractive Pound and the aura of the Pre-Raphaelite and Victorian poetry he brought to their meetings. Heydt, her analyst, asks why reading her notes excites her, and she replies, referring to the time of her infatuation with Pound, "it's the *fiery moment* but it's all so long ago." She recalled that she once wrote, "The perfection of the fiery moment can not be sustained—or can it?" And she remains indecisive: "Ezra was not consciously a love-image. But perhaps he lurked there, hid there."[21]

When Heydt, feeling that she was not telling him everything, asked what she was hiding, she brought forward the deeply embarrassing moment when her father caught her with Ezra in the armchair. Her insistence that the importance of the first embrace "cannot be overestimated" and her confessions that the "mariage du ciel et de la terre" was an ideal that "filled my fantasies and dreams, my prose and poetry for ten years" were certainly based on the "fiery moment" of her youthful affair with Pound. But Pound himself is lost in the cloud of a more abstractly imagined figure as she adds that all this has been tempered by later experience that ultimately renders "the poet" harmless.

In her study of the sexual themes H.D. drew from Romantic and Pre-Raphaelite sources, Cassandra Laity formulates the shifting relationships to Pound that H.D. refers to in *End to Torment* as a "Bloomian triad" in which the acolyte successively admires, rejects, and finally accepts a dominant precursor. Considering this relation within the context of her view that by this time H.D. was reinterpreting the male figures of her earlier life as Romantic or Pre-Raphaelite figures, Laity finds that H.D. first admired Pound within a Romantic aura; then, in her novels, saw him as the patriarchal "type of anti-Romantic male modernity"; and finally, after his imprisonment, thought of him sympathetically as a victim who shared the female experience of oppression. It was in this phase, no doubt, that she could see him as "harmless." Laity attributes this shift in her "myth" of Pound to a reversion to the period of their Pre-Raphaelite and Romantic readings. Having portrayed him as an overbearing, harshly masculine character in her novels, Laity says, she now reconfigured him, and brought him closer to herself as a feminized Romantic who shared the ostracism of all Romantic artists. As Laity recognizes, throughout these changes and throughout the years, she remained loyal to Pound, adopting a "father/brother" relationship with him, and identifying him with the Pre-Raphaelite figures she admired, such as the red-haired Swinburne.[22]

Perhaps the most painful of the memories recalled in *End to Torment* was that of Pound's departure for Europe in 1908. Writing in 1958, which she regarded as an anniversary of that event, she linked the suspense she felt in waiting for letters to the "intense apprehension" she had felt fifty years before. She was "selfishly frustrated," she says, when she learned that Pound and his wife were returning to Italy after his release from St. Elizabeths because it recalled the same "first break, when Ezra left, on a cattleship . . . for Venice." She still felt this as a desertion, for she had illogically depended on his support, while rejecting his proposals of marriage, and felt, as she told a friend, that "every disappointment or shock, is superimposed on another."[23]

Ezra, she says, separated her from "my friends, my family, even from America." When we recall the strong attachment to her family and their traditions H.D. displays in such works as *The Gift*, it is clear that her youthful commitment to Pound had been accompanied by intense conflict. Now, again, in 1958, a similar conflict arose. When friends who had suffered during the war condemned Pound for his wartime behavior, she replied, perhaps in her own mind, "But . . . You catch fire or you don't catch fire," and wrote, "We who have profited by his inspiration must take our stand—here, now."[24]

H.D. may have been the first of Pound's critics to attempt the difficult task of separating the man and the poet from his political opinions. She was pained to learn that the newly freed Pound was exposing the folly of his unchanged political ideas in interviews with reporters, but she turned to her recollections of their youth to declare: "There is a reserve of dynamic or daemonic power from which we may all draw." She felt that power in Pound's latest poem, for she added: "He lay on the floor of the Iron Cage and wrote the *Pisan Cantos*."[25]

End to Torment is related to two texts, the "Weekend with Ezra Pound" article and the *Cantos*. H.D. seems to have been especially fixated by Rattray's reports about Sheri Martinelli, whom Pound had dubbed "Undine." Rattray described Pound displaying much affection for this young woman, hugging and kissing her, and running his hand through her hair. Martinelli told Rattray that Pound had devoted a passage in the "Rock Drill" section of the *Cantos* to her, and he quotes her as saying: "Grandpa loves me. It's because I symbolize the spirit of Love to him, I guess." This remark is not entirely inaccurate, since the poetry about love as a form of worship that begins in Canto 90 seems to have been inspired by Pound's infatuation with Martinelli.[26]

The Canto opens with a Latin epigraph declaring that the soul delights with the love flowing from it, rather than with itself, and the theme continues through the following Cantos, eloquently forging a bond between love and religion, a more mature reversion, perhaps, to the young Pound's idealization of H.D. as "Is-Hilda." A line in Canto 90, "the curled stone at the marge," is an allusion to the surviving base of a vanished statue of Venus whose restoration, Pound declared, would be "worth more than any metaphysical argument."[27] Martinelli herself enters in Canto 91: "Thus Undine came to the rock, / by Circeo," a line that has her approaching the site of this statue and thus merging with the goddess of love. The connection is supported by the line that soon follows about "Helen of Tyre," a figure Pound believed to be an acolyte of Venus. The sacredness of love is perhaps definitely pinned down in the line "ichor, amor," identifying the fluid in the veins of the gods with love.

Pound addresses Martinelli directly in Canto 93:

> (Yes, my Ondine, it is so god-damned dry on these rocks)
> "The waves rise, and the waves fall
> But you are like the moon-light:
> Always there!"[28]

It seems clear that Martinelli aroused feelings that led Pound to write some of his best poetry in these Cantos. But she also engaged H.D.'s emotions. H.D., following her tendency to identify herself with any woman that interested Pound, wrote "Undine is myself *then*," referring to the time of the parting of 1908 and the

Imagist period. She painstakingly, and no doubt painfully, copied Rattray's sentences describing Pound's hugs and kisses into the text of her book. A rather incoherent entry mingles "Undine" with some of her own most trying experiences; it contains lines from Swinburne's "Itylus" associated with her friendship with Frances Gregg, and "Aztec, Aztlan," words with a long history in her "legend" that refer to female sacrifice, brought to mind because Martinelli had proposed going to Mexico to paint a temple. And it refers again to Pound's traumatic departure for Europe in 1908, when H.D. adds: "This is 1958. The year's division divideth us? No," denying that the intervening years have "divided" her from Pound.[29]

After 20 June, the *End to Torment* entries are very much occupied with "Undine" because Martinelli had established a relationship with both Pearson and H.D. She sent them a photo of herself and examples of her art work and professed great admiration for H.D. H.D. was interested enough to obtain a book of Martinelli's pictures with an introduction by Pound, and she and Pearson both answered her requests for money. H.D.'s entry of 25 June—"Poor Undine! They don't want you . . . How shall we reconcile ourselves to this?"—refers to the fact that Pound dropped Martinelli abruptly after his release in April.[30] This was due to Dorothy's insistence and the discovery that Martinelli was addicted to drugs. But H.D. remained sympathetic with her for some years, and specified her place in her imaginative life by writing: "Undine is imposed or super-imposed on Frances [Gregg] Josepha."[31] The identification does not simplify her feelings about either Martinelli or Pound, for Gregg, we recall, was not only her lover but also a rival for Pound's love.

The pages of *End to Torment*, like H.D.'s thoughts of Pound at this time, are deeply penetrated by H.D.'s ambiguous attitude toward the *Cantos*, and show that she had to overcome intense psychological disturbance before seeing it clearly. Her knowledge of it began early, for she reports in her memoir that she felt "shock" when she saw early Canto "variations" in unconventional printed form when they were all living in Holland Place about 1913. The recollection seemed to arouse overwhelming feelings about the history of her relations with Pound, for her allusion to the incident is followed by: "Black-out . . . Chthonian darkness—the black-out. I don't pretend to understand. We have gone through some Hell together, separately."[32] She had not seen Pound for twenty years, yet thoughts of his poem plunged her into unconsciousness and confusion on the one hand, but also evoked the feeling that they were somehow united in the separate trials each had suffered.

She read passages from the *Cantos* to Heydt and said that she had only recently "dared" to try reading it through. The experience seemed to frighten her. But when some lines of her own poetry came to her, they "laid the ghost, as it were," and she realized that "I had developed along another line, in another dimension—only the opposites could meet in the end." She expressed the same idea after reading about Jean Cocteau's observation that the artist was a prison from which the work of art escaped. Pound's imprisonment, she thought, was their generation's model of the prison of the Self. But, in the following entry, no doubt with her own case in mind, she speaks of "an intermediate place or *plane*" that lives on after passion has imposed its control over the Self, and becomes a paradise of freedom to write as one wishes. In what sounds very much like a description of her relationship as a poet to Pound, she says: "Make no mistake. Poles apart, two poles made communication possible, Establish the poles. Others may use our invention, extension, communication. We don't care any more."[33] She felt, it seems, that she and Pound would understand each other best by firmly recognizing their different contributions to poetry, the contributions that others now used. The parting, she believed, would lead ultimately to a meeting.

She was able, therefore, to study the *Cantos* attentively. The impression of reading Canto 90 was that of "trying to see a whirling kaleidoscope." She resisted at first, and could not see clearly, she said, but could *hear* the words as she read them aloud, and could "at last accept the intoxication" they offered, an acceptance also of what Pound was doing.[34]

She followed up the lines about Vidal in Canto 4 by consulting a critical work, and, with characteristic independence, fashioned her own interpretation of the legend about the troubadour who wore the skins of wolves to woo his lady and was eaten by his hounds. She speculated that Pound himself had adopted the wolf-trappings of Rome, whose founder had been fed by a wolf, by allying himself with Italy in his broadcasts, and had been consumed by his critics. The idea led her to think of the word "lycanthropy," which she associated with a Greek word resembling "Lynx," and this reminded her of the lynx lyric in Canto 79.

She recalled this passage while telling Heydt about the time her father had discovered her and Pound in the armchair. In writing *End to Torment* more than fifty years later, she recalled that their lovemaking had aroused her passion, transforming her into one of the wild women of the pagan orgiastic rites: "*Maenad, bassarid.*" Although, as we have seen, she was probably mistaken in thinking the lynx lyric was about her, it nevertheless revived her passionate and contradictory feelings about Pound. "God save us from Canto LXXIX," she said, praying to be spared the memory of his infidelity. She then addressed the young Pound again: "Mr. Pound, with your magic, your 'strange spells of old deity,' why didn't you complete the metamorphosis? Pad, pad, pad . . . come along, my Lynx. Let's get out of here. You are suffocating and I am hungry. You spoke of grapes somewhere—you were starving."[35] She is asking, it seems, why Pound had not accomplished the "metamorphosis" of overcoming her reluctance to marry him, and she invites him, in imagination, to the fulfillment she thinks both have missed. These sentences reflect the imagined union by braiding echoes from her early poems and those of Pound together. The "strange spells" are from Pound's "Cino"—"Dreams, words, and they are jewels, / Strange spells of old deity." The grapes are from H.D.'s early poem, "Orchard"—"stripped late of their green sheaths, grapes, red-purple . . . I bring you as offering." The "Pad, pad" sentences, imagined as spoken by Pound to H.D. when he has changed her into the lynx of the Canto, offer to let her breathe, and seek out those grapes.

She echoes the lynx passage again when, overjoyed after a correspondent passed on a compliment Pound had written about her, the aged H.D. surrendered control of herself in a remarkable poetic ecstasy: "I danced in the garden in the moonlight like a mad thing. *Maenad and bassarid.* It is not necessary to understand."[36]

Other parts of the *Cantos* came to mind as she wrote the entries for *End to Torment*. On Palm Sunday, she copied the variant of François Villon's line, "Le Paradis n'est pas artificiel," which appears in the *Pisan Cantos*, and wrote that she identified Leucothea, the goddess who helped Odysseus, with Pound's wife, Dorothy. (This seems to be her first identification, through implication, of Pound with Odysseus.) She quoted the lines from Canto 4 about Vidal and noted that the Canto was published in 1919, the year of Pound's visit to her room in the nursery after the birth of Perdita.

End to Torment did not accomplish the catharsis that Heydt and Pearson hoped might free H.D. from her obsession with Pound. She not only continued her correspondence with him when he went back to Italy but sent him what she was writing for criticism, including *End to Torment*. And she reviewed her passionate attachment to him in one of her finest poems, the "Coda" to *Helen in Egypt* that was titled *Winter Love*.

10

Modern Epics

> . . . the nature of one, in achieving his art, is different
> from the nature of another.
> Marianne Moore, "Ezra Pound," in *Predilections*

Greek literature was a lifelong topic of agreement and disagreement between the two poets. They agreed in condemning the work of academic classicists, but they favored different Greek authors. H.D's Greece was that of the *Greek Anthology,* the lyrics of Sappho, and the plays of Euripides, especially the choruses, while Pound turned to Homer and, to a far lesser extent, to Sophocles. Pound's major Greek source was the *Odyssey,* and H.D.'s favorite Greek figure was Helen. Since Pound's father was named Homer, and H.D.'s mother was named Helen, Freud might have seen unconscious motives behind these preferences. H.D.'s immersion was more thorough and more personal than Pound's. Much of her poetry is translation or paraphrase from the Greek, and her poetic world is essentially a transcription of parts of the Greek heritage.[1] The Homeric element in the *Cantos,* on the other hand, while crucial, is only one of a vast array of intertextual effects, and most of these allusions are fragmentary. The exception is Canto 1, an extended translation of a passage from Book 11 of the *Odyssey*. It first appeared in draft form in a series of articles about translations from Greek texts that Pound contributed to the *Egoist* in

1918–19, most of them dealing with versions of Homer. It was then incorporated into the *Cantos* as an opening announcement of one its major themes, that of cultural renewal.

Pound approved of H.D.'s Greek strain at first, describing the Imagist poems he sent to *Poetry* as being "straight talk, straight as the Greek" (as if he knew that they were, in fact, translations or paraphrases). In defending the Imagist practice of *vers libre* in a 1913 article, "The Tradition," a short and grudging review of H.D.'s translations, Pound had referred to certain passages of Euripides as precedents. However, his comment that he is not sure Euripides offers the best entry to Greek drama is a sign of dissent, for Euripides was H.D.'s lifelong enthusiasm, and a source of *Helen in Egypt*.[2] He was publicly approving in 1918, when he said in a review of H.D.'s "Choruses from Euripides" that they were "a great relief from other windy and verbose translators." Pound admitted that he had not given them the praise they deserved and added a reprinting of H.D.'s "Chorus of the Women of Chalkis."

In a review contributed to *The Egoist* in 1916, H.D. referred to "our present day literary Alexandria." This was an effort to equate what was being written at that time with the Greek poetry associated with Hellenistic Alexandria of the 3rd century B.C., concentrated poems characterized by sensuality, delicacy, decadence, and syncretism. Much of it was preserved in the *Greek Anthology*, which H.D. and Aldington had studied and used as a source of translations. This was the "polubendius" Hellenism that had led Pound to stop and laugh in the street when they were all in Venice in 1913. By 1920 he had become so impatient with H.D.'s enthusiasm for these poets, that he declared, in a letter to William Carlos Williams, that H.D.'s ideas were "Alexandrine bunk." And as late as 1939, as we have seen, he urged her to abandon what he called her "schoolroom hellenism." He may have had this debate with H.D. in mind when, in *ABC of Reading* (1960), he expressed reservations about the merits of Greek drama, and said there was little in "Alexandrine epigram" that could not be found in earlier authors.

Though both Pound and H.D. accepted the Hermetic tradition and the occult ideas stemming from ancient Greece, Pound turned to the high classical period and its Renaissance interpreters in contrast to H.D.'s deep interest in the later poets. "There is something to be said," he wrote, "for old Hellenism and for Renaissance Hellenism revived."[3] H.D. also admired the high classical period, even though "it has been so mossed over and distorted by the academicians," for "It is modern enough, and near 'cosmic' race-consciousness."[4]

Pound eventually changed his views about the Hellenistic poets, however. Callimachus, a leader of the Alexandrian school, and an advocate of the concise and delicate poem, was important to the young H.D., and would no doubt have been included in Pound's disapproval of her "Alexandrine bunk." But, many years later, in a letter of 1953, he urged her to turn to him, writing from St. Elizabeths "get a KALLIMAXOS / ever bathe in ole KAL?" sent her a fine edition with French translation that he expected her to translate, and later reproached her for not carrying out this assignment.

Pound tended to underestimate H.D.'s knowledge of the Greeks. In December 1949, he recommended that she read the Greek geographer Pausanias as a guide on her planned visit to Greece. She replied that she was familiar with him, having written some essays on his work many years before, after World War I. She rather apologized to Pound for writing these, and said, referring to that time, when she had contributed to Aldington's *Poets' Translation Series,* that "the Greek translations in general were taking me out of my path; but they were stepping-stones and I treasure my memory of them."[5] This does not accurately reflect the importance of Greek translation as a factor in all of her poetry, including *Helen in Egypt,* but was no doubt intended to mollify Pound.

Pound and H.D. had somewhat differing views of the Greek gods, and these attitudes subtly tone their treatment of the deities in their poems. For H.D., the gods are associated with the elements and processes of nature, so that in her poem "Adonis," she says to the god, "each of us like you / has passed through the drift of wood leaves, / cracked and bent / and tortured and unbent / in the winter frost."[6] For Pound, on the other hand, a god was "an eternal state of mind," a psychological or emotional condition that becomes "manifest" through human consciousness.

Helen in Egypt brings forward Pound's and H.D.'s contrasting approaches to the Trojan War. In *H.D. and Hellenism,* Eileen Gregory observes that Pound admired Aeschylus's *Agamemnon* for its force and energy, and for the vortex-like drive of the *Oresteia* as a whole. H.D., on the other hand, was occupied, throughout her career, with Euripides. During World War I, when, as Gregory points out, battles on the shores of the Dardanelles were taking place at or near the site of the Trojan War, she translated parts of Euripides' *Iphigenia in Aulis,* and often turned to him later in her career. Gregory notes that H.D. was attracted to Euripides' lyrical expressions of the grief caused by war, especially the lamentations of women. However, the passages H.D. chose to translate from *Iphigenia in Aulis* end on a heroic note after acknowledging the dark dictates of fate, and the intense emotions of her *Hippolytus* translation have, of course, nothing to do with war. Gregory's larger point is that H.D. was demonstrating independence by preferring the Greek dramatist who was "unfashionable" and associated with "progressive heterodoxies."[7]

With *Helen in Egypt,* her major work, H.D. resumed the poetic dialogue with Pound, for she referred to it as "my Cantos," as though her poem were in some sense a reply to the *Pisan Cantos.*[8] She said that it had been "simmering" for three years, which was the period after she had first seen the *Pisan Cantos.*[9] Her enthusiasm for the *Cantos* wavered while she was writing *Helen in Egypt,* but she was always conscious of it. In a letter of 12 June 1954, when her poem was almost completed, she told Pearson that conversations with people at the sanatorium led her to think about Pound's poem again.

While *Helen in Egypt* was in progress, both H.D. and Pearson thought of it in some relation to Pound's poem, for they usually referred to the series of lyrics H.D. was writing as "cantos." At one point in 1953, H.D. said that her poem could "go on forever à la

E.P.'s cantos" and that she did not know if she would continue with "the so-called Cantos." When she sent Pearson sections of her poem in 1954, she called them "Cantos" in quotation marks. Later, musing on the relations between *Helen in Egypt* and Pound's epic, she wrote: "I completed my own *cantos* as Norman called them again in the Greek setting."[10]

Helen in Egypt does resemble the *Pisan Cantos* in its positioning of autobiographical elements against a background of war. When she was preparing to have it printed, H.D. wrote to Pearson: "It is really so exoteric (difficult word—all war-problems) as well as being strictly INNER and esoteric and personal."[11] And, in fact, it is a blending of two of H.D.'s customary modes, disguised autobiography and adaptations from Greek sources.

In the dialogue we have been tracing, Pound had long since ceased to learn anything from H.D.'s work, which he did not always see. But H.D., after developing her own method and interests, now turned to the *Cantos* to see if she could profit from them. She wrote to Pearson, after receiving a friendly letter from Pound, that "I am rather tempted to study the P[isan] C[antos] sections & I want to get on with *Helen*."[12] Pearson followed her work on her "cantos" closely, and in a letter of 1953 responded enthusiastically to the news that she was continuing it. He once linked it with Pound's work by referring to the reappearance of Helen in the "Leuké" section of *Helen* as a "metamorphosis as Ezra would call it." He advised her to follow the method of the sculptor Pound described in Canto 25, quoting the lines:

> as the sculptor sees the form in the air
>> before he sets hand to mallet,
> and as he sees the in, and the through,
>> the four sides
> not the one face to the painter
> As ivory uncorrupted:

Pearson added: "That is the way Ezra puts it."[13]

When she had completed her poem, and was planning its publication, H.D. told Pearson that she felt great satisfaction and mentioned, among those who had encouraged her, "Ezra, of course, in the beginning."[14] She said she wanted to reread the *Cantos*—"but the manner is a bit 'catching.' I am sure E. would revile the *Helen* technique!"[15] As it turned out, however, she was mistaken about Pound's reaction.

In *End to Torment,* she acknowledged that there was a relationship in her mind between the two poems. "Thinking of Ezra's work, I recall my long *Helen* sequence. Perhaps there was always a challenge in his creative power. Perhaps even, as I said to Erich, there was unconscious—really unconscious—rivalry."[16] She had reason to believe that Pound lingered in her subconscious, for she once reported: "I dream of Ezra last night. I seldom dream of Ezra . . . I say to someone, 'He is fascinating but so kind.'"[17] Throughout their careers, she had responded to Pound's greater poetic success by regarding it as a "challenge" that moved her to respond with courageous new efforts. Now this idea was no longer "unconscious," and there is reason to believe that she had been aware of it much earlier.

H.D. did turn to her planned study of the *Pisan Cantos* when her poem was finished, and in a letter of 24 November 1955, she reported that she had read "Pisa" several times. She added that she hoped to give more time to it, and that she had seen articles and translations relevant to it. She made progress in coming to terms with it. In *End to Torment,* she reports that by reading a part of Canto 90 aloud to Heydt, she gained "a new power" over it, that it lifted her above cares, and that she could accept the "intoxication" of its devotional lines, even though unwelcome thoughts of Pound and war intervened.[18]

H.D.'s idea of using the story of *Helen in Egypt* may well have been suggested by her reading many years earlier of *Divine Fire,* a novel by May Sinclair, who had befriended the Imagists. In Sinclair's novel, a young working-class poet writes a "neo-classic drama" called *Helen in Leuce,* never published but deeply admired by his friends. In it, a chorus rehearses the history of Helen's lovers and the Trojan war, and Helen arrives on the "enchanted isle"

of Leuce where she is joined by Achilles — all features found in
H.D.'s epic. We are told that the poem praises the character of
Helen, for, through all her adventures, "the godhead in her re-
mained pure, untouched, holding itself apart."[19]

While the work of the fictional poet may well have lingered in
H.D.'s mind during the years since she had read Sinclair's book,
the most immediate source of *Helen in Egypt* is Euripides' *Helen*,
a play that H.D. studied carefully over a long period.[20] She found
in the Greek play a rationale for redeeming the figure of Helen,
and a basis for telling the story of her own quest for the ideal
lover. Euripides' *Helen* was written in the shadow of Athens's long
and disastrous war against Sparta, and can be seen as a protest
against the evils of war, like the poems of Pound and H.D. written in the shadow of World War II. His play makes use of the legend that Helen of Troy was a phantom double of the real Helen,
who was sent to Egypt. It finds Helen in Egypt after the fall of
Troy, condemned against her will to marry the Egyptian king.
When the shipwrecked Menelaus, her husband, arrives after hiding the figure he believes to be his faithless wife in a cave, he is
astonished to encounter the real Helen. She explains that the goddess Hera, jealous of Paris's decision to award the Apple of Dis-
cord to Aphrodite, fashioned a false Helen for Paris to take to
Troy, while Zeus sent her, the real Helen, to Egypt, where she remained faithful to her marriage vows. The ironies are multiple. It
is revealed that the Trojan War was fought over a phantom, a
pointed comment on the futility of war. The hateful Helen of
Troy — "reviled" by "all Greece" in H.D.'s early poem based on a
line from Euripides' play, and briefly glimpsed at the beginning of
Pound's Canto 7 in lines from the *Iliad* — was the false one, and
the true Helen, hidden in Egypt, is innocent of the suffering
caused by the war.

According to H.D.'s record, she began to write *Helen in Egypt*
in September 1952 in the tearoom of the Hotel Bristol in Lugano.
She began the second section after going to Küsnacht in 1953, and
completed the last in Lugano in the summer of 1954, after interruptions by the two hospital stays in connection with her opera-
tion. Pearson suggested that she write an explanation of her poem,

and when H.D. recorded parts of it, she read prose captions that were included, as a necessary evil, when the poem was published.

The sequence of events is indistinct and inconsecutive, secondary to Helen's meditations on past events and their meaning for her. We first encounter her in Egypt, where Achilles, her lover, has joined her, and she recalls how, coming from the Trojan War, he attacked her, but then relented when she called upon his mother, Thetis. Afterward, he leaves her with a riddling question about her identity. Helen, seeking to determine the meaning of her life with regard to the war and her former lovers, recalls such events of the war as Achilles' rebellion and the sacrifice of Iphigenia, which Achilles approved. She wanders in an Egyptian temple, a recollection, no doubt, of H.D.'s visit to Luxor, and, beset by inner conflicts and Achilles' question, reflects that she would like to forget the past and bring the Egyptian religion to Greece. The scene then shifts to a shepherd's cottage on the island of Leuké, a transcendental realm beyond death, where her former lover, Paris, comes and tries to free her from her love for Achilles. After him, another lover, Theseus, comes to counsel her, and she thinks she finds peace by reconciling her warring memories with each other. She then returns to Egypt, waking from what has apparently been a dream, to the real world and its unfathomable mystery.

While H.D. may have thought of her poem as a counterpart of the *Pisan Cantos,* her immediate motivation for writing it was elsewhere. She said that she wrote the first section after learning of Lord Dowding's marriage, and Dowding, she said, in "Compassionate Friendship," was the "dynamic liberator or inspiration" for what she called her "Greek epic." This statement explains much about what she meant by saying that her poem was "INNER" and "personal." While it cannot be reduced to autobiography, it is formed on an autobiographic armature whose characters are identifiable with people in H.D.'s life. H.D.'s persistent idea that her life was a "legend" is reflected early in the sequence as Helen realizes that the Egyptian hieroglyphs she is unable to read encompass her, so that *"She herself is the writing."* Helen is, of course, H.D. herself; Theseus, the master of the labyrinth, is a good Freud; Menelaus has the position of Aldington as a former husband; Paris has much advice for Helen, and so recalls Heydt; and Chiron is a fount of wisdom, as H.D. took Havelock Ellis to be. Nevertheless, these men are presented primarily as the figures of the myths, only secondarily as people from H.D.'s life.

What is remarkable, from the reader's point of view, is that Pound is nowhere to be seen in the disguised review of H.D.'s lovers.[21] H.D. amended this omission by casting him as Odysseus in *Winter Love*, the "Coda" she added to *Helen in Egypt*. But the Odysseus mentioned in *Helen in Egypt* is only a member of the Greek leadership, who is allied with Achilles, not one of Helen's lovers.

The passionate relation between Helen and Achilles is the center of the story. Their love had its paradoxical origins in the Trojan War, and when Achilles, or his ghost, comes to join Helen on the island of Leuké, they speak of the lives lost at Troy, and he tries to strangle her, evidently because she was the cause of the war in which he lost his life.[22] Nevertheless, she continues to love him, as her other lovers appear to recall the episodes of the war and to predict its aftermath, and she wonders throughout the poem what relation toward them he bears in her mind. One can perceive dimly through this recasting of the myth the outlines of the Dowding–H.D. relation, their concern for the dead pilots, their violent disagreement about clairvoyance, and, above all, H.D.'s continued infatuation with the "Air Marshall."

Helen in Egypt is not an imitation of the *Cantos* but rather a riposte to it, treating the effects of war on an individual spirit in an entirely different poetic style and on a different level of experience. It consists of lyrics written in uniform triplets that disguise the fluent, shifting narrative on which it is based, with a prose gloss for each lyric. Like *Trilogy*, it is divided into a regular number of parts: three large sections with all but one consisting of seven "books," and each containing exactly eight separate lyrics. It consists mainly of Helen's interior monologue and conversations between Helen and her lovers in which Helen gropes toward an understanding of the dichotomies that divide her world. Like *Trilogy*, and in contrast to the *Cantos*, it is written in complete sentences, and most of these are the speeches of identifiable characters.

Nevertheless, the poem is clouded with obscurity as characters, places, times, the living and the dead, dream and reality, and nearly all its determinants are constantly shifting, so that the underlying narrative is overlaid by a kind of free association, as Helen and the others reflect on their relationships with each other.[23] Mortals and gods are merged, and past events change their meaning as they are recollected, so that the violence of the Trojan War is seen as the origin of the love between Helen and Achilles. In H.D.'s later ruminations about the poem, these identifications remained flexible—for example, she thought, in hindsight, that she had "poetically" married her mother, named Helen, to Achilles, the surrogate of Dowding, leaving her poem as their offspring.

The myth of the phantom Helen provided H.D. with a counterpart to the feelings of division she expressed as early as her novel *HERmione*, whose heroine feels that she is neither in the world nor out of it. Hermione's impulse to "clutch toward something that had no name yet" foreshadows Helen's search for a final truth, and her arrival at a kind of maturity is an early version of Helen's insight that contradictions are part of a larger unity. In the *Pisan Cantos*, the imprisoned Pound expressed a similar vague hope for some sort of finality: "out of all this beauty something must come."

Helen in Egypt does not present the ragged irregularity or the awareness of contemporary events seen in the *Cantos*. Nevertheless, there are similarities near the surface arising from the influences of Imagist doctrines on Modern poetry, especially as they affected the long poem, and from their subjects, minds thrown into chaos by the vicissitudes of war. Although many of the lyrics employ narrative, H.D.'s disciplined language and structure are strongly controlled by Imagist principles, and recall the early days of her association with Pound, as she deploys isolated images drawn from memory to suggest Helen's feelings about the past.

Helen's recollection of an encounter with Achilles on a beach is recalled as "we walk, heel and sole / leave our sandal-prints in the sand," a silent anticipation of the scene of combined love and violence that is to follow.

Both poets had some notion of writing an epic suitable for the times, and this meant an abandonment of such conventions as consecutive narrative in favor of a structure based on mental life.[24] Nevertheless, both poems maintained a vital relation with traditional Homeric epic, the *Cantos* with the *Odyssey, Helen in Egypt* with the *Iliad.* Their subjects are roughly similar: the displacements of war drive their protagonists to an agonized quest for their true identities by weighing past experience. They tangle with the irreconcilable contradictions created by war, reaching toward a transcendental resolution that is never found. The *Cantos* briefly names men lost in World War I, and *Helen* has passages of mourning for the dead of the Trojan War. Both poems are thronged with unstable or multiple characters treated as mythic presences rather than individuals.

By putting her poem into a Homeric framework, H.D. achieved a degree of detachment that corresponds to that of the earlier Cantos, although, as we have seen, it is a deceptive detachment. For *Helen,* like H.D.'s fiction and memoirs, is a version of her "legend," the quasi-mythical story that she conceived her life to be. It is clear, from the fact that H.D. called her quasi-autobiographical *Helen* her "cantos," that she read the *Pisan Cantos* and perhaps the *Cantos* in general as something similar—as a record of Pound's mind. But while the mind of the *Helen* poet is enveloped in myth, the poet of the *Cantos* is in touch with a wide spectrum of literature in many languages, with history as well as myth, and, above all, with the contemporary world. It is a difference between depth and breadth: H.D. plunges deep into her feelings to emerge with a complex vision of her rôle as a woman and a legend, while Pound, except for a few remarkable visionary passages in the *Pisan Cantos,* seeks to define himself in terms of the world he surveys.

When it is aligned with H.D.'s poem, the *Pisan Cantos,* like *Helen in Egypt,* can be seen as a personal testament on the part of "ego scriptor" to the spiritual destructiveness of war. But the whole *Cantos*, with its wide-ranging visits to all sorts and conditions of men, has a broad ethical dimension that contrasts with the interior monologue that occupies most of *Helen in Egypt*. Such passages as the attacks on usura, the French soldier's protest against war, and the fragment in Canto 76 about the blinded soldier who came home to feel the ribs of his cow are specific expressions (misguided though some of them may be) of a spirit that vibrates throughout the *Cantos*. That is a spirit of concern for the suffering and misadventures of humans in general, a massive will, spurred by Pound's colossal egotism, to expose and correct the disorders of civilization.

The protagonist of *Helen in Egypt*, on the other hand, pursues truth by trying to unravel the mysteries of her life. She tries to discover her true identity by clarifying her relationships to her various lovers, a task rendered impossible by the fact that these figures tend to blend with each other and to shift their positions in her story. The bloodshed of the Trojan War is no more than an episode of the past with which she struggles; in fact, she suspects that the war was ordained so that she and Achilles could meet as lovers, that the gods have decreed that "Love should be born of War." Toward the end of the poem, she admits that a woman cannot know the emotions that drive men to war, "man's passion and birthright." For Helen, contraries such as Trojan and Greek, Love and Death, and dream and reality are inseparable from each other. After asking numerous unanswerable questions that lead her deeper into the labyrinth of her tangled feelings, she concludes that there is a "simple path," and that "the dart of Love / is the dart of Death . . . there is no before and no after / there is one finite moment."[25]

This cancellation of time and the conflicts it encompasses is completely different from the tumultuous procession of the *Cantos*. For in spite of the complaint that "Time is the evil," the *Cantos* raids the past and present to exploit histories, chronicles, wars, politics, and crowds of actual men and women. The two poets had contrasting notions of a Modern epic: Pound's is inclusive, varied, sweeping over vast extents of time and space; H.D.'s is focused, psychological, probing for ultimate truth in the depths of a single consciousness. But the contrast is not complete. There is an important parallel as Pound, in the *Pisan Cantos,* turns briefly to Helen's method of introspection in an effort to decipher the truth of his existence. And, as we have seen, both epics look toward a final deliverance that is never attained.

There is another struggle toward some sort of resolution as H.D. turns to her relation with Pound in the "Coda" she added to *Helen in Egypt,* but that also ends in an unsatisfactory and self-contradictory ambiguity. If the reason for this spiritual failure in the *Helen* poems is the baffling complexity of the heroine's feelings, there may be a different reason, a structural one, for the obvious incompleteness of the *Cantos.* In 1958 Pound, writing from Brunnenburg, sent Pearson an important comment about the *Cantos.* "Cantos won't be finished," he wrote, "until my demise, shd / always reserve possibility of death bed swan."[26] Apparently, Pound had given up hope of completing his sprawling poem and did not even desire it, because it would forestall a significant death bed effort. He seemed to be anticipating a move that would intertwine the end of his life and the end of the *Cantos* with each other, in order to give the poem the status of an intellectual autobiography and make some final statement that would bring it to a significant conclusion.

Helen in Egypt, though completed in 1955, was not published until 1961. H.D. had written to Pound about it, but he admitted that he had not answered immediately. In a note hastily added to the margin of a letter dated 1958, some months after his return to Italy, Pound said that he was behind in answering his mail and added: "never got round to word re / yr / poEM [*sic*] etc."[27] He later asked her to send a copy, and H.D. sent one in November 1959, urging him not to hurry to read it or to write to her about it. And he does not seem to have expressed his opinion of *Helen* until after H.D.'s death.

11

Last Years

Theirs was, in fact, a friendship that, despite silences
and differences, never died.
                    Raffaelle Baccolini, "Pound's Tribute to H.D."

H.D.'s ambivalent attitude toward the *Cantos* and its poet continued after she had completed *Helen in Egypt*. In a remarkable
double-edged passage in the unpublished "Compassionate Friendship," dated 24 February 1955, she says that she went to find a copy
of the *Cantos* and read Canto 21. She admits she was not atten-
tive enough but says, nevertheless: "There is beauty in every paragraph or stanza or page, somewhere, a dynamic, indissoluble
beauty. The world and time are blasted, dynamited, shattered."
While she envies Pearson's students, who have the chance to
study this text, she is, as always, doubtful about her own relation
to Pound: "But long ago, I stepped out of the track of this particular whirlwind, this psychic landslide." Nevertheless, she has "always credited Ezra with my own first awakening." There follows
a brief recollection of the British Museum tearoom scene, where
Pound shaped her poems into the "then unfamiliar free-verse."
And she adds: "He did not like my later work—and told me so."[1]

In a later entry, she says she reread Canto 20, which she had
known earlier from *Tre Cantos,* Mary de Rachewiltz's Italian
translation, and occasionally compared it with the English text.

These Cantos and the pictures of Pound accompanying them in the book were a constant presence, for "I carried this tiny book in my hand-bag." She said that this made her feel that she was back at the tearoom with Pound. However, her resistance asserted it-self again: "I took the big volume of the Cantos upstairs again to my attic. I felt it would devitalize me, un-gravitate me somehow." Nevertheless, she says she will continue to carry "Mary's little book" until she is "reconciled to the bulkier volume." Apparently, H.D. kept two reminders of Pound with her, for her handbag also contained one of the "Yogi books" he had given her many years before. However, it seems as if she needed the intervention of Mary's translation to shield her from Pound's symbolic presence, for, as she wrote later, "Ezra's theories had distressed me. I could not follow them, & I am always unhappy at the thought of his tragedy."[2]

Pound was released from St. Elizabeths and H.D. completed *Helen in Egypt* in the same year—1958. They continued to correspond after Pound went to live with his daughter and her family in their castle in the Italian Alps; H.D. continued to live in Dr. Brunner's clinic, except for the period in 1958 when she was recovering from her fall in the Hirslanden clinic in Zürich. Now that he was comparatively close to Küsnacht, Pound thought of visiting her, but she was not encouraging about this plan, or future plans like it.

In the following three years, the restless Pound did considerable traveling. He went back to Rapallo for a time, moved about Italy, and visited an old friend in Rome. H.D. interrupted her seclusion in Switzerland to travel to New York in the summer of 1960 to receive an award from the American Academy of Arts and Letters. These were productive years for her, as well as years of recognition. During this time, she wrote the group of poetic sequences ultimately published as *Hermetic Definition*, as well as the sequence, *Sagesse*, and *Winter Love*, the addition to *Helen in Egypt* initially called "Coda" that is addressed to Pound.

As the two poets entered their seventies, ailing and disabled in different ways, their relations entered a new phase. H.D. now asked for Pound's opinion of her current work, and he in turn showed interest in it and asked to see it. She wrote to him in January 1959 to say that she had written "a sort of tribute on E.P." consisting of fifty-seven typed pages, the project called, at Pearson's suggestion, *End to Torment*. It was written, she said, for Pearson, to whom it was dedicated, and not intended for publication. Fearing that Pound would not understand it, she nevertheless offered to send him a carbon copy and said that he could make pencil comments on facing pages — a dangerous invitation.[3] Pound replied: "Yes, glad to satisfy curiosity as to how the hell you cd / have covered 51 [*sic*] pages (typescript, I hope) with my glories. Of course rectification of error has its uses."[4]

A copy of H.D.'s manuscript — or part of it — was sent to Mary de Rachewiltz in 1959, but Pound did not read it until November, when he turned a new page in their relationship by sending H.D. rather inconsistent but surprisingly favorable comments. He said he had torn up a letter protesting about "something toward the end," possibly an objection to Pearson's account of the Pounds' departure for Italy in 1958, which H.D. quoted to close her book. But he quickly added, "there is a great deal of beauty (pages 1-55)."

However, he also turned to "rectification of error," expressing some skepticism and disagreement. He felt that H.D. had not realized the full truth of Rattray's report about the food he supplied his followers — he suspected Rattray of having put a stop to it. He unkindly questioned the accuracy of her memories, though he did say that he saw nothing seriously wrong up to page 66. Then, he said, "you risk unjustness."[5] This may well be the section about Martinelli; Pound threatened to correct it with "facts," and wrote some notes that H.D. said she would forward to Pearson. It is surprising that he had nothing to say about H.D.'s sometimes lyrical and often ambivalent accounts of her relationship with him, although he may have reserved comments of this kind for the conversation he hoped to have with her on his projected visit to Küsnacht that never took place. H.D. said changes were possible, but also told Pearson that the book could not be revised. There were several suggestions, in the letters exchanged in 1959 and 1960, that the two poets, no longer far apart geographically, might see each other again. At a time when Aldington was planning to come to Küsnacht for a medical checkup, Pound expressed a desire to come to see him. But the reunion of the three Imagists never took place, for Aldington came, but Pound did not. Bryher was firmly opposed to any reunion with Pound, and said she would leave if he came.

In his letter, which devoted much space to Martinelli's problems, Pound turned aside for a moment to say that he was deeply depressed. He made an admission to his old friend that he would probably not have made to anyone else: "I am no longer pleased with my past life, and the moments of extreme blindness and insensitivity have been PHEnomenal."[6] However, this remorse does not seem to relate to his long-standing political and economic views, but rather to his treatment of the people around him.

The comment in a letter written about a week later, "Torment title excellent, but optimistic," suggests that Pound was still depressed, but H.D.'s manuscript seems to have put him into a nostalgic mood. The letter recalls some scenes of their happy youth together: "the 2000 memories. creek bank straripido, i.e., Hokusai-wave over reach, breaking, you playing the fool on the edge, Willow-Grove scenic railway, ten years of beauty . . . and the Gods can envy."[7]

Pound continued the literary exchange by sending H.D. a copy of his new Cantos, *Thrones de las Cantares,* which H.D. listed among her books received in 1959. In a letter written in the spring of 1959, Pound grumbled, "I dont know much of what has gone on in your head for the past 40 years."[8] But he was now ready to continue exchanging information about ongoing work. He wrote enigmatically from Rapallo in June 1959: "You once said: Serenitas Dieudonne [*sic*] Imagist, Imagiste or whatever dinner," adding, "I have just made a draft line for a canto from it."[9] H.D. replied that she did not know what she could have said that would be a suitable line for the *Cantos.* Pound was referring to an event that had occurred forty-five years earlier, the Vorticist dinner in 1914 at the Dieudonné restaurant to which Amy Lowell had been invited shortly after her arrival in England. H.D. had used the Latin word to praise Aldington's translation of Sappho's "Atthis." The event is encapsulated in Canto 113 of the "Drafts and Fragments":

> H.D. once said "serenitas"
>> (Atthis, etc.)
>   at Dieudonné's
>>> in pre-history.[10]

There is no emotional depth here, but Pound's feeling, late into old age, is suggested in another fragment, "Notes for 111":

> The eyes holding trouble—
>> no light
>>> ex profundis—
> naught from feigning.
> Soul melts into air,
>>> anima into aura,
>>>> Serenitas.[11]

The eyes recall those seen in Pound's tent in Canto 81, and H.D.'s word, recollected years afterward, is joined with them to convey the feeling that the soul is entering some region of transcendental truth. Pound may have had little to say directly about his feeling for H.D. in these latter years, but the imagery of these lines eloquently testifies that his memories of her—the "2000 memories"—brought him peace after the contentious years of their separation.

Continuing the renewed dialogue, H.D. said in a letter of 15 October 1959, that she had written "a sort of '*Coda*' to her "long, long *Helen* sequence" and felt that she should send it to Pound for his reaction to what she called her "*altmodisch*" manner, an acknowledgment that her style now differed sharply from that of the *Cantos*. She invited him to "slash it to pieces & return." as a "*divertissement.*"[12] Her invitation is a reversion to the scene in the tearoom in 1912, when, as H.D. described it in *End to Torment*, Pound "slashed with a pencil" at her first poems before sending them to *Poetry* for publication. After many years, she apparently still valued the surgical critical discrimination that Pound had employed to shape the first Imagist poems and submitted herself to his guidance again—or pretended to do so in order to please him.

Pound replied that revising *Winter Love* would not be a *"divertissement,"* for he now had difficulty reading, but he did read it twice, and approved of it. He wrote: "At any rate there is your imprint," then said, flatteringly, that he had struggled for an hour to add "a line that will not be an assumption," and asked if she really did want her poem "slashed." Instead of the violent criticism she had feared, he acknowledged that "I think it is written better than you have done." He did, however, suggest a small revision, which H.D. passed on to Pearson.[13] A new harmony descended on their literary relations as H.D. said that she was happy that he had "accepted the *Winter Love*" and that Pearson, too, would be pleased.

Pearson was pleased, of course, and also recognized its structural resemblance to the latest part of Pound's epic. "I keep calling things your Cantos. This Winter Love section is really like the Pisan section, calling up what goes before—as in a moment of stasis which is climactic. I liked *Helen* before; I like it twice as much with the *bon chance* of Winter Love."[14]

Winter Love, H.D. replied, "explained so much to me & was (& is) a comfort ." She had described it as "the first (conscious) poem I ever wrote E[zra] P[ound], Odysseus here."[15] Her poetic sequence is, in fact, nothing less than a review of her relationship with Pound, encoded as a version of Helen's story, and a passionate expression of her tormented feelings about him. It briefly recapitulates the sequence of Helen's lovers in *Helen in Egypt,* this time including Odysseus, a figure based on Pound, as the dominant lover.

The drafts in the Beinecke Library tell us something about H.D.'s method and the development of the poem. The first draft is written in pencil in a small blue notebook, with a label reading "Espérance, Virgo (cancelled), Winter Love, H.D." The first leaf identifies this as the first rough copy and is dated, like the published version, 3 January to 5 April 1959. It corresponds in general to the final printed text, although there were to be two more manuscript copies and some revisions. Some of these may have been made at the suggestion of Pearson, who read these drafts. Her assurance that she would achieve satisfactory results in a first draft that required little change contrasts with H.D.'s youthful practice of writing automatically and rejecting all but a few lines.

In this notebook, the early sections, consisting of the speeches of Helen, are written in prose form, and the divisions into lines of verse are indicated by vertical slashes, which seem to be darker, as if written later. The choruses addressed to Helen, however, are written as verse, with some cancellations and changes, and Helen's speeches continue as verse until a later return to the slashed prose mode. The prose form suggests that H.D. was composing Helen's recollections with great spontaneity, and waited until later to mark the rhythms and pauses that she already had in mind. Later in April, she wrote a more legible copy in ink in a similar notebook, adding six lines to the end of section 17, and then made a typed copy. Two revisions were made in this final copy. The last lines of Antistrophe 18, which originally read "the Paradise / the Ring / Pass-Not," were changed to read "reality of the white sand, / the meadow . . . / *Parthenos*." The new lines apparently recall the scenes of Helen's violent encounter with Achilles in *Helen in Egypt* and her loving one with Odysseus. H.D. had originally planned to use an epigraph from Nikos Kazantzakis that would have identified the poem with her conception of her own life: "and dull life burst with stars / and turned to fabled myth." These lines were canceled in the typed manuscript.

Winter Love consists mainly of lyrics spoken by Helen in a voice that is unquestionably that of H.D. She begins by saying that for ten years—presumably the period of the Trojan War—she did not think of Odysseus and did not know of the women he encountered in his wanderings. In the third section, Helen declares, "Now there is winter-love," in a scene that recalls the secluded snowbound shepherd's den subtly sketched as the scene of her colloquy with Theseus in *Helen in Egypt*. Episodes of Pound's life are suggested as she says, "you married your Princess"—Dorothy—and "you left Ithaca for another *Helen*"—Olga. H.D.'s passionate recollections of her youthful love scenes with Pound emerge as Helen recalls that she was with Odysseus "in Calypso's cave," where the "first kiss" left "unsatisfied desire," and she then asks, "how could I love again, ever?" When Helen, expecting to meet Odysseus, is told that he left on a ship, it seems clear that H.D. is again recalling Pound's 1908 departure for Europe, which she had described in *End to Torment* as an enduring wound.

A sequence of choruses then exchanges views about Helen's fate, leading to the advice that she must ignore death and enjoy the blessing that her misfortunes will be enshrined in myth.

The themes of the shepherd's hut and the departure by ship are brought together in a series of lyrics in which Helen imagines that she might be sharing the cold den with Odysseus as a "reality" opposed to the dream of her other lovers. She was willing to share "the moment of fulfillment" with Odysseus, but was called back and then learned that he had left. Thinking of this, she cries out: "Comfort me, then, Odysseus, King of Men." Nevertheless, she expects to find her own comfort in the cold and darkness through memory, for "love built on dreams / of the forgotten first unsatisfied embrace, / is satisfied," a spiritual recovery based on memories of the youthful Pound in H.D.'s far past.[16]

A chorus advises Helen to let her three lovers, Odysseus, Paris, and Achilles, go their ways, and to turn to her myth—"it was from Song, you took the seed." Within that framework, she possesses all three men and their respective attributes and can find happiness. But an antistrophe counters this, and defines her as "bereft," lost, and guilty—a barefoot, widowed figure wandering a seacoast. Helen then recalls a time when Odysseus saved her from the sterile luxury of Menelaus's palace, with the repeated line: "There was a Helen before there was a war." Lyric 24 opens a new theme: that of the child that Helen bore, or thought she bore, on Leuké, the island where she encountered Achilles. Her feelings toward the child and Achilles are desperately divided, for love has plunged her into an unbearable dilemma.

Winter Love is H.D.'s final effort, after her novels and early poems, to formulate her feelings about Pound. Appropriately, the poet finds that her own medium of encoded Greek myth, now refined and perfected, is the best way of expressing these complicated emotions. The actual events of H.D.'s emotional life are only thinly veiled by the mythic materials, but the mythic setting gives the poet a number of advantages. It links the personal events to which H.D. covertly refers to the great, echoing arena of the Trojan War, so that they acquire the consequential status of the "legend" she took her life to be. They provide her with figures and images—some borrowed from the myth, some improvised—that she fashions into effective poetic resources. And perhaps most important, the supernatural atmosphere, inhabited by gods, and alive with memories and imagined events, enables her to convey the illogical and tormenting contradictions from which she suffered after a life of many conflicting emotional demands.

While she was writing it, H.D. described *Winter Love* as a "*great comfort,*" but after more than a year had passed, she was less satisfied with it. She wrote to Pearson: "The whole atmosphere of the *Coda* (the provisional title) somehow contradicts the real psychic or spiritual achievement of the *Helen in Egypt.*"[17] While it is hard to know what H.D. meant by this, it is possible that she felt that the passionate tone of her sequel was not sufficiently distanced from what she had once called her "real self." The longer poem, as I have said, projects an air of detachment, as H.D. frames her story as a legend. In it, Helen finds satisfaction in thinking of herself as the material of myth and in reaching the "psychic" insight that the contradictions she faces cannot be resolved. But *Winter Love* is, in great part, a love poem that ends in a prayer for deliverance from the cruelty of love. These seem to be direct transcriptions from H.D.'s feelings about Pound, and they do not lead to the pacifying insight seen at the end of *Helen in Egypt.*

There are two direct links to Pound in *Winter Love* that bypass his disguise as Odysseus, and they are, in turn, linked to each other. When H.D. writes of "Helen's breasts . . . and the wine-cup that they wrought,"[18] she is picking up a legend mentioned in the *Pisan Cantos.* Pound first referred to the legend in 1917 in a dialogue called "Aux Étuves de Wiesbaden," where one of the speakers, when asked whether he would prefer to be without an ideal, tells of a cup of "white gold" cast from one of Helen's breasts and says that it led him to feel dissatisfied with "human imperfection."

This symbol of perfection turns up in Pound's thoughts in the DTC, Canto 79, where it follows an oath taken in the name of the two breasts of Tellus, the earth goddess, which leads to:

> as from the breasts of Helen, a cup of white gold
> 2 cups for three altars . . .[19]

These lines are followed by a repetition of the goddess's name, so that the cup is associated with the theme of fertility, which the *Cantos* often takes as the object of worship. The cup is mentioned again in Canto 106:

> How to govern from the time of Kuan Chung
> but the cup of white gold at Patera
> Helen's breasts gave that.[20]

Through this link with the Chinese emperor who emphasized agriculture, the cup is again seen as a source of fertility. H.D., however, characteristically associates it with the love theme that dominates her poem, as she thinks of the famous cup after a chorus reminds her of the time when Odysseus kissed her breast.

That love scene leads to a second and more far-reaching connection with Pound, for the child, *Espérance*, was conceived at that time. The child figure of *Winter Love* is a final expression of a preoccupation that had been in H.D.'s mind nearly all her life.[21] It takes us back to 1919, to the scene, recorded in *End to Torment*, where H.D. reported that on the day before Perdita was born, Pound appeared at the nursing home at a time of "grave crisis in my life" to declare: "my only real criticism is that this is not my child." Recalling the incident nearly forty years later, she said that Pound had displayed no "tenderness," only "passion and regret."

Pound's "only real criticism" about the child is enigmatic enough. He and H.D. were married to other people at that time, and had had other sexual partners, and he had shown no interest in a sexual relation with her since their Pennsylvania days, seven years earlier. He may have meant that the literary and romantic partnership of those times should have continued, and should have produced some such result as the child. This flicker of possessiveness was to be more than reciprocated in future years.

There is reason to believe that Pound's protest corresponded with H.D.'s own wish, for, as we have seen, her writing and behavior strongly suggest that she was obsessed throughout her life by a similar desire, and used the figure of a "child" as a private symbol of her attachment to Pound. The hypothetical child continued to live in her imagination as the symbol of a union she found both irresistible and impossible. It is striking that her real child, Perdita, seemed to have no relevance to this image.[22]

Pound had not told H.D. about the birth of Mary Rudge, his daughter by Olga Rudge, in July 1925, although she was fully informed about his life with Olga. H.D. was highly indignant at having been kept ignorant of the child's existence until learning about her from a conversation with someone during her trip to America in 1937–38. She also managed to pick up rumors about Mary's birth and the family who cared for her, but Pound discounted these and denied that he had wanted a boy. He blustered, "WOT wd / I have done with a male offspring / It wd / have indubitably been philistine of worst type or gone to the bowwows."[23] However, Omar Pound had been born in 1926, and H.D. reported, in a letter hypothetically dated 1929, that she had seen him.

In the spring of 1938, H.D. suggested that a balance equivalent to about eighteen pounds that she had in an Italian bank be transferred to Rudge through Pound. In the three-way correspondence among H.D., Pound, and the Banca Nazionale del Lavoro, Pound questioned Olga's need for the money, and H.D. justified the grant by declaring, in a significant outburst, that "O. is as it were ME." Following her tendency to identify with Pound's lovers, she felt that Olga Rudge was her surrogate as Pound's sexual and artistic partner. She followed this up by identifying herself with their child: "and twice-doubly, mathematically so is (more so) the Marienkind." By this logic, Olga is also her surrogate as the mother of the child. It was in this letter reproaching Pound for never telling her about the birth of the child that she repeated Pound's words, claiming that she was "'Ezra's oldest femaile [*sic*] relative' your phrase with a change of gender one day back in 1919."[24]

When Pound sent photos of Mary, H.D. offered to become her legal guardian in case of need, and to set up a bank account for her. This echo of the fantasy that she might bear a child fathered by Pound, implanted in H.D.'s mind by his reproach at the time her own daughter was born, is a significant expression of her lasting emotional attachment to Pound himself.[25] A dream recorded by the Freud-trained H.D. in the Hirslanden journal on 11 February 1957, may be connected with this theme. It begins abruptly with "An enchanting child," and after some typically confused dream imagery, continues: "I find an enchanting child, my child, who is both my lover-husband's child and my lover-father's child, and we have *Oedipus,* or one of the fabulous exciting *Borgia* incest stories or plays." The child here seems to be the fruit of her union with the composite male figure of her unconscious desires.

End to Torment continues the theme. In her entry of 16 March 1958, H.D. recalls a moment when she was in the Zürich train station with Heydt to begin her trip to America in 1956. She caught sight of a little boy with "short red-gold curls" who deeply impressed her. An entry made about a month later identifies the boy with "the 'fiery moment' incarnate." Pound, we recall, had red hair, and "fiery moment," as we have seen, is the term H.D. frequently used in referring to her youthful affair with him. About three weeks after her initial entry, she mysteriously notes that while she was discussing Rattray's article about Pound with some friends the child image came to mind—"the Child was with us," she wrote. Her preoccupation continues in the entry of 10 May, as she links the image of the child with the scene from the nursing home, declares that it "manifested" in the station, and adds that perhaps Pound's visit also "manifested," that it may have been a psychic phenomenon.

Two days later, her writing wanders from a defense of Pound's practice of borrowing from other sources to a series of associations connected with the child figure including Venice churches; the child at the station, now identified with *Séraphita,* the mystical Balzac novel Pound had shared with her; Pound's daughter; his granddaughter; and her own daughter and grandchildren. She asks, "What am I hiding?" Several days later, after exploring her thoughts, she gives the answer she has found. It is: "The Idol that should have been . . . the *Wunderkind*." Included in this composite of her imagination is the child from the station; the pianist Van Cliburn, of whom she had recently read; and "Ezra at one time." The child image, therefore, was not identified solely with Pound, but was a kind of framework housing H.D.'s idealism where Pound had a place.[26]

Winter Love, written in the following year, 1959, powerfully revives the child image. The child's name, *Espérance* (which, of course, means "hope" in French), appears as the poem's subtitle, and so positions the theme as a central one. When the child image appears in section 24, there are different stories about the identity of the father. In her journal, H.D. said that her poem ended with the reconciliation of the four "kings" of the Helen legend: Odysseus, Achilles, Paris and Menelaus, her lovers, who underwent "reconciliation" in accordance with her tendency to blend the figures in her imagination, as joint fathers of the child. "The imaginary or actual child or children," she wrote, "is here symbolized by Euphorion or *Espérance*, the child of the essence of Helen's love-life & of the four 'kings' equally."[27] According to her journal, therefore, the child figure, embodies Helen's (and H.D.'s) capacity for love and hope, a power of imagination that enfolds the four lovers within it.

In H.D.'s poem, however, the child has a single father: the Pound figure, Odysseus. In a scene that recalls the one in *HERmione* where the Pound figure paws at the girl "like a great tawny beast," Helen reports that there was "a wild moment that begot a Child, / when long ago, the *Virgo* breasts swelled / under the savage kiss of ravening Odysseus." This child figure has its roots both in reality and in H.D.'s desire, for on the one hand, his "cap-crown of bright hair" suggests his relationship with Pound, and on the other, he is associated with the fulfillment of an ideal, for "Euphorion, *Espérance* the infinite bliss / lives in the hope of something that will be / the past made perfect."[28] In the final section, the poet, knowing that the hope the child represents, like that implied by Odysseus's love, is futile, calls on the midwife to take it away because she wants to rest and is unwilling to be brought back to life. The "cruel, cruel midwife" is reproached for undressing her so that Odysseus can caress her and for putting the child in her arms. She complains that all that has been sweet is now painful, "cruel, cruel the thought of Love," and looks forward to a paradoxical death. Yet she cannot finally bring herself to part with the child and cries out: "I die in agony whether I give or do not give." The sequence closes as she calls on the child to live again, and "so slay me."[29]

Winter Love is surely H.D.'s most unrestrained expression of the intolerable conflict between love and fear that Pound aroused in her. If the figure of the child embodies these feelings, it is a vital metaphoric expression of her insight that she is passionately drawn to him still, but realizes, as she has throughout her life, that surrendering to him or joining him would be fatal to her independence as a woman and as a poet.

Winter Love represents a mini-genre that guided H.D. in the poetry she was to write in the last two years of her life: lyric sequences with strong personal references and shifting settings and levels of reality. *Sagesse,* written about two years earlier, moves through conversations at a zoo, scenes in a plebeian household, conversations with Heydt, and prayers to angels. However, its point of departure is the picture of a caged owl seen in a magazine, and H.D.'s lines about its caged grandeur are suggestive of her feeling about Pound, who was still in St. Elizabeths when the poem was written. The three sequences of *Hermetic Definition* are, like *Winter Love,* open and rather passionate acknowledgments of H.D.'s infatuation with two men who had impressed her deeply during her 1960 visit to New York: the *Newsweek* reporter Lionel Durand and the French poet St.-John Perse. The difference is that this sequence ends on a positive note, as the poet paradoxically finds a release and a recovery of her identity in the death of Durand, so that even in mourning, "Night becomes Day."

Pound had expressed scorn for H.D.'s novels in earlier years, but responded with enthusiasm when he was sent *Bid Me to Live: A Madrigal,* her autobiographical novel set in the World War I period, which was published in March 1960. The title is taken from the first line of Robert Herrick's "To Anthea, who may command him anything." H.D. says, in another novel, "The Sword Went Out to Sea," that a musical setting of Herrick's poem was sung by a character based on Aldington, no doubt an incident from real life. An undated sheet that, unlike Pound's typed letters, is written in his large, looping script, seems to be a spontaneous burst of praise for *Bid Me to Live*. It reads: "Marvelous, marvelous evocation—that you shd have remembered them in such detail—the beauty of yr mind thru it all, permeating—the marvelous retention of visual detail—& abundance & innocence, blessed innocence—detail of later life, stuffed with memories of the then."[30]

As if to reciprocate, H.D. responded with praise when Pound sent her a copy of his translations of the collection of poems called the *Chinese Classic Anthology* (*Shih-Ching*), which he had written in 1949 while he was in St. Elizabeths. She said she was "enchanted" with the book, and quoted back to Pound two lines from the section called "The Adorned but Immature Gallant" that, she said, reflected Heydt's impression of Sheri Martinelli. Another opportunity for revisiting the past came to her when she read Charles Norman's biography of Pound, and said that the book gave her "the sense of *continuity and finality*."[31]

In a last effort to enlist H.D. in one of his projects, Pound asked her, early in January 1961, to edit "some 40 pages" by Nagao Ariga, the scholar who had assisted Fenollosa in his Chinese translations, a project Pound had postponed since 1916. He accompanied the request with grudging flattery: "You have had sense to be comprehensible even at danger of going flat, whereas I have sunk into crypto,"[32] a comment strongly suggesting that Pound was beginning to recognize the difficulties of his recent *Cantos*.

The long friendship ended when H.D. died in the Hirslanden clinic in September 1961. *Helen in Egypt* had just been published, and she was given a copy, but probably was not aware of it. Pound learned of her death in a joint letter from Perdita, her husband, John Schaffner, Bryher, and Pearson, which reached him at Brunnenburg. The letter quoted some exquisite lines from H.D.'s

Sagesse, beginning "arise, arise, re-animate / O Spirit this small ark, this little body."[33]

When he saw this letter, Pound rushed to his room, lay down on his bed, and began to translate H.D.'s lines into Italian, but soon interrupted himself. He wrote the following:

> Surge surgete, reanimate
> O Spirito, quest arca picciolina
> > > questo corpo cosi <u>non</u> grande
> quest identita separata;
> > > dei mortal' mondani,
> > ~~fate un uno imortal~~
> > > ~~vi~~
> fanno qu'un immortal, ma sveglia un solo,
> per
> > > Translate this for Vanni
> > > or some current
> > > obit of H.D.
> or I will if my signature is
> of <u>use</u>,
> > > set dead pyre flaming
> la pyra morta
> > > in fiammegia
> > > folgorante
> que, ~~Phoe~~ Fenice, Venere, Venere
> > > > Mercurio
> ~~in fiammare~~
> > > ~~in cen~~ in fiamma il
> > > > mondo d'estasi
> con l Amore que dimentica
> > I nostri
> > > mancanze
> con l Amore, que   I perduti
> amore Amore-Amore unico[34]

This document curiously resembles a passage from the *Cantos,* as it juxtaposes apparently unrelated and incongruous materials joined by an underlying theme—the purpose of commemorating H.D.'s death. After translating a few lines, Pound turns to English to ask Mary to find a place for these lines in an Italian obituary with the publisher Vanni Scheiwiller or elsewhere. This is followed by an English phrase quoted from H.D.'s lines, and Pound then returns to the Italian translation, correcting as he goes. The confusion of spontaneous composition reflects his passionate eagerness to see that H.D. was not forgotten.

In a letter to Pearson written on 28 September 1961, about a month after H.D.'s death, Pound expressed admiration but, notably, no affection. He tells Pearson that he was unable to write about her death, and then adds, "besides she isn't @ all," which seems to mean that he regards her as still alive, in some sense. He says he couldn't cover the sixty years of their friendship in cold "condolences," as if Pearson, but not he himself, were a bereaved survivor. Not quite coherently, he says he meant to write to her about her work, but was not sure he sent it. Of *Tribute to Freud*, he says, "very well written = steady = integrity from 'pools of fir' to splendid Helen in Egypt," bracketing H.D.'s life work between her early poem, "Oread," and her late epic. He has some "matter for crit" about *Helen in Egypt*, but needs to have a typewriter brought to him in the hospital. (He was in the Martinsbrunner clinic in Merano at the time.) This "matter" is not extant but must have been at least partly favorable, for at the top of the letter, he wrote: "Helen in Egypt a marvel." In the publicity he had written for *Helen in Egypt*, Pearson had said that it was "epic in stature," and Pound may have recalled this when he wrote, at the end of the letter, "H in Egt *the* real epic," seeming to concede its superiority to his own *Cantos*. But an added note raises doubt about whether he had read the whole poem, for he adds that the prose glosses were not with "the fragment I had seen."[35] Pearson replied that he was "deeply moved" by Pound's letter, and kindly added: "she kept always your cantos and your poems in her room wherever she was. She would say to me, picking the books up, how they sang as true poetry."[36]

Pound lived on, in ill health, often bedridden and in hospitals, but surprisingly active. He was in the care of Olga Rudge, who gave up her work as an administrator at the Accademia Musicale in Siena to devote herself to him. She lived with him in Sant'Ambrogio and Venice, and frequently took him traveling. He sometimes fell into spells of deep depression, maintaining an unnerving silence. Nevertheless, he gave a number of interviews to journalists and critics, including a famous one with Allen Ginsberg. When T. S. Eliot died in 1965, Rudge took him to the memorial service in Westminster Abbey, and suggested a side trip to Dublin. They went to the annual Festivals of the Two Worlds in Spoleto, where Pound read before the audience. In 1969 they came to New York to attend the exhibit of *The Waste Land* manuscript at the New York Public Library, and joined Pound's publisher, James Laughlin, who took him to his old college, Hamilton. He also continued to write Cantos, and produced the final group known as "Drafts and Fragments." There is no evidence that he gave any thought to H.D. during these years. Rudge was holding his hand when he died in his sleep in the Venetian hospital of Santi Giovanni e Paolo on 1 November 1972.

Pearson had been present at H.D.'s funeral in her hometown of Bethlehem, Pennsylvania. While helping to bury her ashes, he read from her poems during the Moravian service. He put a yellow rose into the grave, a duplicate of the one H.D. had sent the Pounds when they left for Italy in 1958, as if he meant to seal the bond between the two poets in the earth.

Notes
References
Index

Notes

Preface

1. Michael King, foreword to *End to Torment: A Memoir of Ezra Pound by H.D.*, ed. Norman Holmes Pearson and Michael King (New York: New Directions, 1979), x.

2. For discussions of Pound's and H.D.'s publishing histories, see Lawrence Rainey, *Institutions of Modernism: Literary Elites in Public Culture* (New Haven: Yale University Press, 1998). Rainey shows how both poets isolated themselves by adopting strategies intended to protect the Modernist project from a popular culture contaminated by market values. In this respect, he says, "They are exemplary fables of modernism's fate" (170).

3. Claire Buck, *H.D. and Freud: Bisexuality and a Feminist Discourse* (New York: Harvester, Wheatsheaf, 1991), 6.

1. Two Poets

1. William Carlos Williams, *Autobiography* (New York: Random House, 1951), 58.

2. Ibid., 68–70. Writing to Dorothy Pound in her old age, H.D. vigorously protested Williams's portrait of her and her family in this book. He reported that she stained herself with ink before writing, but H.D. declared that she always wrote in pencil. However, she does not deny that the seaside episode occurred. Undated letter [October 1951], Lilly Library, Indiana University.

3. Quoted from a letter by H.D. to Norman Holmes Pearson, 12 March [1950], in Donna Krolik Hollenberg, ed., *Between History and Poetry: The Letters of H.D. and Norman Holmes Pearson* (Iowa City: University of Iowa Press, 1997), 94.

4. H.D., *End to Torment: A Memoir of Ezra Pound by H.D.*, ed. Norman Holmes Pearson and Michael King (New York: New Directions, 1979), 4.

5. *End to Torment*, 18–19, 26, 12.

6. Susan Stanford Friedman, *Penelope's Web: Gender, Modernity, H.D.'s Fiction* (Cambridge: Cambridge University Press, 1990), 105.

7. For H.D. and Swinburne and the Pre-Raphaelites, see Cassandra Laity, *H.D. and the Victorian Fin de Siècle: Gender, Modernism, Decadence* (Cambridge: Cambridge University Press, 1996).

8. Undated letter, H.D. to Pound [1950?], Lilly Library, Indiana University.

9. Letter dated 11 April 1958, in Hollenberg, *Between History and Poetry*, 220.

10. These poems have been published as an addition to *End to Torment*, 67–84. The original notebook is in the Harvard University Library. It came into the possession of Frances Gregg, who gave it its title.

11. *End to Torment*, 38.

12. Letters of February (undated) and 7 March 1908 from H.D. to Williams (Poetry/Rare Book Collection, State University of New York at Buffalo). The misspelling may have been habitual with H.D. It occurs again in a letter written many years later.

13. *End to Torment*, 54.

14. Letter dated June 3 [1958], H.D. to Pearson, in Hollenberg, *Between History and Poetry*, 227. And she also thought his abandonment of Martinelli at this time as a "super-imposition" on the event of 1908. In an earlier letter discussing her emotional difficulties, she refers to the pain caused by the same event: "I went on after E (1908) went to Venice." Letter dated April 11 [1958], ibid., 220.

15. Frances Gregg Wilkinson, *The Mystic Leeway* (Ottawa: Carleton University Press, 1995), 84, 91. Gregg also says that Pound led her to read Freud, a figure he opposed in later years.

16. "Redondillas," *Collected Early Poems of Ezra Pound*, ed. Michael John King (New York: New Directions, 1976), 218.

17. Ezra Pound, "Portrait d'Une Femme," *Personae: The Shorter Poems of Ezra Pound* (New York: New Directions, 1990), 57.

18. I will be using "Modern" and related words as a term to refer to avant-garde works of the early twentieth century, corresponding to such period terms as Augustan, Romantic, etc. For the problems related to this word, see Robert Bechtold Heilman, *The Professor and the Profession* (Columbia: University of Missouri Press, 1999), 281–86.

19. H.D., *Asphodel,* edited with Introduction and Biographical Notes by Robert Spoo (Durham: Duke University Press, 1992), 70.

20. Caroline Zilboorg, "H.D.'s Influence on Richard Aldington," in *Richard Aldington: Reappraisals,* ed. Charles Doyle (Victoria: University of Victoria, 1990), 28.

21. *End to Torment,* 15.

22. *End to Torment,* 17. Barbara Guest, in *Herself Defined* (Garden City, N.J.: Doubleday, 1984), says that Walter Rummel told H.D. that Pound was engaged to Dorothy (49), and implies that this news led to Margaret Cravens's suicide. However, in H.D.'s *Asphodel,* it is the character based on Cravens who tells her about it (93).

23. H.D., Manuscript Diary, Paris, 1912, Beinecke Library, Yale University. On the cover page is written "Hilda Doolittle, Dec. 23, 1911," and in large, angry letters, "Destroy H." cancelled with two light lines and below, "Paris, 1912." Many of the individual words in this diary are illegible.

24. Letter dated 12 December [1937], H.D. to Pearson, in Hollenberg, *Between History and Poetry,* 10.

25. Richard Aldington, *Life for Life's Sake* (New York: Viking Press), 111.

26. Letter dated 16 March [1938], H.D. to Pound, Beinecke Library, Yale University.

27. For information about Powys and Gregg, see Oliver Marlow Wilkinson, "Frances Gregg: First Hand," in *The Mystic Leeway,* 17–43.

28. H.D., *Paint It Today,* ed. Cassandra Laity (New York: New York University Press, 1992), 33–38.

29. See *Ezra Pound and Margaret Cravens: A Tragic Friendship 1910–1912,* ed. Omar Pound and Robert Spoo (Durham: Duke University Press, 1988).

30. H.D., in *The Cantos of Ezra Pound: Some Testimonies* (New York: Farrar and Rinehart, 1933), 19. The odd form of seeing Pound "plain" is an allusion to a visit to a lady who had once "seen Shelley plain," which is in turn an allusion to the first line of Browning's "Memorabilia": "Ah, did you once see Shelley plain?"

2. Imagism

1. Aldington, *Life for Life's Sake*, 133.

2. Letter dated 20 March 1929, *Richard Aldington and H.D.: The Later Years in Letters*, ed. Caroline Zilboorg (Manchester: Manchester University Press, 1995), 17.

3. Pound, "Prologomena," *Poetry Review* 2 (February 1912): 72–76 (reprinted in *Ezra Pound's Poetry and Prose: Contributions to Periodicals*, prefaced and arranged by Lea Baechler, A. Walton Litz, and James Longenbach, 10 vols. [New York: Garland Publishing, 1991], 1:59–61). The misspelling of the Latin title is Pound's.

4. Letter dated [18] August 1912, in Ezra Pound, *Letters, 1907–1941*, ed. D. D. Paige (New York: Harcourt, Brace and World, 1950), 10.

5. H.D., *End to Torment*, 18. The date of this event is in dispute. Pound says it occurred in "spring or summer." Guest places it in September, when the poets returned from France. Pondrom gives the date as 18 October. Since Pound came back from southern France in August, and the poems were sent to *Poetry* in October, late summer or early fall seems to be the likely period. H.D. says the event took place in the "Museum tea room," but Aldington, who acknowledges that his memory is vague, says it occurred in a Kensington tea shop, a site that has been identified as Ella Abbott's tea shop on Holland Street. (Aldington, *Life for Life's Sake*, 135). Pearson's report is quoted from his manuscript in Friedman, *Penelope's Web*, 37.

6. Pearson's notes quoted in Friedman, *Penelope's Web*, 37, and Aldington, *Life for Life's Sake*, 134–35. For the importance of Pound's influence at this time, see *Penelope's Web*, 103–4.

7. Letter dated October 1912, in Pound, *Letters, 1907–1941*, 11. H.D. never knew of this praise of her early poems until she saw the quotation in a biographical note that Pearson sent her in 1957. She had apparently been unwilling to show her poems to Pound. He wrote that "it was only by persistence that I got to see it at all."

8. Letter to H.D. dated 6 June 1929, *Richard Aldington and H.D.: The Later Years in Letters*, 45.

9. The note is reprinted in Noel Stock, *The Life of Ezra Pound* (New York: Pantheon Books, 1970), 115–16. In the letter of 18 August first mentioning "Imagiste," Pound also says that he is dealing with the proofs of *Ripostes*, so it is clear that the term was on his mind at that time.

10. *Poetry* 1 (November 1912): 65.

11. T. E. Hulme, "Romanticism and Classicism," *The Collected Writings of T. E. Hulme,* ed. Karen Csengeri (Oxford: Clarendon Press, 1994), 70.

12. Hulme, "Notes on Language and Style," *The Collected Writings of T. E. Hulme,* 25.

13. Hulme, "A Lecture on Modern Poetry," *The Collected Writings of T. E. Hulme,* 54.

14. "A Retrospect," *Literary Essays of Ezra Pound,* ed. T. S. Eliot (New York: New Directions, 1968), 3. As the reprint in *Ezra Pound's Poetry and Prose* shows, the section of "Imagisme" containing these principles, as it appeared in the March 1913 issue of *Poetry* (1, 6, 198–200), was signed by Flint, and the following section, "A Few Don'ts by an Imagiste," 200–206, was signed by Pound. The original article made no mention of H.D. and Aldington as co-inventors of these principles. Their names were added when several articles were grouped and reprinted in 1918 in Pound's *Pavannes and Divisions* under the title, "A Retrospect." Pound's influence is shown by the fact that the new statements echo the ideas he expressed in the section "Credo" from the article, "Prologomena," published a few months earlier in the *Poetry Review.*

15. See, for example, L. K. Goodwin, *The Influence of Ezra Pound* (London: Oxford University Press, 1966), and Marjorie Perloff, "The Contemporary of Our Grandchildren," *Poetic License: Essays on Modernist and Postmodernist Lyric* (Evanston: Northwestern University Press, 1990).

16. H.D., "Orchard," *Collected Poems, 1912–1944,* ed. Louis L. Martz (New York: New Directions, 1983), 28.

17. Aldington, "Hermes, Leader of the Dead," *The Complete Poems of Richard Aldington* (London: Allen Wingate, 1948), 30.

18. Aldington to H.D., 6 January 1953, *Richard Aldington and H.D.: The Later Years in Letters,* 191, and a quotation from a letter by H.D. on 229 n.3.

19. Pound, "Vorticism," *Fortnightly Review* 573 (1 September 1914): 461–71 (reprinted in *Ezra Pound's Poetry and Prose,* 1:275–85).

20. "Ortus," *Personae: The Shorter Poems of Ezra Pound* (New York: New Directions, 1990), 85.

21. Undated letter [9 May 1913], *Ezra Pound and Dorothy Shakespear: Their Letters 1909–1914,* ed. Omar Pound and A. Walton Litz (New York: New Directions, 1984), 226.

22. Letter to Harriet Monroe dated January [1915], in Pound, *Letters, 1907–1941,* 49.

23. Undated letter [? January, 1917], in Pound, *Letters, 1907–1941*, 107.

24. *The Cantos of Ezra Pound* (New York: New Directions, 1983), 469.

25. John Gould Fletcher, *Life Is My Song* (New York: Farrar and Rinehart, 1937), 146–52.

26. Humphrey Carpenter, *A Serious Character: The Life of Ezra Pound* (London: Faber and Faber, 1988), 252–53.

27. Letter to Alice Corbin Henderson dated May 1916, *The Letters of Ezra Pound to Alice Corbin Henderson*, ed. Ira Nadel (Austin: University of Texas Press, 1993), 142.

28. Letter dated 9 August [1915], *Letters of Ezra Pound to Alice Corbin Henderson*, 118.

29. Letter dated 26 September 1927, in Pound, *Letters, 1907–1941*, 213.

30. "Écrevisse?," a piece in Italian by Pound that appeared in a periodical called *Il Mare* in 1933 (reprinted in *Ezra Pound's Poetry and Prose*, 3:23–24). The original reads: "H.D. poetessa nel gruppo dei primi imagisti; si può anche dire che l'imagismo fu formulato quasi per dare un'enfasi a certe qualità che essa possedeva in massimo grado: un senso mito-poetico profondo, vero, della natura." There is an odd puzzle about Pound's title. The article begins by reporting that Natalie Barney had said that the feminine of *écrivain* was *écrevisse* or "crawfish." The pun also appears in H.D.'s story, "Mira-Mare," where the narrator, asked what her profession is by an official of the Monte Carlo casino, almost says "écrevisse" instead of "écrivain." "Mira-Mare" was written in 1930 and privately published in 1934, while Pound's article appeared in March 1933. The pun was apparently in general circulation among American expatriates in France.

31. H.D., *The Egoist* 3, 8 (August 1916): 118.

32. Letter dated 27 July 1916, in Pound, *Letters, 1907–1941*, 88, 90.

33. Letter dated 9 August 1915, *Letters of Ezra Pound to Alice Corbin Henderson*, 120.

34. Letter dated 8–9 August 1913, *Letters of Ezra Pound to Alice Corbin Henderson*, 53.

35. Letter dated 13 April 1917, *Letters of Ezra Pound to Alice Corbin Henderson*, 106.

36. John T. Gage has attacked the idea of autonomy and objectivity in Imagism, contending that images cannot fail to insinuate some statement, that the choice of images is controlled by the poet's feeling, that objectivity is a route to subjective emotion, etc. See his *In the Arresting Eye: The Rhetoric of Imagism* (Baton Rouge: Louisiana State University Press, 1981).

37. *Poetry* 2, 1 (April 1913): 12 (reprinted in *Ezra Pound's Poetry and Prose*, 1:37). When he sent the poem to the editor, Pound wrote: "In the 'Metro' hokku, I was careful, I think, to indicate spaces between the rhythmic units, and I want them observed." (Letter dated 30 March [1913] to Harriet Monroe, in Pound, *Letters, 1907–1941*, 17.) However, the poem is invariably reprinted without the spaces, as in *Personae*.

38. "Papyrus," *Personae*, 112. For comment on this poem, see Hugh Kenner, *The Pound Era* (Berkeley: University of California Press, 1971), 5–6.

39. "Hermes of the Ways," *Collected Poems, 1912–1944*, 39.

40. "Heather," *Personae*, 112.

41. However, Friedman detects surrealist and dream-work effects in some of H.D.'s fiction written before her contact with Freud, and possibly attributable to the influence of the experimentalism of the first two decades of the century. See especially her comments on *Hedylus* in *Penelope's Web*, 253–59.

42. Robert Duncan, "Beginnings," chapter 1 of "H.D. Book," *Coyote's Journal* 5–6 (1966): 13, 21.

43. Ernest Fenollosa, *The Chinese Written Character as a Medium for Poetry*, ed. Ezra Pound (San Francisco: City Lights Books, 1936), 23.

44. H.D., *Collected Poems, 1912–1944*, ed. and with intro. by Louis L. Martz (New York: New Directions, 1986), 509.

45. H.D., *Helen in Egypt* (New York: New Directions, 1961), 23, 31.

46. Pound, "A Few Don'ts by an Imagiste," *Poetry* 1, 6 (March 1913): 200 (reprinted in *Ezra Pound's Poetry and Prose*, 1:120).

47. Duncan, "Rites of Participation, II," *Caterpillar* 1 (October 1967): 149.

48. Janice S. Robinson, *H.D.: The Life and Work of an American Poet* (Boston: Houghton Mifflin, 1982), 29–35. Robinson regards these poems as steps in H.D.'s rejection of Pound's influence.

49. Rebecca West, "Imagisme," *New Freewoman* 1, 5 (15 August 1913): 86.

50. Friedman, *Penelope's Web*, 130–31.

51. H.D., *Collected Poems, 1912–1944*, 5.

3. The First War

1. See Gary Burnett, "A Poetics Out of War: H.D.'s Responses to the First World War," *Agenda* 25, 3–4 (autumn–winter 1987–88): 54 ff.

2. Pound, "Through Alien Eyes," *New Age* 12 (16 January 1913): 252 (reprinted in *Ezra Pound's Poetry and Prose*, 1:114).

3. Iris Barry, "The Ezra Pound Period," *Bookman* 74, 2 (October 1931): 159–71.

4. Letter dated 12 August 1918, *Richard Aldington and H.D.: The Early Years in Letters*, ed. Caroline Zilboorg (Bloomington: Indiana University Press, 1992), 124. These letters, mostly from Aldington, together with the editor's introduction, give an excellent view of the confusion of this time.

5. Pound, "Lament of the Frontier Guard," *Personae*, 133.

6. Ibid., 188.

7. *Literary Essays of Ezra Pound*, 444.

8. Monroe Spears, *Dionysus and the City: Modernism in Twentieth-Century Poetry* (New York: Oxford University Press, 1970), 63.

9. See Wendy Stallard Flory, *Ezra Pound and "The Cantos"* (New Haven: Yale University Press, 1980), 89–93.

10. H.D., "The Tribute," in *Collected Poems, 1912–1944*, 59–68.

4. Postwar Years

1. H.D., "Writing on the Wall," in *Tribute to Freud. Writing on the Wall. Advent* (New York: New Directions, 1984), 57.

2. Quoted in *Richard Aldington and H.D.: The Early Years in Letters*, 34.

3. H.D., *End to Torment*, 7–8.

4. Aldington to H.D., *Richard Aldington and H.D.: The Later Years in Letters*, 28.

5. For a detailed account of the Pound-Rudge relationship, see Anne Conover, *Olga Rudge and Ezra Pound* (New Haven: Yale University Press, 2001).

6. Robert McAlmon, *Being Geniuses Together, 1920–1930* (Garden City, N.J.: Doubleday, 1968), 100.

7. J. J. Wilhelm, *Ezra Pound in London and Paris, 1908–1925* (University Park: Pennsylvania State University Press, 1990), 338.

8. Undated letter ("Friday" [1929]), Beinecke Library, Yale University.

5. Vision and Sexuality

1. Quoted from a letter to Harriet Monroe in James Longenbach, *Stone Cottage* (New York: Oxford University Press, 1988), 22.

2. Robert Duncan, "Two Chapters from H.D.," *TriQuarterly* 12 (spring 1968): 80.

3. Ibid., 67, and "Rites of Participation," *Caterpillar* 1 (October 1967), 28. Among Duncan's many statements linking the two poets to the occult tradition: "H.D. and Pound in the Imagist period cannot be separated from the reawakened sense of the meaning and reality of the gods in the contemporary studies of the mystery cults" ("Two Chapters from H.D.," 80). The studies Duncan mentions are those of Jane Harrison and G. R. S. Mead.

4. Leon Surette, *The Birth of Modernism* (Montreal: McGill-Queen's University Press, 1993), 36. For H.D.'s mysticism, see her *Notes on Thought and Vision* and Barbara Guest's *Herself Defined.*

5. These books are usefully identified in William French and Timothy Materer, "Far Flung Vortices and Ezra's 'Hindoo' Yogi," *Paideuma* 11, 1 (spring 1982), 39–43. See also Demetres Tryphonopoulos, *The Celestial Tradition,* 64–67, which emphasizes the point that "Pound's and H.D.'s initiation into things occult took place on American soil during their youth and . . . this interest endured for both of them." Tryphonopoulos's book and Leon Surette's *The Birth of Modernism* are thorough explorations of Pound's occult themes.

6. Letter dated 13 March [1957], in Hollenberg, *Between History and Poetry,* 204.

7. Honoré de Balzac, *Séraphita,* trans. Clara Bell (New York: Hippocrene Books, 1989), 95.

8. "I Gather the Limbs of Osiris, IX, On Technique," *New Age* 13 (January 1912): 297–99 (reprinted in *Ezra Pound's Poetry and Prose,* 1:57).

9. "The New Sculpture" *Egoist* 1, 4 (16 February 1914) (reprinted in *Ezra Pound's Poetry and Prose,* 1:222).

10. Tryphonopoulos, *The Celestial Tradition,* 27. For information about Pound's response to serious scholars of the esoteric tradition, see Tryphonopoulos's chapter 3, "Pound's Occult Education."

11. See Longenbach, *Stone Cottage,* for the influence of Yeats's ideas on Pound.

12. Longenbach, *Stone Cottage,* 88.

13. James Longenbach, *Modernist Poetics of History* (Princeton: Princeton University Press, 1987), 19, 21. Longenbach cites Eliot's comment about the sudden inspirations writers may experience: "You may call it communion with the Divine, or you may call it a temporary crystallization of mind." 226, quoted from *Selected Essays,* 358.

14. Quoted in Friedman, *Penelope's Web,* 34.

15. H.D., *Tribute to Freud,* 35.

16. H.D., *Notes on Thought and Vision,* 37.

17. For a description of the frescoes and an account of their relation to the *Cantos,* see Guy Davenport, *Cities on Hills: A Study of I–XXX of Ezra Pound's Cantos* (Ann Arbor: UMI Research Press, 1983), 80–92.

18. *Cantos,* 531.

19. Ibid., 606.

20. H.D., *Notes on Thought and Vision,* 41–56.

21. Ibid., 42.

22. H.D., Hirslanden Journal, entry of 2 February 1957, 3, 27–28. Beinecke Library, Yale University.

23. Ibid., entry of 8 February 1957, 3, 14.

24. Ibid., entry of 4 February 1957, 3, 4–7.

25. H.D., "The Walls Do Not Fall," *Collected Poems, 1912–1944,* 531.

26. Ibid., 535–36.

27. "Tribute to the Angels," *Collected Poems, 1912–1944,* 570.

28. "The Flowering of the Rod," *Collected Poems, 1912–1944,* 602.

29. Ronald Bush, "Modernism, Fascism and the Composition of Ezra Pound's *Pisan Cantos,*" *Modernism Modernity* 2, 3 (September 1995): 75–76.

30. Ibid., 73–74.

31. *Cantos,* 520. According to Flory, in this passage, the poet first sees the eyes as a spiritual manifestation, but then realizes that there are three pairs of eyes of different colors belonging to three women, namely Olga Rudge, Dorothy, and Bride Scratton. See *Ezra Pound and "The Cantos,"* 216–17.

32. *Cantos,* 425.

33. *Confucius,* trans. Ezra Pound (New York: New Directions, 1969). The quotations are from 99, 101, 183.

34. H.D., *Notes on Thought and Vision,* 21.

35. For the medieval and Chinese traditions behind Pound's identification of the brain and seminal fluid, see Jean-Michel Rabaté, *Language, Sexuality and Ideology in Ezra Pound's "Cantos"* (London: Macmillan, 1986), 217–18. In *Pound Revised* (London: Croom Helm, 1983), Paul Smith builds a strong case for Pound's phallocentrism, especially in the *Cantos.* See chapter 3, "Towards Veracity."

36. Kendra Langeteig, "Visions in the Crystal Ball: Ezra Pound, H.D., and the Form of the Mystical," *Paideuma* 25, 1/2 (spring–fall 1996): 55–82. Eileen Gregory attributes another value to H.D.'s crystal imagery. She sees it as H.D.'s symbol of artistic perfection, embodying

the brilliance, clarity, and enduring qualities of Pater's "hard, gem-like flame," a view that recalls H.D.'s praise of Marianne Moore's poems. However, H.D. later objected to the term "crystalline" applied to her early poems. See Eileen Gregory, *H.D. and Hellenism* (Cambridge: Cambridge University Press, 1997), 85–88.

37. *Cantos*, 238.

38. Langeteig, "Visions in the Crystal Ball," 48.

6. Between the Wars

1. Letters dated 6 April [1938] and 31 July [1938], Beinecke Library.

2. Letter dated 27 August 1928, Beinecke Library.

3. Undated letter ("Friday" [1929]), Beinecke Library.

4. Letter dated 13 September 1916, *Iowa Review* 16, 3 (1986): 136.

5. Undated letter [1929], Beinecke Library.

6. *Cantos*, 11, 25.

7. H.D., "Thetis," *Collected Poems, 1912–1944*, 160.

8. Letter dated 24 March [1933], Beinecke Library.

9. H.D. copied this part of Pound's letter in a letter to Pearson, 10 June [1934], in Hollenberg, *Between History and Poetry*, 156–57. She was disturbed by the letter, which contained some other gratuitous criticism, and showed it to her two psychiatrists, who apparently advised her not to take it as seriously as she did.

10. "Écrevisse?" *Il Mare* 26, 1253 (18 March 1933): 3, 23–24 (reprinted in *Ezra Pound's Poetry and Prose*, 3:23–24).

11. H.D., *Tribute to Freud*, 14, 35.

12. Information about Pearson and H.D. is from Hollenberg, *Between History and Poetry*.

13. Guest, *Herself Defined*, 246–47.

14. Letter dated 7 August [1939], Beinecke Library.

15. H.D., "Fragment Forty," *Collected Poems, 1912–1944*, 174.

16. H.D., "Epigram 1," *Collected Poems, 1912–1944*, 172.

7. Pound in H.D.'s Fiction

1. From a letter quoted in Friedman's *Penelope's Web*, 34. *Asphodel* covers the period of H.D.'s life also covered by novels published earlier, often giving a different emphasis to the events, and including episodes omitted from them. See *Penelope's Web*, 170–213, for a thorough analysis of the relationships among these texts.

2. H.D., *HERmione* (New York: New Directions, 1981), 28.

3. Ibid., 85.

4. Ibid., 148–49.

5. Ibid., 218.

6. Friedman, *Penelope's Web*, 115.

7. *HERmione*, 161. Friedman fails to quote this, but does quote Fayne's subsequent remarks: "Your writing is the thin flute holding you to eternity. Take away your flute and you remain, lost in a world of unreality." Whether this is a favorable comment on the writing is dubious.

8. Friedman, *Penelope's Web*, 116 ff.

9. *HERmione*, 197, 223.

10. Ibid., 70, 82.

11. Ibid., 119. "Aum" or "Om" is an incantatory word used in Indian religions in connection with mystic meditation. Hermione has said that she has been reading "Wisdom of the East books." These would seem to be the "Yogi books" by Yogi Ramacharaka that Pound brought to H.D. in Pennsylvania.

12. *HERmione*, 158.

13. See Cassandra Laity, *H.D. and the Victorian Fin de Siècle*. For the influence of Swinburne on *HERmione*, see 32–42.

14. H.D., *Paint It Today*, ed. Cassandra Laity (New York: New York University Press, 1992), 7.

15. Ibid., 22–23.

16. In her unpublished journal, "Compassionate Friendship" (Beinecke Library), H.D. says that "Hipparchia" is "much the same story as the later *Madrigal*." *Madrigal* is H.D.'s temporary name for the autobiographical *Bid Me to Live*. There is no Pound figure in *Bid Me to Live*, but the appearance of one in "Hipparchia" suggests that he is behind the scenes in that novel as well. For details about the historical setting of "Hipparchia" and its anachronisms, see Eileen Gregory, *H.D. and Hellenism* (Cambridge: Cambridge University Press, 1997), 60–61.

17. H.D., *Palimpsest* (Boston: Houghton Mifflin, 1926), 95. There are misspellings and typographical errors in this edition, which is based on the one printed in France by Maurice Darantiére in Dijon, the same firm that printed the error-filled *Ulysses*, and I have not made corrections in quoting from it.

18. H.D., *Palimpsest*, 101–2.

19. Ibid., 85, 87.

20. Ibid., 111–12.

21. Ibid., 114.

22. Ibid., 115.

23. Ibid., 131.

24. H.D.'s comment is quoted from "Compassionate Friendship" in Robinson, *H.D.: The Life and Works of an American Poet*, 270. Pound's comment is from a letter to Homer L. Pound. 11 April [1927]. See Pound, *Letters, 1907–1941*, 210.

25. H.D., *Palimpsest*, 165.

26. *Asphodel*, 57. A corresponding picture of Pound is Alvin Langdon Coburn's photograph, to be seen, among other places, in Humphrey Carpenter, *A Serious Character: The Life of Ezra Pound* (London: Faber and Faber, 1988).

27. Undated letter [December 1949?], Lilly Library.

28. "The Sword Went Out to Sea," part 2, 158, 166, etc., Beinecke Library. The play was *Iphigenia in Tauris*, performed at the University of Pennsylvania in April 1903. There is a photo of the chorus in Humphrey Carpenter's *A Serious Character*.

29. "The Sword Went Out to Sea," part 1, 128–29, Beinecke Library.

30. Ibid., part 1, 142.

31. Ibid., part 3, 125.

32. In a study that examines H.D. through the psychoanalytic theories of Melanie Klein, Susan Edmunds declares that "the visionary politics of H.D.'s long poems cannot be reconciled with the liberal-feminist and post-structuralist-feminist agendas currently attributed to them." *Out of Line: History, Psychoanalysis and Montage in H.D.'s Long Poems* (Stanford: Stanford University Press, 1994), 5.

33. Quotation from "H.D. by Delia Alton," in Friedman, *Penelope's Web*, 144–45.

34. L. S. Dembo, "Norman Holmes Pearson: An Interview," *Contemporary Literature* 10, 4 (autumn 1969): 441, 445. Pearson also remarked that H.D.'s use of multiple metaphors was learned from the modern poets, including specifically Pound.

35. "Compassionate Friendship," 35 (March 15) and 24 (February 24), Beinecke Library.

36. Rachel Blau DuPlessis, "Romantic Thralldom in H.D.," *Contemporary Literature* 20, 2 (spring 1979): 178–203.

37. Friedman, *Penelope's Web*, 16.

8. The Second War

1. H.D., *Tribute to Freud*, 93–94.

2. H.D., *The Gift*, ed. Jane Augustine (Gainesville: University Press of Florida, 1998), 222.

3. H.D., "The Walls Do Not Fall," *Collected Poems, 1912–1944,* 543.

4. Hirslanden Journal, 3, 2, and 4 February 1957, Beinecke Library.

5. For a thorough account of Pound's thinking at this time, see chapter 3, "Pound and Mussolini," 82–130, in Flory, *The American Ezra Pound.*

6. Friedman regards *Trilogy* as a reply on H.D.'s part to Freud's rationalism and materialism. See *Psyche Reborn: The Emergence of H.D.* (Bloomington: Indiana University Press, 1981), 101–9. Cyrena N. Pondrom's comparative study of *Trilogy* and Eliot's *Four Quartets,* especially "Little Gidding," helps to illuminate the similar but less marked relation between H.D.'s poem and the *Pisan Cantos.* See "*Trilogy* and *Four Quartets:* Contrapuntal Visions of Spiritual Quest," *Agenda* 25, 3–4 (autumn–winter 1987–88): 155–65.

7. H.D., "The Walls Do Not Fall," *Collected Poems, 1912–1944,* 523.

8. There is an annotated English translation by Massimo Bacigalupo in *Paideuma* 20, 1–2 (spring–fall 1991): 9–41.

9. H.D., *Collected Poems, 1912–1944,* 513.

10. "H.D. by Delia Alton," 184, entry of 14 December 1949.

11. The rod symbol H.D. had in mind is probably based on the passage in the Book of Numbers, 17, where the Lord commands the Israelites to write the name of each tribe upon a rod, and "the man's rod whom I shall choose shall blossom." He blesses the rod of Aaron, which "budded, and brought forth buds and bloomed blossoms and yielded almonds." However, section 3 of "The Walls Do Not Fall" refers to the Caduceus as "the rod of power," a pagan symbol that displays snakes and not flowers.

12. *Cantos,* 530. The manuscript originally read: "whose eyes are like the clouds over Taishan / When some of the rain has fallen / and half remains yet to fall" (see Ronald Bush, "Modernism, Fascism, and the Composition of Ezra Pound's *Pisan Cantos,*" *Modernism Modernity* 2, 3 [September 1995], 69–78). Pound identified one of the mountains visible from the DTC with Taishan, the sacred mountain of China.

13. *End to Torment,* 17.

14. Friedman and DuPlessis believe that this passage is echoed in H.D.'s *Winter Love,* which would mean that H.D. replied in turn to Pound. See "I had two loves separate" in *Signets: Reading H.D.,* ed. Susan Stanford Friedman and Rachel Blau DuPlessis (Madison: University of Wisconsin Press, 1990), 225.

15. *Cantos,* 473.

16. Fenollosa, *The Chinese Written Character,* 22.

17. Jerome J. McGann, "The Cantos of Ezra Pound, the Truth in Contradiction," *Critical Inquiry* 15 (autumn 1988): 1–25.

18. Roland Barthes, "Writing Degree Zero," *A Barthes Reader*, ed. Susan Sontag (London: Jonathan Cape, 1982).

19. Michael Alexander, *The Poetic Achievement of Ezra Pound* (Berkeley: University of California Press, 1981), 19.

9. After World War II

1. Letter dated 20 July [1950], in Hollenberg, *Between History and Poetry*, 95.

2. Letter to Pound, 23 February [1955?], Beinecke Library.

3. Letters dated 23 August, 22 September, and 8 October 1948, H.D. to Pound, Lilly Library.

4. Letter dated 25 September 1951, H.D. to Dorothy Pound, Lilly Library.

5. Letter dated 9 August [1950], H.D. to Pound, Beinecke Library.

6. Letter dated 6 October [1958], Pound to H.D., Beinecke Library.

7. Letter dated 18 September 1952, Aldington to H.D., quoted in *Richard Aldington and H.D.: The Later Years in Letters*, 183, and letter dated 20 December 1952, ibid., 186.

8. Letters to Pound dated 23 September [1956] and 16 October [1956], Beinecke Library.

9. Letter dated 23 August 1948, H.D. to Pound, Lilly Library.

10. Letter dated 22 September 1948, H.D. to Pound, Lilly Library.

11. Letter dated 3 January 1949, H.D. to Pound, Lilly Library.

12. Letter dated 17 October [1948], H.D. to Aldington, *Richard Aldington and H.D.: The Later Years in Letters*, 132.

13. Letter dated 21 October [1948], H.D. to Aldington, *Richard Aldington and H.D.: The Later Years in Letters*, 133.

14. The information in the following paragraphs is based mainly on letters exchanged between Pearson and H.D. between 30 March and 4 May 1958, *Richard Aldington and H.D.: The Later Years in Letters*, 213–24.

15. Letter dated 6 July 1958, H.D. to Pound, Lilly Library.

16. Undated letter [1959], Beinecke Library.

17. Letter dated 11 April [1958], H.D. to Pearson, in Hollenberg, *Between History and Poetry*, 220.

18. Undated letter [26 June 1959], Pound to H.D., Beinecke Library.

19. Letter dated 3 April [1958], in Hollenberg, *Between History and Poetry*, 216.

20. Letter dated 3 April [1958], in Hollenberg, *Between History and Poetry*, 216–17.

21. *End to Torment*, entries of 21 March 1958, 27; 16 March, 24; 14 March, 17.

22. Cassandra Laity, *H.D. and the Victorian Fin de Siècle*, 151–52, 158–61.

23. Hirslanden Journal, 7 October 1957, 4, 5.

24. *End to Torment*, 5 April, 34, and 7 May 1958, 43.

25. Ibid., 9 May 1958, 44.

26. For Martinelli in these Cantos, see Flory, *Ezra Pound and "The Cantos,"* 239 ff.

27. The "curbed stone" echoes an admiring reference to the "well-curb of Terracina" in "Terra Italica," *Selected Prose, 1909–1965*, ed. William Cookson (New York: New Directions, 1973), 58. The argument for the metaphysical value of the monument appears both in "Paideuma," *Selected Prose*, 320, and as an epigraph to "Religio," *Selected Prose*, 45.

28. *Cantos*, 623–24.

29. *End to Torment*, 6 June, 53.

30. Ibid., 25 June, 57.

31. Ibid., 2 July, 59.

32. Ibid., 21 March, 26.

33. Ibid., 19 July, 56.

34. Ibid., 27 March, 30.

35. Ibid., 14 March, 17.

36. Ibid., 15 April, 39.

10. Modern Epics

1. I am indebted for much of the following discussion to Eileen Gregory's *H.D. and Hellenism*, a thorough and detailed study of H.D.'s use of Greek literature. She offers a survey of H.D.'s devotion to the Alexandrian school and its principles.

2. Pound, "H.D.'s Choruses from Euripides," *Little Review* 5, 7 (November 1918): 16–20 (reprinted in *Ezra Pound's Poetry and Prose*, 3:224–25). In a later article in this series, Pound again expressed his dislike for Euripides by saying: "Aristophanes was needed as acid for Euripides."

3. B. H. Dias, "Art Notes" *New Age* 22, 16 (15 August 1918): 255–56 (reprinted in *Ezra Pound's Poetry and Prose*, 3:169).

4. Letter dated 5 March [1937], H.D. to Pound, Beinecke Library.

5. Letter dated 8 October 1948, H.D. to Pound, Lilly Library.

6. H.D., "Adonis," *Collected Poems 1912–1944*, 47.

7. Gregory, *H.D. and Hellenism*, 22–28.

8. Friedman, who emphasizes Helen's opposition to the military "Command" of the Greeks, suggests another relation between H.D.'s poem and Pound's: "Her 'Cantos' recall Pound's *Cantos* in more ways than one: her attack on fascism as a 'death-cult' is perhaps an answer to Pound's espousal of fascism in Italy and his celebration of the patriarchal, Confucian world view." *Psyche Reborn*, 260.

9. Letter dated 26 November [1955], H.D. to Pearson, in Hollenberg, *Between History and Poetry*, 180. See Guest in *Herself Defined*, 290–93: "There is no doubt that these cantos [the *Pisan Cantos*] were the ferment on both the conscious and subconscious levels of what would become H.D.'s own book of cantos, *Helen in Egypt* . . . Ezra's unseen hand would make the corrections on the new page. His genius would challenge her into competition, his evocation of the past would become a lure . . . The book gathers its distinction . . . from the inspired *Pisan Cantos* of Pound."

10. *End to Torment*, 31 March 1958, 32.

11. Letter dated 26 November [1955], in Hollenberg, *Between History and Poetry*, 180.

12. Letter dated 24 July [1954], in Hollenberg, *Between History and Poetry*, 159.

13. Letter dated 17 September 1953, in Hollenberg, *Between History and Poetry*, 144–45.

14. Letter dated 26 November [1955], in Hollenberg, *Between History and Poetry*, 180.

15. Quoted from a letter of 12 June 1954, H.D. to Pearson, in Hollenberg, *Between History and Poetry*, 158.

16. *End to Torment*, 23 April [1958], 41.

17. "Compassionate Friendship," entry of 7 April 1955, 72, Beinecke Library.

18. *End to Torment*, 27 March [1958], 30.

19. May Sinclair, *Divine Fire* (New York: Henry Holt and Company, 1904), 137. H.D. might also have been attracted by the fictional poet's description of his Helen as "the eternal Beauty, the eternal Dream. Beauty, perpetually desirous of incarnation, perpetually unfaithful to flesh and blood; the Dream that longs for the embrace of reality, that wanders, never satisfied until it finds a reality as immortal as itself," etc. (148).

20. For a thorough analysis of the relation of *Helen in Egypt* to the plays of Euripides, see the section "Eidolon: Helen in Egypt," 218–31, in

Gregory, *H.D. and Hellenism*. There were other sources and inspirations for *Helen;* see, for example, Guest, *Herself Defined*, 290–93.

21. Robinson, however, feels that Pound appears frequently in *Helen in Egypt* in a variety of disguises. Her argument is interesting, but unconvincing. See *H.D.: The Life and Work of an American Poet*, 420–30.

22. H.D. might originally have derived the idea of the union between Helen and Achilles from Pausanias's *Description of Greece*. He repeats the legend that Achilles' spirit was taken to the island of Leuké, known as the White Island, where he married Helen, and the two were seen by a man from Croton who went to Leuké for a cure. However, the idea that Helen was in Egypt originated, as H.D. says, in the gloss on her first lyric, in the Pallinode of Stesichorus, who was blinded for criticizing her, but had his sight restored when he recanted. This episode, oddly, is mentioned in Edmund Spenser's sixteenth-century poem, "Colin Clout Comes Home Again": "And well I wote that oft I heard it spoken, / How one that fairest *Helen* did revile: / Through judgment of the Gods to been ywroken / Lost both his eyes and so remayned long while, / Till he recanted had his wicked rimes, / And made amends to her with treble praise."

23. Pearson's jacket copy for H.D.'s book read in part that "the subject is the inner world of a woman in her quest to understand her experiences, to define her sense of reality and time, to resolve the conflict between the rational and the irrational, to consider the problem of guilt, and to establish the relationship between love and death. *Helen in Egypt* exemplifies H.D.'s own definition of a poem." Letter dated 6 July 1961, Pearson to H.D., Beinecke Library.

24. See Friedman, *Psyche Reborn*, 67–69, for a relevant discussion of *Helen in Egypt*.

25. H.D., *Helen in Egypt* (New York: New Directions, 1947), 303.

26. Letter dated 5 December [1958], Pound to Pearson, Beinecke Library.

27. Letter dated 22 November 1958, Pound to H.D., Beinecke Library.

11. Last Years

1. "Compassionate Friendship," 26–27, Beinecke Library.

2. "Compassionate Friendship," 22–24, 129.

3. Letters dated 2 January and 7 January [1959], H.D. to Pound, Beinecke Library.

4. Undated letter [mistakenly dated 1958], Pound to H.D., Beinecke Library.

5. Letter dated 6 November [1959], Pound to H.D., Beinecke Library. Pound's page numbers are puzzling, considering that the manuscript is supposed to consist of 57 pages.

6. Letter dated 6 November [1959], Pound to H.D., Beinecke Library.

7. Undated letter [13 November 1959], Pound to H.D., Beinecke Library. The incident of the "Hokusai-wave" may well be the one reported by Williams, when H.D. was taken out of the water unconscious.

8. Undated letter [1959], Pound to H.D., Beinecke Library.

9. Undated letter [26 June 1959], Pound to H.D., Beinecke Library. In this letter, he also recalls that she said "not if you were the last man," apparently referring to her rejection of a marriage proposal.

10. *Cantos*, 787.

11. Ibid., 783.

12. Letters dated 15 October and 4 November [1959], H.D. to Pound, Beinecke Library.

13. Undated letter [1959] and 6 November [1959], Pound to H.D., Beinecke Library. This correction is mentioned in H.D.'s letter to Pearson of 21 November. It apparently concerned the last three lines of Antistrophe 18.

14. Letter dated 16 June [1959], in Hollenberg, *Between History and Poetry*, 259, n.144.

15. Letters dated 17 May and 19 June [1959], H.D. to Pearson, in Hollenberg, *Between History and Poetry*, 239, 241. H.D.'s "Conscious" is significant, and possibly inaccurate. As we have seen, there were earlier poems, such as "To the Piraeus" probably written with Pound in mind many years before.

16. H.D., *Winter Love* in *Hermetic Definition* (New York: New Directions, 1972), 100, 103.

17. Letter dated 10 October [1960], H.D. to Pearson, in Hollenberg, *Between History and Poetry*, 281.

18. *Winter Love* in *Hermetic Definition*, 97.

19. *Cantos*, 487.

20. Ibid., 752.

21. See Donna Krolik Hollenberg, *H.D.: The Poetics of Childbirth and Creativity* (Boston: Northeastern University Press, 1991), 224–26.

22. In *Pound Revised*, Paul Smith follows Freudian doctrine in interpreting H.D.'s desire for a child as penis envy. This leads to her

unconscious attachment to the father, who, Smith believes, was identified in H.D.'s mind with Pound. See 112, 115.

23. Undated letter [1938], Pound to H.D., Beinecke Library.

24. Letter dated 16 March [1938], H.D. to Pound, Beinecke Library.

25. See Hollenberg, *H.D.: The Poetics of Childbirth and Creativity*, 224–26.

26. *End to Torment*, 16 March 1958 to 23 May, 21 to 52.

27. Hirslanden Journal, 25 April 1959, 4, 26. "Euphorion" is the name of the child of Helen and Achilles in *Helen in Egypt*.

28. *Winter Love* in *Hermetic Definition*, 112.

29. Ibid., 117.

30. Undated letter [1960?], Pound to H.D., Beinecke Library.

31. Letter dated 19 November [1960], H.D. to Pearson, in Hollenberg, *Between History and Poetry*, 283.

32. Letter dated 9 January 1961, Pound to H.D., Beinecke Library.

33. H.D.'s lines may owe something to these lines from a sonnet by John Donne: "arise, arise / From death you numberless infinities / Of soules, and to your scattered bodies goe."

34. Raffaelle Baccolini, "Pound's Tribute to H.D.," *Contemporary Literature* 27, 4 (winter 1986): 434–39. The article is accompanied by a reproduction of Pound's manuscript.

35. Letter dated 1 November [1961], Pound to Pearson, Beinecke Library.

36. Letter dated 23 November 1961, Pearson to Pound, Beinecke Library.

References

Manuscript Sources

Beinecke Library, Yale University

H.D. "Compassionate Friendship." YCAL MSS 24, Series 2.

H.D. Diary, Paris, 1912. YCAL MSS 24, Series 1. Photocopy.

H.D. Hirslanden Journal, 1957: 1, 10-12 January; 2, 26 January–3 February; 3, 4-14 February; 4, September 1957–February 1960. YCAL MSS 24, H.D. Papers -Writings, Series 2. Photocopies.

H.D. Papers, YCAL MSS 24, Series 1. Photocopies.

H.D. "The Sword Went Out to Sea," by Delia Alton. YCAL MSS 24.

H.D. "Winter Love," draft notebook 3 January–5 April 1959.

Norman Holmes Pearson. Letters to H.D. YCAL MSS 43, Series 1, and YCAL MSS 53.

Ezra Pound Papers. YCAL MSS 43 Series 1. Photocopies.

Lilly Library, Indiana University

Pound, Ezra. Pound MSS II. Photocopies.

Published Sources

Agenda 25, 3-4 (autumn–winter 1987-88). H.D. Special Issue. Edited by Diana Collecott.

Aldington, Richard. *The Complete Poems of Richard Aldington*. London: Allen Wingate, 1948.

———. *Life for Life's Sake*. New York: Viking Press, 1941.

Alexander, Michael. *The Poetic Achievement of Ezra Pound.* Berkeley: University of California Press, 1981.

Ambelain, Robert. *Dans l'Ombre des Cathédrales.* Paris: Éditions Adyar, 1939.

Barry, Iris. "The Ezra Pound Period." *Bookman* 74, 2 (October 1931): 159–71.

Bryher. *The Days of Mars: A Memoir, 1940–1946.* New York: Harcourt Brace Jovanovich, 1972.

Bush, Ronald. "Modernism, Fascism, and the Composition of Ezra Pound's *Pisan Cantos.*" *Modernism Modernity* 2, 3 (September 1995): 69–87.

Carpenter, Humphrey. *A Serious Character: The Life of Ezra Pound.* London: Faber and Faber, 1988.

Conover, Anne. *Olga Rudge and Ezra Pound.* New Haven: Yale University Press, 2001.

Davenport, Guy. *Cities on Hills. A Study of I–XXX of Ezra Pound's Cantos.* Ann Arbor: UMI Research Press, 1983.

DuPlessis, Rachel Blau. "Romantic Thralldom in H.D." In *Signets: Reading H.D.,* edited by Susan Stanford Friedman and Rachel Blau DuPlessis, 406–29. Madison: University of Wisconsin Press, 1990.

Edmunds, Susan. *Out of Line: History, Psychoanalysis, and Montage in H.D.'s Long Poems.* Stanford: Stanford University Press, 1994.

Fenollosa, Ernest. *The Chinese Written Character as a Medium for Poetry.* Edited by Ezra Pound. San Francisco: City Lights Books, 1936.

Fletcher, John Gould. *Life Is My Song.* New York: Farrar and Rinehart, 1937.

Flory, Wendy Stallard. *The American Ezra Pound.* New Haven: Yale University Press, 1989.

———. *Ezra Pound and "The Cantos": A Record of Struggle.* New Haven: Yale University Press, 1980.

Friedman, Susan Stanford. *Penelope's Web: Gender, Modernity, H.D.'s Fiction.* Cambridge: Cambridge University Press, 1990.

———. *Psyche Reborn: The Emergence of H.D.* Bloomington: Indiana University Press, 1981.

Gibson, Mary Ellen. *Epic Reinvented: Ezra Pound and the Victorians.* Ithaca: Cornell University Press, 1995.

Goodwin, K. L. *The Influence of Ezra Pound.* London: Oxford University Press, 1966.

Gregg, Frances. *The Mystic Leeway.* Edited by Ben Jones. Ottawa: Carleton University Press, 1995.

Gregory, Eileen. *H.D. and Hellenism.* Cambridge: Cambridge University Press, 1997.

Guest, Barbara. *Herself Defined.* Garden City, N.J.: Doubleday, 1984.

Harmer, J. B. *Victory in Limbo: Imagism 1908–1917.* New York: St. Martin's Press, 1975.

H.D. *Asphodel.* Edited with introduction and biographical notes by Robert Spoo. Durham: Duke University Press, 1992.

——. *By Avon River.* New York: Macmillan, 1949.

——. *Collected Poems 1912–1944.* Edited with introduction by Louis L. Martz. New York: New Directions, 1986.

——. *End to Torment: A Memoir of Ezra Pound.* Edited by Norman Holmes Pearson and Michael King. New York: New Directions, 1979.

——. *The Gift.* Edited by Jane Augustine. Gainesville: University Press of Florida, 1998.

——. "H.D. by Delia Alton," *Iowa Review* 16, 3 (fall 1986):180–221.

——. *Helen in Egypt.* New York: New Directions, 1961.

——. *Hermetic Definition.* New York: New Directions, 1979.

——. *HERmione.* New York: New Directions, 1981.

——. *Notes on Thought and Vision and the Wise Sappho.* San Francisco: City Lights Books, 1982.

——. *Paint It Today.* Edited by Cassandra Laity. New York: New York University Press, 1992.

——. *Palimpsest.* Boston: Houghton Mifflin, 1926.

——. *Richard Aldington and H.D.: The Early Years in Letters.* Edited by Caroline Zilboorg. Bloomington: Indiana University Press, 1992.

——. *Richard Aldington and H.D.: The Later Years in Letters.* Edited by Caroline Zilboorg. Manchester: Manchester University Press, 1995.

——. *Tribute to Freud. Writing on the Wall. Advent.* (1956). New York: New Directions, 1984.

Hemingway, Ernest, et al. *The Cantos of EP: Some Testimonies.* New York: Farrar and Rinehart, 1933.

Hollenberg, Donna Krolik. *H.D.: The Poetics of Childbirth and Creativity.* Boston: Northeastern University Press, 1991.

Hollenberg, Donna Krolik, ed. *Between History and Poetry: The Letters of H.D. and Norman Holmes Pearson.* Iowa City: University of Iowa Press, 1997.

Hulme, T. E. *The Collected Writings of T. E. Hulme.* Edited by Karen Csengeri. Oxford: Clarendon Press, 1994.

Iowa Review 16, 3 (1986). H.D. Centennial Issue. Edited by Adalaide Morris.

Laity, Cassandra. *H.D. and the Victorian Fin de Siècle*. Cambridge: Cambridge University Press, 1966.

Langeteig, Kendra. "Visions in the Crystal Ball: Ezra Pound, H. D., and the Form of the Mystical." *Paideuma* 25, 1–2 (spring–fall 1996): 55–82.

Longenbach, James. *Stone Cottage*. New York: Oxford University Press, 1988.

McAlmon, Robert. *Being Geniuses Together, 1920–1930*. With chapters by Kay Boyle. Garden City, N.J.: Doubleday, 1968.

Perloff, Marjorie. "The Contemporary of Our Grandchildren." In *Poetic License: Essays on Modernist and Postmodernist Lyric*. Evanston: Northwestern University Press, 1990.

Pondrom, Cyrena N. "H.D. and the Origins of Imagism." *Sagetrieb* 4, 1 (spring 1985): 73–97.

———. *The Road from Paris: French Influence on English Poetry 1900–1920*. London: Cambridge University Press, 1974.

Pound, Ezra. *The Cantos of Ezra Pound*. New York: New Directions, 1983.

———. *Collected Early Poems of Ezra Pound*. Edited by Michael John King. New York: New Directions, 1976.

———. *Ezra Pound and Dorothy Shakespear: Their Letters 1909–1914*. Edited by Omar Pound and A. Walton Litz. New York: New Directions, 1984.

———. *Ezra Pound's Mauberley*. Edited by John Espey. Berkeley: University of California Press, 1955.

———. *Ezra Pound's Poetry and Prose: Contributions to Periodicals*. Prefaced and arranged by Lea Baechler, A. Walton Litz, and James Longenbach. 10 vols. New York: Garland Publishing, 1991.

———. *Letters, 1907–1941*. Edited by D. D. Paige. New York: Harcourt, Brace and World, 1950.

———. *The Letters of Ezra Pound to Alice Corbin Henderson*. Edited by Ira Nadel. Austin: University of Texas Press, 1993.

———. *Literary Essays of Ezra Pound*. Edited by T. S. Eliot. New York: New Directions, 1968.

———. *Personae: The Shorter Poems of Ezra Pound*. New York: New Directions, 1990.

———. *Selected Prose, 1909–1965*. Edited by William Cookson. New York: New Directions, 1973.

Pratt, William, and Robert Richardson. *Homage to Imagism.* New York: AMS Press, 1992.

Rabaté, Jean-Michel. *Language, Sexuality, and Ideology in Ezra Pound's "Cantos."* London: Macmillan, 1986.

Riddell, Joseph N. "H.D. and the Poetics of 'Spiritual Realism,'" *Contemporary Literature* 10, 1 (autumn 1969): 447-73.

Robinson, Janice. *H.D.: The Life and Work of an American Poet.* Boston: Houghton Mifflin, 1982.

Signets: Reading H.D. Edited by Susan Stanford Friedman and Rachel Blau DuPlessis. Madison: University of Wisconsin Press, 1990.

Smith, Paul. *Pound Revised.* London: Croom Helm, 1983.

Surette, Leon. *The Birth of Modernism.* Montreal: McGill-Queen's University Press, 1993.

Tryphonopoulos, Demetres P. *The Celestial Tradition.* Waterloo: Wilfrid Laurier University Press, 1992.

Wilhelm, J. J. *Ezra Pound in London and Paris, 1908-1925.* University Park: Pennsylvania State University Press, 1990.

———. *Ezra Pound: The Tragic Years, 1925-1972.* University Park: Pennsylvania State University Press, 1994.

Williams, William Carlos. *Autobiography.* New York: Random House, 1951.

Index